THE STORY OF THE
BOOK OF ABRAHAM

THE STORY OF THE BOOK OF ABRAHAM

Mummies, Manuscripts, and Mormonism

H. Donl Peterson

Deseret Book Company
Salt Lake City, Utah

Library of Congress Cataloging-in-Publication Data

Peterson, H. Donl.
    The story of the Book of Abraham : mummies, manuscripts, and Mormonism / H. Donl Peterson.
        p.   cm.
    Includes bibliographical references (p. xxx–xxx) and index.
    ISBN 0-87579-846-2
    1. Book of Abraham—Criticism, interpretation, etc. 2. Pearl of Great Price—Criticism, interpretation, etc. 3. Lebolo, Antonio, 1781–1830. 4. Smith, Joseph, 1805–1844. I. Title.
    BX8629.P53P49   1994
    289.3'2—dc20   94-7534
                                                                   CIP

Printed in the United States of America

10   9   8   7   6   5   4   3   2   1

CONTENTS

PREFACE

Searching, researching, and teaching classes on the history and doctrine of the Pearl of Great Price has been an exciting adventure spanning nearly thirty years. Preparing this manuscript on the historical aspects has been very tedious and demanding. On some segments of the story my files and folders are quite adequate, while on others my knowledge and documents range from meager to woefully lacking.

In 1989 I presented a paper in a Brigham Young University summer lecture series in which I explained how my intense interest in this topic began:

> When I began teaching classes in the Pearl of Great Price in 1965 at Brigham Young University, I spent little class time discussing the historical background of this book of scripture because only limited information was available, particularly about the Book of Abraham. It was commonly believed that the mummies and papyri that came from Egypt via Ireland were sold to the early Church leaders by a Michael H. Chandler, a nephew of the excavator. Joseph Smith had translated some of the papyrus manuscripts; then all were reportedly burned in the great Chicago fire of 1871. Little more was known. This much I had learned in a graduate class on the Pearl of Great Price taught by James R. Clark, author of *The Story of the Pearl of Great Price.* He had meticulously detailed all that was known in those days relative to the Abrahamic history. He was plowing new ground and establishing a solid foundation upon which others could build.[1]

The Latter-day Saint community was startled by an announcement in November 1967 that the Church had obtained from the Metropolitan Museum of Art in New York City eleven fragments of Egyptian papyri that had once been in the hands of the Prophet Joseph Smith. This announcement piqued the interest of students, and soon the number of young people who registered for Pearl of Great Price classes skyrocketed. I, along with my colleagues, was unprepared to field the many questions that were forthcoming because of the find. We didn't know even the most basic things about the historical background of the Book of Abraham, as indicated by these typical questions and answers:

1. Since all the papyri did not burn in the Chicago fire, is it possible that more papyri may be in existence?

Answer: I don't know.

2. Who was Sebolo or Lebolo or whatever his name was? Where was he from? Why was he in Egypt?

Answer: I don't know.

3. Where were the mummies and papyri exhumed in Egypt?

Answer: I don't know.

4. How did the mummies get to the United States?

Answer: I don't know.

5. How accurate is the Michael H. Chandler account of the origin of the mummies and papyri as recorded in the *History of the Church?*

Answer: I don't know.

6. Where is Sebolo's or Lebolo's will? Does it detail his giving the antiquities to his Irish nephew Michael H. Chandler?

Answer: I don't know.

My lectures were filled with too many "I don't knows." The sudden fervor of student interest and questions stirred me to probe for answers to questions that previously had not even been asked. I was very uncomfortable with the void in our understanding, and because we were caught without facts, controversy flourished among various factions.

Jay M. Todd, then an editorial associate on the *Improvement Era* staff, wrote an excellent article that appeared in January 1968. It detailed Dr. Aziz Atiya's find of the eleven papyri fragments and the bill of sale between the buyer, A. Combs, and the owners—Emma Smith Bidamon, the prophet's widow; Lewis C. Bidamon; and Joseph Smith III.[2]

Jay's article intrigued me, as did other events that year. During that summer, I attended a BYU Land of the Scriptures workshop led by Dr. Daniel H. Ludlow, during which we visited Pit Tomb 33 on the west bank of the Nile near Luxor, Egypt. This tomb, Dr. Ross Christensen of Brigham Young University had hypothesized, was where Lebolo had exhumed the eleven mummies.[3]

The tour concluded in Florence, Italy, so I stopped at the Latter-day Saint mission home there and visited with Elder R. Brent Bentley, a young friend of mine from BYU who had researched the Antonio Lebolo story. Jay Todd had written to the mission president, President Duns, to ascertain what information could be located about Antonio Lebolo. In response, President Duns, who was unable to go himself, sent Elder Bentley and two other elders to Lebolo's birthplace, Castellamonte. The elders had found Lebolo's birth recorded in the parish register of the local Catholic church, and they had also located Lebolo's large home. Although I was unable to leave the tour to go to Castellamonte myself, my interest was further stirred to follow up on the elders' findings.

Jay Todd published Elder Bentley's findings and photographs in the July 1968 *Improvement Era*. In 1969 Jay performed another great service by publishing his fascinating and insightful book, *The Saga of the Book of Abraham*.

I was hooked by the intrigue of this story and began to plan how I might untangle the details of this saga. I began by corresponding with anyone who might know something about Lebolo. Occasionally, as I directed travel study tours to Israel, Europe, and the Middle East, I would bid the homeward-bound participants farewell in Rome or Athens and then hurry to northern Italy, Paris, or Dublin to continue the research.

In 1982 I was appointed the Pearl of Great Price director in the Religious Studies Center at Brigham Young University, which had funds for research. In the fall of 1984, I was granted a professional development leave. Having both time and funds, I traveled in company with a research assistant to Philadelphia, New York, Dublin, London, Paris, Turin, Castellamonte, Venice, Trieste, and, briefly, Egypt to continue research. In addition, Jay Todd, as a friend, generously shared his files on his Book of Abraham research. His book accompanied me on nearly every research journey, and it has greatly influenced my efforts.

Thanks to all the research carried out, the questions answered with "I don't know" are less numerous today than they were twenty-five years ago.

I hope that this work will aid some in acquiring a basic understanding of this topic and challenge others to set the record straight by producing facts that will fill in the missing pieces of the puzzle, or correcting errors where my exuberance rushed ahead of my judgment.

Overall, it's been a great adventure visiting the tombs and backroads of Egypt; many great libraries, archives, and museums of the United States, Europe, and Egypt; LDS Church history sites in New York, Pennsylvania, Ohio, and Illinois; and meeting many fascinating personalities along the way. My colleagues and research assistants have been and are some of the most intelligent and dedicated scholars in the Church and in the academic community.

How exciting it is to learn, to be challenged, to grasp a new concept, or to painfully release an old favorite! I hope that your exposure to this work provides many enjoyable hours for you. This quest was pursued not merely to piece a story together but to actually trace the whereabouts of some prophetic writings from their ancient origin nearly four millennia ago to their arrival in this final dispensation, referred to as the *restoration*—"the restitution of all things, which God hath spoken by the mouth of all his holy prophets since the world began." (Acts 3:21.)

FOREWORD

The purpose of a foreword is to provide information that is likely to be of interest, but that is not absolutely essential for understanding the book itself. It is customary also that the foreword not be composed by the author of the book but by someone acquainted with the subject matter and also with the author. It is therefore with humility and a sense of honor that I record a few items concerning H. Donl Peterson's definitive and informative work: *The Story of the Book of Abraham*, which, although written by Professor Peterson, is being published posthumously.

This new book is the result of original research by Dr. Peterson, much of it never published before, that can be found nowhere else in collected and usable form. Such research was an on-going, magnificent obsession for Donl over a period of at least thirty years and took him to the eastern portions of the United States, to Europe, especially Italy, and to the archaeological remains in the Valley of the Kings in ancient Egypt.

Donl was untiring and meticulous. Because in his continuing investigation and careful searching of documents and records, many of which were previously untouched by LDS researchers, the Church and the world will have a clearer understanding of the history of the Pearl of Great Price, and particularly of the papyri associated with the Book of Abraham. Donl's studies have given us a clearer view of Antonio Lebolo, who was responsible for getting the papyri, along with some mummies, out of Egypt. Eventually they found their way to the

United States and into the hands of the Prophet Joseph Smith. The entire historical background of the Book of Abraham will be plainer to readers today because of Dr. Peterson's work.

The discovery by Dr. Aziz Atiya of fragments of the papyri in 1967 in New York's Metropolitan Museum generated a lively interest among Latter-day Saints. Often the Book of Abraham seems surrounded in an aura of mystery. As a consequence, Jay M. Todd, an editorial associate of the *Improvement Era*, responded to a need and published an informative book, *The Saga of the Book of Abraham* (Deseret Book, 1969). However, as Brother Todd explained, there were many unknowns about Antonio Lebolo and Michael Chandler, and also the historical background and journey of the papyri scrolls. Donl Peterson's research continues to draw back the curtain and allows the light to shine where previously there was darkness. Not all the facts are known even now, but because of *The Story of the Book of Abraham*, readers will gain a clearer and more complete comprehension of the story behind the Book of Abraham than has been possible heretofore.

H. Donl Peterson, a family man, was assisted often by his wife, Mary Lou, and she sometimes accompanied him in his travels. After his untimely passing in 1994, his six children (Terry, Diane, Jaqueline, Scott, James, and Michael), enabled Mary Lou to bring this work to publication. The book is rich in facts, photos, maps, and charts. It will be a boon to all who seek to know the fascinating history of the Pearl of Great Price, and especially the sacred writings of Abraham.

Because the Pearl of Great Price is one of the standard works of The Church of Jesus Christ of Latter-day Saints, this monumental work is of considerable significance.

Robert J. Matthews
Former Dean of Religious Instruction
Brigham Young University

ACKNOWLEDGMENTS

Through the years many individuals provided invaluable assistance, information, and encouragement as the author searched for answers to the intriguing story behind the Book of Abraham in the Pearl of Great Price. Gratitude is expressed for colleagues in the Department of Religious Studies at Brigham Young University; graduate assistants and researchers; staff members at libraries and archives in many areas of Africa, Europe, and the United States; and untold others who contributed in various ways. Dr. Peterson passed away in March of 1994, soon after the manuscript was completed and submitted to Deseret Book Company. Eleanor Knowles, executive editor at Deseret Book, and Kent Ware, designer, worked in consultation with Mary Lou Peterson, Dr. Peterson's wife, and his daughter Jacque to bring the book to publication.

1
ANTIQUITIES IN KIRTLAND, OHIO

Near the end of June 1835, a large, creaking wagon with a mysterious cargo slowly wended its way down the rutted roads of Kirtland, Ohio. The curious freight was thousands of miles away from the cargo's distant point of origin. Michael H. Chandler, an Irish immigrant who had settled in Pennsylvania, was responsible for the wave of excitement that resulted when he registered at the Riggs Hotel and announced he would be in town for several days to display four Egyptian mummies and some ancient papyri. He also expressed interest in visiting with the Mormon prophet, Joseph Smith, concerning his collection.

Mr. Chandler had previously contacted several linguists at reputable academic institutions in the eastern states for their opinions on and possible interpretation of the writings on the papyrus. In 1822 the young French genius Jean Francois Champollion, with the aid of the trilingual Rosetta Stone, had first deciphered the ancient hieroglyphic writings in France, but his dictionary of Egyptian hieroglyphics would not be published in Europe until 1841.[1] Hence, the American academicians whom Chandler consulted in 1833–35 were unable to read the papyrus records. At best, they could only speculate on the meaning of some of the symbols when they could reach consensus on them.[2]

Mr. Chandler had heard of Joseph Smith's skill in translating from the Egyptian. However, most of the informers apparently made light of the Prophet's claim of having translated the Book of Mormon from a "reformed" Egyptian language.

When Chandler arrived in Kirtland, he probably placed copies of two different placards, or handbills, in conspicuous locations to promote his exhibit. One placard, referred to as the "certificate of the learned," was signed by seven prominent Philadelphia medical doctors who had visited the exhibit while in Philadelphia and who recommended the exhibit of mummies and papyri to the public.[3] The other placard was printed after Chandler's original collection of eleven mummies had dwindled to four. It read:

EGYPTIAN ANTIQUITIES

These Mummies, with seven others, were taken from the Catacombs of Egypt, near where the ancient, and we may say, almost unparalleled city of Thebes once stood, by the celebrated French traveller Antonio Lebolo; at a great expense, under the protection of the French Consul, by consent of Mehemet Ali, the Viceroy of Egypt. It is to be noticed that several hundred Mummies, differently embalmed were found in the same catacomb, but only the eleven in a state to be removed. The seven have been sold to gentlemen for private museums, and in consequence are kept from the public.— They have been exhibited in Philadelphia and Baltimore, to crowded audiences; in the latter place, although only engaged for two weeks, the exhibition was prolonged to *five weeks,* with attraction. Of all the relics of the ancient world that time has left, the Mummy is the most interesting. It is a well known fact, recorded in both sacred and profane history that men were embalmed, which science has attracted the learned for ages. All other antiquities are but the work of man, but *Mummies* present us with the men themselves—they are the personages, preserved in human form, for the gaze and attraction of people who are occupying down the stream of time centuries from those—they have certainly been conspicuous actors in those mighty scenes of which the history of Egypt is full. An hundred generations have passed away, and new empires have began since this flesh was animated—since these eyes were bright, and this tongue was eloquent, and the heart beat within this breast. These strangers illustrious from their antiquity, may have lived in the days of Jacob, Moses, or David, and of course some thousand years have elapsed since these bodies were animated with the breath of life! History records the fact, that the higher class concealed their knowl-

edge from the lower, in figures and hieroglyphic characters—
A few of those, upon papyrus, used by the Egyptians for writing, will be exhibited with the Mummies.[4]

When Chandler registered at the Riggs Hotel, he requested
that Gideon Riggs, the proprietor, send his son John to Joseph
Smith's house to invite him and his family to attend the exhibition that evening. The Prophet informed John Riggs that he was
unable to attend because of a previous commitment. John Riggs
was sent a second time to Joseph's home with a note from Mr.
Chandler requesting an interview with the Prophet. Joseph
replied that he would come to the hotel at eight o'clock the following morning.

The young messenger was present when the Prophet first
saw the papyrus the next morning. He later recalled that
"Joseph was permitted to take the papyrus home with him,
Father Riggs vouching for its return, and the following morning
Joseph came with the leaves which he had translated, which
Oliver Cowdery read, and Mr. Chandler then produced the
translation of Professor Charles Anthon as far as the professor
could translate it." Young Riggs, who was also present at the
reading, stated that the translations of the Prophet and the professor agreed to a point, but "there was one language Professor
Anthon could not translate which the Prophet did."[5]

When Did Chandler Arrive in Kirtland?

There are slight discrepancies in the various accounts as to
the exact day of Chandler's arrival in Kirtland.

Oliver Cowdery wrote that Chandler visited Kirtland "the
last of June, or first of July, at which time he presented bro.
Smith with his papyrus."[6]

The *History of the Church* reads: "On the 3rd of July, Michael
H. Chandler came to Kirtland to exhibit some Egyptian mummies. There were four human figures, together with some two
or more rolls of papyrus covered with hieroglyphic figures and
devices."[7]

A letter from W. W. Phelps to his wife Sally favors Oliver

Cowdery's earlier date concerning Chandler's initial visit to Kirtland. Phelps had left his wife and six of his seven children behind in Missouri in order to go to Kirtland to work on the temple, and had written the following letter to his wife:

Kirtland, Ohio
July 19 and 20, 1835

Beloved Sally:

Last evening we received your first letter after an absence of twelve weeks and twelve hours. Our tears of joy were the witness of its welcome reception. By these things we learn the value of each other's society and company, and friendship, and virtue. Taking the letter altogether, with all its candor and information and remembered names, it is, by all who have read it, called a very good one. Brother Joseph remarked that it was as easy to shed tears while reading that letter as it was when reading the History of Joseph in Egypt. . . .

The last of June four Egyptian mummies were brought here; there were two papyrus rolls, besides some other ancient Egyptian writings with them. As no one could translate these writings, they were presented to President Smith. He soon knew what they were and said they, the "rolls of papyrus," contained the sacred record kept of Joseph in Pharaoh's Court in Egypt, and the teachings of Father Abraham. God has so ordered it that these mummies and writings have been brought in the Church, and the sacred writing I had just locked up in Brother Joseph's house when your letter came, so I had two consolations of good things in one day. These records of old times, when we translate and print them in a book, will make a good witness for the Book of Mormon. There is nothing secret or hidden that shall not be revealed, and they come to the Saints.[8]

In a letter written six months later to a man named William Frye, Oliver Cowdery explained that Joseph Smith showed Chandler, on the morning they met, a number of characters copied from the gold plates, and that there were some points of resemblance between the Nephite characters and the characters on the papyrus.[9] Joseph Smith reported:

As Mr. Chandler had been told I could translate them, he brought me some of the characters, and I gave him the inter-

pretation, and like a gentleman, he gave me the following
certificate:

Kirtland, July 6, 1835.

This is to make known to all who may be desirous, concerning the knowledge of Mr. Joseph Smith, Jun., in deciphering the ancient Egyptian hieroglyphic characters in my possession, which I have, in many eminent cities, showed to the
most learned; and, from the information that I could ever
learn, or meet with, I find that of Mr. Joseph Smith, Jun., to
correspond in the most minute matters.

> Michael H. Chandler
> Traveling with, and proprietor of,
> Egyptian mummies[10]

Oliver Cowdery, in the Frye letter, added the following
explanation pertaining to Chandler's certificate: "The foregoing
is *verbatim* as given by Mr. C. [Chandler] excepting the addition
of punctuation, and speaks sufficiently plain without requiring
comment from me. It was given previous to the purchase of the
antiquities, by any person here."[11]

Apparently Oliver wanted to make it clear to those inclined
to censure that Chandler's certificate substantiating Joseph
Smith's credentials as a translator was not induced by a promise
to purchase the artifacts.

Additional light is shed on this story by Orson Pratt, a member of the newly organized Quorum of the Twelve Apostles. The
following sermon was given in Salt Lake City forty-three years
later while Elder Pratt, then a senior member of the Twelve, was
also serving as Church historian. Some may question his accuracy in recalling events that occurred so long before, but other
accounts attest to its correctness.

After receiving the mummies he [Chandler] began to take
off some of the ancient covering or wrapping, and to his astonishment he found upon the breast of one of these mummies a
record written upon ancient papyrus in plain characters, written both in black and red inks, or stains, or colors. And the
mummies and the records were exhibited by Mr. Chandler, in
New York, Philadelphia, and many of the Eastern States of our

Union; and thousands of people saw them, and among them many learned men; and these characters were presented to them, and not unfrequently was Mr. Chandler referred to "Joe" Smith as they used to term him, who, they said, pretended to have translated some records that he found in the western part of New York, and that if Mr. Chandler would go and see him perhaps he would translate those ancient characters. Many of these references were made with the intention of ridiculing Mr. Smith; but it so happened that in traveling through the country, he visited Kirtland, Ohio, where the Prophet Joseph Smith resided, bringing the mummies and the ancient papyrus writings with him. Mr. C. had also obtained from learned men the best translation he could of some few characters, which however, was not a translation, but more in the shape of their ideas with regard to it, their acquaintance with the language not being sufficient to enable them to translate it literally.[12]

The Records and Mummies Are Purchased

While exhibiting the antiquities in Cleveland, Ohio, three months before he visited the Saints in Kirtland, Chandler had announced in a newspaper article that he was interested in selling the four remaining mummies and the ancient documents.[13] After viewing the artifacts, Joseph Smith told Chandler that he had no interest in purchasing the mummies, only the papyrus. According to Orson Pratt, Chandler replied that "he would not sell the writings unless he could sell the mummies, for it would detract from the curiosity of his exhibition."[14]

Accounts vary as to the amount paid for the artifacts and also how the money was raised. N. L. Nelson wrote in 1885 that the Prophet paid "about $2000."[15] At the other extreme, Josiah Quincy, a prominent Bostonian, reported that the cost was $6,000.[16] This last figure, which is far from accurate, is probably based upon a related story that will be explained later. In a letter to Joseph Smith that was dated January 1, 1844, Joseph Coe, the Prophet's former business agent who had by then apostatized, said that the four mummies cost the Church $2,400.[17] The bill of sale, which came into the hands of the Church in 1967, confirms that $2,400 was the correct amount.[18]

Twenty-four hundred dollars was a large sum of money to the impoverished Saints in Kirtland. In 1993 that sum would equate to about $35,000.[19] Many financially destitute families had recently immigrated to Kirtland to unite with their "fellow-citizens" in the Church. Construction of the temple there demanded nearly all of the free time and resources the faithful could spare after acquiring their daily bread. Reports vary as to how the Church raised such a large sum of money to buy the mummies and manuscripts. Parley P. Pratt, a member of the Twelve Apostles, wrote: "An event, of a nature so extraordinary, was of course soon noised abroad, when a number of gentlemen in the neighborhood, not connected with the Saints, united together, and, purchasing the record altogether with some or all of the mummies, made MR. SMITH a present of them."[20]

On the other hand, the *History of the Church* reports that "some of the Saints at Kirtland purchased the mummies and papyrus."[21] In his 1844 letter to the Prophet, Joseph Coe mentioned the method used to finance the purchase, which partially explains how both members and nonmembers alike could have been involved:

> I have for a long time been anxious to receive some communication from you in relation to my interest in the Mummies etc. but having failed hitherto of learning anything satisfactory on the subject I have thot proper to drop you a line as the most ready means of exchanging sentiments on this subject. Permit me here to sketch the history of the purchase etc. in order to bring the subject fresh to your recollection. When the subject of purchasing that concern came up I was somewhat involved and unable to sustain a heavier burthen any great length of time. but having all confidence in the utility of the collection, and being assured by yourself that the burthen would be but temporary; that the profits coming from the work when translated would be more than adequate to the defraying all the expense which might accrue by the purchase. I therefore managed the business in relation to the purchase with the same confidence that I had previously done business which I thought would result in the good of the church. Previous to closing the contract with Chandler, I made arrangements with S. Andrews for to take one third part and

your self & Co. one third leaving one third to be borne by myself.[22]

Joseph Coe and Simeon Andrews each raised $800, while Joseph Smith "and company" raised the balance of $800. Possibly many people, members and nonmembers alike, assisted in purchasing the mummies by contributing funds under Joseph Smith's name to raise his share of the amount.

It is not known when Joseph first realized what the contents of the papyrus were. If it was not while Chandler was in Kirtland, it was made known to the Prophet a few days later. One thing seems clear: Providence was directing his servant. Joseph's account in the *History of the Church* states:

> Soon after this [between July 5 and July 9], some of the Saints at Kirtland purchased the mummies and papyrus, a description of which will appear hereafter, and with W. W. Phelps and Oliver Cowdery as scribes, I commenced the translation of some of the characters or hieroglyphics, and much to our joy found that one of the rolls contained the writings of Abraham, another the writings of Joseph of Egypt, etc.,—a more full account of which will appear in its place, as I proceed to examine or unfold them. Truly we can say, the Lord is beginning to reveal the abundance of peace and truth.[23]

2

ABRAHAM AND JOSEPH IN EGYPT

Since Abraham and Joseph of Egypt are such prominent men of God in the scriptures and in this world's secular history, and some of their writings were obtained by the Prophet Joseph Smith in 1835, it seems important to include a brief synopsis of their lives early in this account.

Even though they lived nearly four thousand years ago, their heroics have been told and retold innumerable times to succeeding generations. These are the kind of men parents pray that their sons may emulate and their daughters might marry. These are true heroes, men of testimony, valor, nobility, and integrity.

When Joseph Smith announced he had acquired some writings of these two prophets of God, writings more ancient than any known biblical literature, the faithful wondered and anxiously waited while the skeptics scoffed. A brief review of the lives of these seers, the contributions they made, and the times in which they lived helps us in connecting the story. Some information from the writings of Abraham acquired by Joseph Smith in July 1835 is included in this chapter along with the biblical account.

Abraham: A Preacher of Righteousness

Abraham's early life is unrecorded in holy writ. The biblical account first mentions him living in Ur of Chaldea when he and his brother Nahor "took them wives." (Genesis 11:29.) Several apocryphal records are available relative to Abraham's early life, but the scriptures are silent. The Book of Abraham reports that his "fathers" had apostatized from the gospel, adopted the ways of their idolatrous neighbors, and consented to have Abraham killed upon an altar of sacrifice apparently as a public example. At the very moment he was to succumb in Ur to the sacrificial knife wielded by the priest of Egypt's pharaoh, the Lord interceded and saved his life. (Abraham 1:5–15.)

Abraham was told by the Lord to leave his apostate relatives and that he would be directed to a new home, a "strange land," a promised land, unfamiliar to Abraham (who was known at that time as Abram). The Lord also assured Abraham that he would be blessed with power in the priesthood "as it was with Noah," the great prophet and patriarch who was the presiding prophet of that dispensation. (Abraham 1:16–19.)

A famine prevailed throughout the land. Terah, Abraham's father, experienced great affliction and repented of his evil intent to kill Abraham. In company with his wife Sarah (or Sarai), his nephew Lot, and Lot's wife, Abraham left Ur and traveled to a land they named Haran; his father, he recorded, "followed after me." (Abraham 2:4.) While in Haran, Abraham anxiously taught the gospel of Jesus Christ to those who would listen. However, Terah was not spiritually prepared to benefit from his son's inspired words, for Abraham recorded that after the famine abated, his father "turned again unto his idolatry." (Abraham 2:5.)

Once again the heavenly veil parted and the Lord appeared to Abraham and commanded him to leave Haran, telling him that he would be directed to the land that the Lord would give to him and to his posterity "for an everlasting possession," conditional on the promise "when they hearken to my voice." (Abraham 2:6.) The Lord further covenanted with Abraham that he would make of him "a great nation," that Abraham's name would be honored among all nations, that his seed should bear this ministry and priesthood unto all nations, that those who accepted the gospel would be known as Abraham's seed, and that through Abraham's posterity "all the families of the earth [would] be blessed with the blessings of the Gospel . . . even [with] eternal life." (Abraham 2:9–11.)

Abraham Had the Gospel of Jesus Christ

The scriptures indicate that the gospel of Jesus Christ was taught to Abraham. Only one gospel, one inspired message of hope, has been revealed by the Lord; that is, the teachings and ordinances that were revealed to Adam in the beginning of time are those that have been taught to all the holy prophets since his day. Nephi, son of Helaman, explained:

"Abraham saw of his [Christ's] coming, and was filled with gladness and did rejoice. . . . Abraham not only knew of these things, but there were many before the days of Abraham who were called by the order of God; yea, even after the order of his Son; and this that it should be shown unto the people, a great many thousand years before his coming, that even redemption should come unto them. And now I would that ye should know, that even since the days of Abraham there have been many prophets that have testified these things." (Helaman 8:17–19.)

The Prophet Joseph Smith commented:

It will be noticed that, according to Paul, (see Gal. iii:8) the Gospel was preached to Abraham. We would like to be informed in what name the Gospel was then preached, whether it was in the name of Christ or some other name. If in any other name, was it the Gospel? And if it was the Gospel, and that preached in the name of Christ, had it any ordinances? If not, was it the Gospel? And if it had ordinances what were they? Our friends may say, perhaps, that there were never any ordinances except those of offering sacrifices before the coming of Christ, and that it could not be possible for the Gospel to have been administered while the law of sacrifices of blood was in force. But we will recollect that Abraham offered sacrifice, and notwithstanding this, had the Gospel preached to him. That the offering of sacrifice was only to point the mind forward to Christ, we infer from these remarkable words of Jesus to the Jews: "Your Father Abraham rejoiced to see my day: and he saw it, and was glad" (John viii:56). So, then, because the ancients offered sacrifice it did not hinder their hearing the Gospel; but served, as we said before, to open their eyes, and enable them to look forward to the time of the coming of the Savior, and rejoice in His redemption. We find also, that when the Israelites came out of Egypt they had the Gospel preached to them, according to Paul in his letter to the Hebrews, which says: "For unto us was the Gospel preached, as well as unto them: but the word preached did not profit them, not being mixed with faith in them that heard it" (see Heb. iv:2). It is said again, in Gal. iii:19, that the law (of Moses, or the Levitical law) was "added" because of transgression. What, we ask, was this law added to, if it was not added to the Gospel? It must be plain that it was added to the Gospel, since we learn that they had the Gospel preached to them. From these few facts, we conclude that whenever the Lord revealed Himself to men in ancient days, and commanded them to offer sacrifice to Him, that it was done that they might look forward in faith to the time of His coming, and rely upon the power of that atonement for a remission of their sins. And this they have done, thousands who have gone before us, whose garments are spotless, and who are, like Job, waiting with an assurance like his, that they will see Him in the *latter day* upon the earth, even in their flesh.[1]

Elder Bruce R. McConkie also wrote about Abraham and the covenant the Lord made with him:

Abraham first received the gospel by baptism (which is the covenant of salvation); then he had conferred upon him the higher priesthood, and he entered into celestial marriage (which is the covenant of exaltation), gaining assurance thereby that he would have eternal increase; finally he received a promise that all of these blessings would be offered to all of his mortal posterity. (Abra. 2:6–11; D. & C. 132:29–50.) Included in the divine promises to Abraham was the assurance that Christ would come through his lineage, and the assurance that Abraham's posterity would receive certain choice, promised lands as an eternal inheritance. (Abra. 2; Gen. 17; 22:15–18; Gal. 3.)

All of these promises lumped together are called the *Abrahamic covenant*. This covenant was renewed with Isaac (Gen. 24:60; 26:1–4, 24) and again with Jacob. (Gen. 28; 35:9–13; 48:3–4.) *Those portions of it which pertain to personal exaltation and eternal increase are renewed with each member of the house of Israel who enters the order of celestial marriage;* through that order the participating parties become inheritors of all the blessings of Abraham, Isaac, and Jacob. (D. & C. 132; Rom. 9:4; Gal. 3; 4.)[2]

Thus, we see that the Abrahamic covenant is another term for the gospel covenant that is the gospel of Jesus Christ, with all its divine teachings and saving ordinances administered by the holy priesthood.

In company with Lot and his wife, along with the converts whom they had "won in Haran" (Abraham 2:15), and with all the substance they had acquired, Abraham and Sarai journeyed south to the land of Canaan. In the land of the idolatrous Canaanites, Abraham built an altar and offered sacrifice, then sought further instructions from the Lord. He recorded: "And the Lord appeared unto me in answer to my prayers, and said unto me: Unto thy seed will I give this land." (Abraham 2:19.)

Because of the severity of the famine in Canaan, Abraham left his land of promise and continued on to Egypt, where the conditions were considerably better.

Abraham in Egypt

As Abraham's caravan approached the borders of Egypt, the Lord reminded him of one of the customs of the Egyptians: "Behold, Sarai, thy wife, is a very fair woman to look upon; therefore it shall come to pass, when the Egyptians shall see her, they will say—She is his wife; and they will kill you, but they will save her alive; therefore see that you do on this wise: Let her say unto the Egyptians, she is thy sister, and thy soul shall live." (Abraham 2:22–24.)

To understand better the predicament Abraham faced, it is necessary to understand Egyptian marriage customs. If a beautiful woman were observed approaching the borders of Egypt, inquiry was made as to her status: Was she single, married, or widowed? If she was single or widowed, she was eligible to be married to the pharaoh or some other man of prominence, provided he selected her and arrangements could be worked out between him and her male family members.

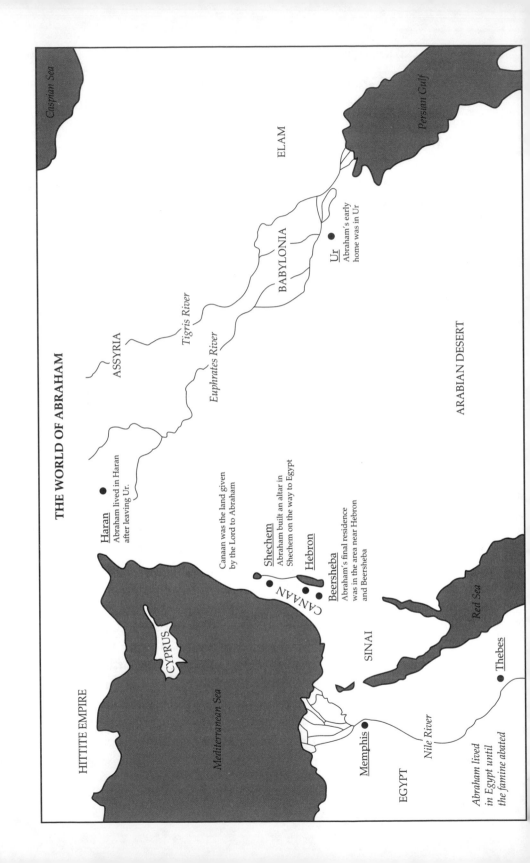

THE WORLD OF ABRAHAM

Caspian Sea

Persian Gulf

ELAM

Ur
Abraham's early
home was in Ur

BABYLONIA

ASSYRIA

Tigris River

Euphrates River

ARABIAN DESERT

Haran
Abraham lived in Haran
after leaving Ur.

Canaan was the land given
by the Lord to Abraham

Shechem
Abraham built an altar in
Shechem on the way to Egypt

Hebron

CANAAN

Beersheba
Abraham's final residence
was in the area near Hebron
and Beersheba

HITTITE EMPIRE

CYPRUS

Mediterranean Sea

SINAI

Red Sea

Memphis

Nile River

Thebes

EGYPT

Abraham lived
in Egypt until
the famine abated

The pharaoh, however, could not marry another man's wife because of the strict laws of the land—unless, of course, the beautiful woman's husband met with an untimely fatal accident as the caravan approached or entered the borders of Egypt. Then she, as a widow, would be free to marry. Besides, who would deny the proposal of the mighty pharaoh, king of Egypt, who would magnanimously provide security and royal status to a sorrowing widow? And who would dare question the particulars of the tragic events that caused her husband's untimely death?

As Abraham had been forewarned by the Lord, the men who earned their living watching female travelers coming to Egypt so they could recommend the desirable ones to the Pharaoh for his harem were impressed with Sarai's beauty. Therefore, she was commended to Pharaoh and taken to the royal palace. According to the biblical account, "the Lord plagued Pharaoh and his house with great plagues because of Sarai Abram's wife." (Genesis 12:17.) When Pharaoh learned that Sarai was married, he was upset, reasoning that his problems came as a result of Sarai, a married woman, being detained in his palace. Reasoning further that Abraham's gods must be superior to his own gods because they had caused such consequences, Pharaoh sent for Abraham and asked: "What is this that thou hast done unto me? why didst thou not tell me that she was thy wife? Why saidst thou, She is my sister? so I might have taken her to me to wife: now therefore behold thy wife, take her, and go thy way." (Genesis 12:18–19.)

Regrettably, the existing records are only fragmentary, but one cannot help but wonder when Pharaoh first learned that the brilliant scientist and holy prophet who stood before him in Egypt was once strapped to a lion-couch altar in Ur, many hundreds of miles away, prepared to be murdered by one of Pharaoh's own priests. Pharaoh's respect, or even fear, of Abraham must have been heightened when he recalled that at the moment Abraham was to have been murdered upon the altar in Ur "after the manner of the Egyptians," the Lord "broke down the altar of Elkenah, and of the gods of the land, and utterly destroyed them, and smote the priest that he died; and there was great mourning in Chaldea, and also in the court of Pharaoh; which Pharaoh signifies king by royal blood." (Abraham 1:11, 20.)

The Bible account has led some to believe that Abraham's visit to Egypt was rather brief, but the Book of Abraham furnishes additional insights. Facsimile 3 provides the explanation that Pharaoh invited Abraham to sit upon his throne and instruct his royal court "upon the principles of Astronomy." The Jewish historian Flavius Josephus, quoting Berosus, referred to Abraham as a man "righteous and great, and skilful in the celestial science."[3]

Josephus recorded that the Pharaoh "gave him [Abraham] leave to enter into conversation with the most learned among the Egyptians; from which conversation, his virtue and his reputation became more conspicuous than they had been before."[4] He continued:

> For whereas the Egyptians were formerly addicted to different customs, and despised one another's sacred and accustomed rites, and were very angry one with another on that account, Abram conferred with each of them, and confuting the reasonings they made use of every one for their own practices, demonstrated that such reasonings were vain and void of truth; whereupon he was admired by them in those conferences as a very wise man, and one of great sagacity, when he discoursed on any subject he undertook; and this not only in understanding it, but in persuading other men also to assent to him. He communicated to them arithmetic, and delivered to them the science of astronomy, for before Abram came into Egypt, they were unacquainted with those parts of learning; for that science came from the Chaldeans into Egypt, and from thence to the Greeks also.[5]

Abraham's own account explains that he was shown some of the marvels of the universe through the use of the "records of the fathers" (Abraham 1:28, 31); the use of the Urim and Thummim (Abraham 3:1); and a personal visitation from the Lord (Abraham 3:12), including Abraham's seeing the creation, the residence of God, Kolob, the star Oliblish, and considerably more.

Abraham came from the land of Ur, home of the wise men of the East, whose interests and expertise in astronomy were widely known and time honored. In the Egyptian Alphabet and Grammar it is recorded that Kolob "signifies the first great grand governing fixed star which is the fartherest that ever has been discovered by the fathers which was discovered by Methusela and also by Abraham."[6]

While Abraham was traveling to Egypt, the Lord gave him the aforementioned visions, which, when told to Pharaoh's court, would help establish his academic and spiritual credentials. The Lord told Abraham, speaking in the visions of the "night time" of the planetary system, "I show these things unto thee before ye go into Egypt, that ye may declare all these words." (Abraham 3:14–15.) The episode of Abraham's having Sarai pose as his sister was the Lord's way of bringing all of this about. How long Abraham stayed in Egypt is unknown— perhaps months, perhaps years. The account in Genesis explains that when he and his followers left Egypt to return to Canaan, he had been entreated well for Sarai's sake; hence, he "had sheep, and oxen, and he asses, and menservants, and maid-servants, and she asses, and camels." (Genesis 12:16.) This account adds that "Abram was very rich in cattle, in silver, and in gold" as he returned to his land of promise. (Genesis 13:2.)

When Abraham was ninety-nine years old, the Lord again appeared to him in the land of Canaan and made further covenants with him. Circumcision was added as a sign of the covenant, so that Abraham's male posterity "may be known among all nations," and "that thou [Abraham] mayest know for ever that children are not accountable before me [the Lord] until they are eight years old." All male babies were to be circumcised at eight days to remind their parents of the grace period all children were in until they were eight years old. (JST, Genesis 17:4, 11.)

The Lord changed Abraham's name from Abram to

Abraham, explaining, "for, a father of many nations have I made thee." (Genesis 17:5.) Sarah's name was also changed from Sarai to Sarah. "I will bless her," the Lord explained, "and I will give thee a son of her; yea, I will bless her, and she shall be blessed, The mother of nations; kings and people shall be of her." (JST, Genesis 17:22; see also Genesis 17:16.)[7]

Abraham, who was ordained to the holy priesthood by the great prophet Melchizedek either in Chaldea or Canaan (see D&C 84:14), had a long life of faithfulness and service. He was blessed with several wives and a large posterity. His great test of faith, when he was asked of the Lord to sacrifice his chosen son, Isaac, on the altar, is widely known and heralded. The greatest individual of all, Jesus Christ, came from his lineage. The Gospel of Matthew begins: "The book of the generation of Jesus Christ, the son of David [the kingly line], the son of Abraham [the Patriarchal order]." (Matthew 1:1.) The faithful in Christ of every generation for the past four millennia have been known as Abraham's seed. The scriptures confirm that Abraham, because of his unwavering faith and devotion, is now a god. (See D&C 132:37.)

Joseph, Son of Jacob

Three great prophets of God—Abraham, Isaac, and Jacob, a father, son, and grandson—are often linked together because of their continued obedience and faith under trying circumstances. Joseph, next in succession, was not one whit behind his three honored forebears. Although he was not literally Jacob's eldest son, Joseph was, in Jacob's mind, the firstborn son of his intended first wife, Rachel. Hence Joseph was entitled to, and prepared to receive, the birthright and family leadership.

For the privilege of marrying Rachel, Jacob, who had fled from Canaan, worked seven years in Haran for his father-in-law, Laban. However, through the trickery of Laban, Rachel's older sister, Leah, was substituted at the wedding. Fortunately Jacob was allowed to marry Rachel a week later, on condition that he serve an additional seven years. He worked for Laban for a total

Jacob blessing his son Joseph

of twenty years, and when he left Haran, he had four wives—
Leah, Rachel, Bilhah, and Zilpah—and eleven sons and some
daughters. Rachel was unable to bear children for several years,
and when Joseph, her firstborn son, was born, he was actually
Jacob's eleventh son. Nevertheless, Jacob considered Rachel his
first wife, and her firstborn son as the family's chosen heir
through the right of primogeniture.

After twenty years in Haran, and at the command of God,
Jacob led his large family back to Canaan. (See Genesis 31:3.)
As the family caravan reached the outskirts of Bethlehem,
Rachel bore another son but died in childbirth. Joseph's younger
brother was named Benjamin.

Inasmuch as Joseph was obviously Jacob's favored son
whom he loved "more than all his brethren," the Bible reports
that his older brothers hated him. (Genesis 37:4.) Not only had
Jacob given Joseph, when he was seventeen years old, a "coat of
many colours," evidence of his favoritism, but Joseph had also
related two dreams to his family that further alienated them
from him.

In the first dream, according to Joseph, "We were binding

House of Israel

Abraham (Sarah)

Isaac (Rebekah)

Jacob or Israel (Leah, Rachel, Bilhah, Zilpah)

Reuben | Simeon | Levi | Judah | Dan | Naphtali | Gad | Asher | Issachar | Zebulon | Joseph | Benjamin

Ephraim | Manasseh

sheaves in the field, and, lo, my sheaf arose, and also stood upright; and, behold, your sheaves stood round about, and made obeisance to my sheaf." In the second dream, he told his brothers, "the sun and the moon and the eleven stars made obeisance to me." Even Jacob rebuked Joseph and inquired, "Shall I and thy mother and thy brethren indeed come to bow down ourselves to thee to the earth?" As Joseph's brothers further envied him, his father wondered what these dreams meant. (Genesis 37:7, 9–11.)

Soon after this, Jacob sent Joseph from their home in Hebron, south of Jerusalem, to Dothan, over seventy miles away, to check on his brothers and the flocks. When his brothers saw Joseph coming toward them, they "conspired . . . to slay him." (Genesis 37:18.) They stripped him of his splendorous coat, which represented to them unwarranted authority and favoritism, and cast him into a dry pit. Reuben, the eldest brother, persuaded the others not to kill Joseph.

Later that day a caravan of merchants traveling to Egypt passed by, and Judah proposed this idea: "What profit is it if we slay our brother, and conceal his blood? Come, and let us sell him to the Ishmeelites, and let not our hand be upon him; for he is our brother and our flesh." (Genesis 37:26–27.) This pleased the brothers, and Joseph was taken to Egypt and sold to Potiphar, one of Pharaoh's officers and captain of the guard. (Genesis 37:36.)

After having dipped Joseph's coat in the blood of a young goat, his conspiring brothers reported to their father that they had found a coat similar to Joseph's that was bloodstained. Upon confirming that it was truly Joseph's coat, and assuming that Joseph had been killed by a wild beast, Jacob mourned for many days, and after considerable attempts by his family to comfort him, he said, "I will go down into the grave . . . mourning." (Genesis 37:35.)

As readers of the Bible know, Joseph prospered in Egypt, and before long Potiphar made him overseer of all his domestic affairs. But when Potiphar's sensuous wife made improper advances toward Joseph, he fled rather than compromise his virtue. In her rejection and humiliation, she reported to her husband that Joseph had attempted to seduce her. Consequently, Potiphar had Joseph incarcerated in the prison where those who had offended Pharaoh were detained.

In prison Joseph's abilities were recognized, and he was soon placed in jurisdiction over the other prisoners. While he was confined in prison, the Lord enabled Joseph to interpret two different dreams: a dream of the chief butler and a dream of Pharaoh's chief baker. Two years later Pharaoh himself had two dreams that troubled him. After his wise men were unable to interpret them, the chief baker volunteered that a young Hebrew prisoner had interpreted a dream of his two years before. Joseph was sent for, and he explained that God, not he, "shall give Pharaoh an answer of peace." (Genesis 41:16.) He explained that both of Pharaoh's dreams meant that there would be seven years of plenty followed by seven years of famine in Egypt. He then counseled Pharaoh to find a man in the kingdom who was "discreet and wise" to implement the necessary preparations for the seven lean years. Pharaoh,

Joseph making grain available to his family in Egypt

accepting the interpretation and impressed with Joseph's wisdom, selected Joseph, "in whom the Spirit of God is," to be second only to himself in his entire kingdom of the Nile. At thirty
years of age, Joseph was made viceroy of Egypt. (Genesis
41:33, 38.)

Joseph wisely prepared for the seven years of famine that
affected not only Egypt but also many adjacent countries. In
neighboring Canaan, Jacob and his large family were severely
afflicted. The touching story in the Bible tells how the family
was reunited after many trials and tests. The dream Joseph had
had at seventeen, of his brothers bowing before him, was fulfilled when his ten older brothers, not recognizing him, knelt
before him and begged sustenance of him, the wise and powerful viceroy of Egypt.

Pharaoh then told Joseph to send for his father and his family so that they could enjoy the prosperity and blessings in
Egypt, and they were given the land of Goshen, "the best of the
land" (Genesis 47:6), in appreciation for Joseph's wisdom.

Jacob, or Israel, as the Lord had renamed him (Genesis
35:9–12), lived in Egypt seventeen years before his death at 147

years of age. After his death, a large cortege consisting of his children, the servants of Pharaoh, and all the elders of the land of Egypt made the trip to Hebron to the cave of Machpelah, where he was buried by the side of his wife Leah; his parents, Isaac and Rebekah; and his grandparents Abraham and Sarah.

Undoubtedly Joseph was ordained to the holy priesthood under the hands of his father, Jacob, during the time Jacob lived in Egypt. The Abrahamic covenant was renewed with Isaac and Jacob. (1 Nephi 17:40.) In the Book of Mormon, the prophet Lehi, after reading the writings of Joseph from the plates of brass and expounding them to his family, commented: "I am a descendant of Joseph who was carried captive into Egypt. And great were the covenants of the Lord which he made unto Joseph." (2 Nephi 3:4.)

The gospel covenant was continued on through Joseph (D&C 27:10), who prophesied to his brothers shortly before his death, "God will surely visit you, and bring you out of this land unto the land which he sware to Abraham, to Isaac, and to Jacob" (Genesis 50:24). Joseph had his brothers swear by an oath that they would take his remains back to Canaan for burial when the Lord allowed them to return to their land of promise. (Genesis 50:25.) After serving as the honored viceroy of Egypt for eighty years, Joseph died at the age of 110.

New Insights through Joseph Smith

The biblical account is silent as to any records being written by Abraham and Joseph. Fortunately, considerable information is found in other authentic sources relative to their literary works. These sources include the writings that came into Joseph Smith's possession in Kirtland, Ohio, in 1835.

The subtitle of the Book of Abraham as it appears in the Pearl of Great Price declare that it is "A Translation of some ancient Records, that have fallen into our hands from the catacombs of Egypt—The writings of Abraham while he was in Egypt, called the Book of Abraham, written by his own hand, upon papyrus."

In this book of ancient scripture, which was translated by the Prophet Joseph Smith, Abraham reports that the ancient records delineating the chronology of the patriarchs beginning with Father Adam were in his possession. He also stated, "I shall endeavor to write some of these things upon this record, for the benefit of my posterity that shall come after me." (Abraham 1:28, 31.) Note that Abraham wrote his account after his name was changed from Abram to Abraham when he was ninety-nine years old, after he had left Egypt to return to Canaan. (See Genesis 17:1–8.) At that time he was explaining things Egyptian to his family in Canaan, who were and would be generally unfamiliar with the customs of the Egyptians. (See Facsimile 1, figure 12, and Facsimile 2, figures 1, 4, and 5.)

The Lord has commanded his prophets since the days of Father Adam to record significant events. Joseph, the son of Jacob, was no exception. The plates of brass, which Lehi's son Nephi took from Laban, were used to enlighten the Nephite nation of the doctrines and prophecies as recorded by prophets of God of the tribe of Joseph. The large plates, first made by Nephi and then continuously kept by the Nephites, a remnant of the tribe of Joseph, were a continuation of the brass plates.

Who initially made and wrote on those is not presently known, but it is clear that they contain many of Joseph's prophecies. One wonders if Joseph himself was not the originator of that sacred text. Nephi, son of Lehi, recorded: "And now, I, Nephi, speak concerning the prophecies of which my father hath spoken, concerning Joseph, who was carried into Egypt. For behold, he truly prophesied concerning all his seed. And the prophecies which he wrote, there are not many greater. And he prophesied concerning us, and our future generations; and they are written upon the plates of brass." (2 Nephi 4:1–2.)

These plates introduce four prophets of the tribe of Joseph who are not mentioned in the Jewish biblical text: Zenos, Zenock, Neum, and Ezias. (See Helaman 8:20; 1 Nephi 19:10; 3 Nephi 10:15–17.)

Abraham and Joseph were men of faith and of learning.

They were prophets and record keepers. Not only were they authorized caretakers of sacred texts, they were also prolific writers of sacred things they had witnessed.

Oliver Cowdery, speaking of the writings of Abraham and Joseph that Joseph Smith purchased, stated: "When the translation of these valuable documents will be completed, I am unable to say; neither can I gave you a probable idea how large volumes they will make; but judging from their size, and the comprehensiveness of the language, one might reasonably expect to see sufficient to develop much upon the mighty of the ancient men of God, and of his dealing with the children of men when they saw him face to face."[8]

One visitor to Kirtland who viewed the mummies and papyrus, an individual who was not a member of the Church, wrote: "They say that the mummies were Egyptian, but the records are those of Abraham and Joseph . . . and a larger volume than the Bible will be required to contain them.[9]

These reports are the only known accounts in which anyone has conjectured about the length of the published writings of Abraham and Joseph. It is safe to conclude, however, that early Church leaders thought that the sacred writings of the two great patriarchs were of considerable length.

THE WRITINGS OF ABRAHAM
AND JOSEPH IN EGYPT

The ancient Egyptians strongly believed in the eternal nature of man. Many understood the fleeting, temporary nature of mortality, which precedes the endless, eternal state of man. At death the bodies of the more affluent were prepared by skilled artisans for their final stage of existence. The entrails were carefully removed and embalmed in separate canopic jars.[1] Then the bodies were dehydrated and wrapped with many layers of linen strips. The entire process between death and burial usually took from forty to seventy days to complete.

When Jacob (Israel), Joseph's father, died and was embalmed in Egypt, according to the scriptures, "Joseph commanded his servants the physicians to embalm his father: and the physicians embalmed Israel. And forty days were fulfilled for him; for so are fulfilled the days of those which are embalmed: and the Egyptians mourned for him threescore and ten days." (Genesis 50:2–3.)

About a thousand years later, Herodotus, the renowned Greek historian of the fifth century B.C., visited Egypt and described the embalming process as he understood it:

> The mode of embalming, according to the most perfect process [first order of burial], is the following:—They take first a crooked piece of iron, and with it draw out the brain through the nostrils, thus getting rid of a portion, while the skull is cleared of the rest by rinsing with drugs; next they make a cut along the flank with a sharp Ethiopian stone, take out the whole contents of the abdomen, which they then cleanse,

washing it thoroughly with palm wine, and again frequently with an infusion of pounded aromatics. After this they fill the cavity with the purest bruised myrrh, with cassia, and every other sort of spicery except frankincense, and sew up the opening. Then the body is placed in natrum for seventy days, and covered entirely over. After the expiration of that space of time, which must not be exceeded, the body is washed and wrapped round, from head to foot, with bandages of fine linen cloth, smeared once with gum, which is used generally by the Egyptians in the place of glue, and in this state it is given back to the relations, who enclose it in a wooden case which they have had made for the purpose, shaped in the figure of a man. Then fastening the case, they place it in a sepulchral chamber, upright against the wall. Such is the most costly way of embalming the dead.[2]

Herodotus explained that the second order of burial was a less expensive process, and the third method was the least expensive, but in all three orders, the body was allowed to "lie in natrum the seventy days."

Those embalmed often had various objects buried in their sarcophagi (coffins) with their bodies, such as jewelry, written records, charms, and amulets. Nobility and others of the economic upper class frequently had papyri documents buried with them. Sometimes the papyrus would be buried "under the bandages, . . . between the hands, on the chest, or under the arms or legs."[3] These were primarily sacred documents that, according to their belief, provided the deceased person with necessary answers to enable them to successfully pass by the angelic guardians at the portals of heaven. If the deceased person valued the sacred words of a prophet of God, it would be appropriate to have such documents buried with him or her in the coffin.

When Did the Church-owned Mummies Live?

Because the present whereabouts of the four mummies and most of the papyri that were in the hands of the Smith family between 1835 and 1856 is unknown, accurately dating all the papyri or the mummies is impossible. However, scholars who have studied the eleven papyri fragments that were once part of the collection and that were returned to the Church in 1967 date that papyri late in Egyptian history. Some Egyptologists have dated Facsimile 1 between the last century before the Christian era and the first century of the Christian era (100 B.C. to A.D. 100).[4]

The original heading of the Book of Abraham published by Joseph Smith in 1842 states that it was "a translation of some ancient Records that have fallen into our hands, from the Catecombs of Egypt, purporting to be the writings of Abraham, while he was in Egypt, called the Book of Abraham, written by his own hand, upon papyrus."[5]

In 1842 Elder Parley P. Pratt published the Book of Abraham in England and the heading remained the same.[6] When the text was republished in England in 1851 in the first edition of the Pearl of Great Price, the heading was unchanged. However, in the 1878 printing of the first American edition of the Pearl of Great Price, the heading was changed from "purporting to be the writings of Abraham" to "the writings of Abraham," deleting the words "purporting to be." It has appeared this way in all editions published since then, including the present 1981 edition.

Commenting on the statement "written by his [Abraham's] own hand, upon papyrus," Dr. Hugh Nibley has written:

> Two important and peculiar aspects of ancient authorship must be considered when we are told that a writing is by the hand of Abraham or anybody else. One is that according to Egyptian and Hebrew thinking any copy of a book originally written by Abraham would be regarded and designated as the very work of his hand forever after, no matter how many reproductions had been made and handed down through the years. The other is that no matter who did the writing originally, if it was Abraham who commissioned or directed the work, he would take the credit for the actual writing of the document, whether he penned it or not.
>
> As to the first point, when a holy book (usually a leather roll) grew old and worn out from handling, it was not destroyed but *renewed*. Important writings were immortal—

for the Egyptians they were "the divine words," for the Jews the very letters were holy and indestructible, being the word of God. The wearing out of a particular copy of scripture therefore in no way brought the life of the book to a close—it could not perish. In Egypt it was simply renewed "fairer than before," and so continued its life to the next renewal. Thus we are told at the beginning of what some have claimed to be the oldest writing in the world, "His Majesty wrote this book down anew . . . His Majesty discovered it as a work of the Ancestors, but eaten by worms. . . . So His Majesty wrote it down from the beginning, so that it is more beautiful than it was before." It is not a case of the old book's being replaced by a new one, but of the original book itself continuing its existence in a rejuvenated state. No people were more hypnotized by the idea of a renewal of lives than the Egyptians—not a succession of lives or a line of descent, but the actual revival and rejuvenation of a single life.

Even the copyist who puts his name in a colophon does so not so much as publicity for himself as to vouch for the faithful transmission of the original book; his being "trustworthy (*iqr*) of fingers," i.e., a reliable copyist, is the reader's assurance that he has the original text before him. An Egyptian document, J. Spiegel observes, is like the print of an etching, which is not only a work of art in its own right but "can lay claim equally well to being the original . . . regardless of whether the individual copies turn out well or ill." Because he thinks in terms of types, according to Spiegel, for the Egyptian "*there is no essential difference between an original and a copy.* For as they understand it, all pictures are but reproductions of an ideal original." . . .

This concept was equally at home in Israel. An interesting passage from the Book of Jubilees [a text unknown before 1850] recounts that Joseph while living in Egypt "remembered the Lord and the words which Jacob, his father, used to read amongst the words of Abraham." Here is a clear statement that "the words of Abraham" were handed down in written form from generation to generation, and were the subject of serious study in the family circle. The same source informs us that when Joseph died and was buried in Canaan, "he gave all his books and the books of his fathers to Levi his son that he might preserve them and *renew* them for his children until this day." Here "the books of the fathers" including "the words of

Abraham" have been preserved for later generations by a process of renewal. Joseph's own books were, of course, Egyptian books.

In this there is no thought of the making of a new book by a new hand. It was a strict rule in Israel that no one, not even the most learned rabbi, should ever write down so much as a single letter of the Bible from memory: always the text must be copied letter by letter from another text that had been copied in the same way, thereby eliminating the danger of any man's adding, subtracting, or changing so much as a single jot in the text. It was not a rewriting but a process as mechanical as photography, an exact visual reproduction, so that no matter how many times the book had been passed from hand to hand, it was always the one original text that was before one. . . . But "written by his own hand"? This brings us to the other interesting concept. Let us recall that that supposedly oldest of Egyptian writings, the so-called Shabako Stone, begins with the announcement that "His Majesty wrote this book down anew. . . ." This, Professor Sethe obligingly explains, is "normal Egyptian usage to express the idea that the King ordered a copy to be made." Yet it clearly states that the king himself wrote it. Thus when the son of King Snefru says of his own inscription at Medum, "It was he who made his gods in [such] a writing [that] it cannot be effaced," the statement is so straightforward that even such a student as W. S. Smith takes it to mean that the prince himself actually did the writing. And what could be more natural than for a professional scribe to make an inscription: "It was her husband, the Scribe of the Royal Scroll, Nebwy, who made this inscription"? Or when a noble announces that he made his father's tomb, why should we not take him at his word? It depends on how the word is to be understood. Professor Wilson in all these cases holds that the person who claims to have done the work does so "in the sense that he commissioned and paid for it." The noble who has writing or carving done is always given full credit for its actual execution; such claims of zealous craftsmanship "have loftily ignored the artists," writes Wilson. "It was the noble who 'made' or 'decorated' his tomb," though one noble of the old kingdom breaks down enough to show us how these claims were understood: "I made this for my old father . . . I had the sculptor Itju make (it)." Dr. Wilson cites a number of cases in which men claim to have "made" their father's tombs, one of them specifically stating that he did so "while his arm was still strong"—with his own hand!

Credit for actually writing the inscription of the famous Metternich Stele is claimed by "the prophetess of Nebwen, Nest-Amun, daughter of the Prophet of Nebwen and Scribe of the Inundation, 'Ankh-Psametik,'" who states that she "*renewed (sma.w) this book* [there it is again!] after she had found it removed from the house of Osiris-Mnevis, so that her name might be preserved. . . . " The inscription then shifts to the masculine gender as if the scribe were really a man, leading to considerable dispute among the experts as to just who gets the credit. Certain it is that the lady boasts of having given an ancient book a new lease on life, even though her hand may never have touched a pen.

Nest-Amun hoped to preserve her name by attaching it to a book, and in a recent study M. A. Korostovstev notes that "for an Egyptian to attach his name to a written work was an infallible means of passing it down throughout the centuries." That may be one reason why Abraham chose the peculiar Egyptian medium he did for the transmission of his record—or at least why it has reached us only in this form. Indeed Theodor Bîhl observed recently that the one chance the original Patriarchal literature would ever have of surviving would be to have it written down on Egyptian papyrus. Scribes liked to have their names preserved, too, and the practice of adding copyists' names in colophons, Korostovstev points out, could easily lead in later times to attributing the wrong authorship to a work. But whoever is credited with the authorship of a book remains its unique author, alone responsible for its existence in whatever form.

There is early evidence for this idea in Israel in the Lachish Letters from the time of Jeremiah in which the expression "I have written," employed by a high official, "must certainly," according to H. Torczyner, "not be meant as 'written by my own hand,' but may well be 'I made (my scribe) write,' as in many similar examples in the Bible and in all ancient literature," even though the great man actually says he wrote it.

So when we read "the Book of Abraham, written by his own hand upon papyrus," we are to understand, as the Mormons always have, that this book, no matter how often "renewed," is still the writing of Abraham and no one else; for he commissioned it or, "according to the accepted Egyptian expression," wrote it himself—with his own hand. And when Abraham tells us, "That you may have an understanding of these gods, I have given you the fashion of them in the figures at the beginning," we do not need to imagine the Patriarch himself personally drawing the very sketches we have before us. It was the practice of Egyptian scribes to rephrase obscure old passages they were copying to make them clearer, and when this was done the scribe would add his own name to the page (289:3), which shows how careful the Egyptians were to give credit for original work only—whatever the first author wrote remained forever "by his own hand."[7]

Facsimile 2, the disk-shaped drawing, is called a *hypocephalus*. Champollion, the French linguist, so named such objects because they were made of metal or linen and usually placed under the head of the deceased (*hypo*, under, and *cephalus*, head). Some modern Egyptologists claim that they were so situated in order to keep the body of the deceased warm.[8] Dr. Nibley explains that the "round cushions" were placed in this way in order to keep the "sleeping dead . . . in touch with the universe."[9]

Hypocephali were used late in Egypt's long history, between the years 600 B.C. and A.D. 200. This dating would place at least one of the four mummies in that late time period and not contemporary with Abraham or Joseph. The twelve surviving papyri fragments and the hypocephalus appear to be documents of a late period.[10]

Record Keeping and Ancient Archives

From the beginning of earth's history, the Lord commanded the faithful to record significant teachings and events and in turn have them teach their posterity to read and write to enable mankind to learn from them. (Moses 6:5–6.) Seven generations after Adam, Enoch reminded the people, "A book of remembrance we have written among us, according to the pattern given by the finger of God; and it is given in our own language." (Moses 6:46.)

Abraham, who lived twenty generations after Adam, wrote:

"I shall endeavor, hereafter, to delineate the chronology running back from myself to the beginning of the creation, for the records have come into my hands, which I hold unto this present time. . . . The records of the fathers, even the patriarchs, . . . the Lord my God preserved in mine own hands; therefore a knowledge of the beginning of the creation, and also of the planets, and of the stars, as they were made known unto the fathers, have I kept even unto this day." (Abraham 1:28, 31.)

The Egyptian civilization was anxious to preserve its story. Extensive writings are found in pyramids and on obelisks, pillars, temple walls, walls of pit tombs, ostraca, and papyrus. Even though some of the well-built tombs and temples and their documents have survived the ravages of time and abuse, the papyri that have survived indicate that the writings were not confined to sacred and kingly matters alone.

John Ruffle states: "Their literature shows them to be a lively people, interested in all forms of human knowledge, experiencing and sharing the whole range of human emotion. Their written documents range from medical treatises to love songs, from philosophy to curt replies to tax demands. Some are written to preserve and pass on knowledge; some to provide propaganda for a failing deity or to prop up a shaky throne; others arise from the unburdening of a heavy heart or delight in a tale well told."[11]

It appears that as soon as there were writings, there were archives. The scribes of Egypt recorded important current events while maintaining the literary and spiritual gems of the past in their archives and libraries. Both Abraham and Joseph left indelible marks on the annals of Egypt, and some of their accomplishments have been preserved.

About 1500 B.C., one of Queen Hatshepsut's obelisk experts and chief adviser, Senmut, left the following inscriptions in his tomb: "I was the greatest of the great in the whole land. . . . The labor of all countries was under my charge. . . . I was a noble who was obeyed. Moreover I had access to all the writings of the prophets; there was nothing which I did not know concerning what had happened since the beginning."[12]

Elmer Johnson and Michael Harris report that an early theological library "was kept in a sacred place and presided over by a priest." They continue:

> Only the most important of the temple officials might have access to this library, and probably only a few of them could read. In most early societies, the scribe or the trained individual who could read and write was a most important person, and often only a few of the temple personnel belonged to this select group. The temple library may have been of the few, and by the few, and for the few, but it preserved the most important literature of a given religion, which was a basic cultural heritage for that particular group. In Egypt, Palestine, Babylon, Greece, and Rome, the temple collection certainly was among the earliest and most important forms of the proto-library.[13]

Ties between the House of Israel and Egypt

The writings of Abraham and Joseph, who spent many years in Egypt, may have been left behind either in sacred archives reserved for the writings of the prophets or in the archives of the royal family, since both spiritual and governmental leaders were renowned among the Egyptian sovereignty.

However, it is possible that the sacred writings of the two prophets were not left behind in Egypt. After Abraham left Egypt, he lived much of the last half of his long life in neighboring Canaan. And though Joseph died in Egypt and his body was placed in a coffin there, his remains were carried back to Canaan by Moses and the children of Israel during the exodus. (See Genesis 50:25–26; Joshua 24:32.) There are no records of any of his possessions or writings being taken to Canaan.

Even if the writings of Abraham and Joseph were not initially left behind in Egypt, however, it is easy to surmise how copies of their writings were later found in Egypt. Consider these possibilities:

• Moses, who was raised as a prince in Egyptian royal splendor, was well aware of his roots. Perhaps he had the writings of his honored ancestors, Abraham and Joseph, preserved in Egyptian archives.

• Solomon, Israel's illustrious king, married the Pharaoh's daughter and took her to Jerusalem to live. (See 1 Kings 3:1.) Did Solomon share copies of his ancestors' writings with his new father-in-law?

• Jeroboam, Solomon's successor in the Northern Kingdom, "fled into Egypt, unto Shishak king of Egypt, and was in Egypt until the death of Solomon." (1 Kings 11:40.)

• The prophet Jeremiah, a contemporary of the prophet Lehi, was taken captive into Egypt after the Babylonian captivity. (Jeremiah 43:6–7.) Could he have taken copies of the records of Abraham or Joseph with him?

• A Jewish colony built a temple patterned after Solomon's temple in southern Egypt on Elephantine Island in the fifth century B.C. Were these devout Jews, who reverently practiced the Hebrew religion, interested in the writings of the two prophets?

• Being warned in a dream, Joseph and Mary took the Christ child and fled to Egypt for safety when Herod issued his edict to kill the babes of Bethlehem. Did the holy family have copies of the patriarchs' writings in their possession?

• If one mummy and some papyri that came into Joseph Smith's hands have been accurately dated as late as the first century A.D., it is possible that the owners were Christian converts who died in Egypt. Tradition has it that Christianity was first introduced into Egypt by Mark, the writer of the second Gospel, soon after the death and resurrection of Christ. Would these early Christian converts have had the writings of Abraham and Joseph?

This list is not an attempt at completeness. Canaan and Egypt shared a common border. Egypt's preeminence, size, large population, water supply, and location made it a haven for numerous Israelites throughout their long intertwined history. There are innumerable ways that the writings of Abraham and Joseph or copies of them could have been entombed and later been discovered in Egypt in the early nineteenth century A.D.

4

LEBOLO AND THE
FRENCH REVOLUTION

The man who excavated the Egyptian mummies and papyrus that were purchased by the Latter-day Saints in Kirtland, Ohio, was Antonio Lebolo. His life story is an integral part of the whole episode, enabling us to piece this complex puzzle together.

Joannes Petros Antonius Lebolo, son of Petri and Marianna Meuta Lebolo, was born January 22, 1781, in Castellamonte in the Piedmont, in what is now northwestern Italy.[1] In his native Italian language, Antonio was known as Giovanni Pietro Antonio Lebolo; in English—John Peter Anthony Lebolo. His father, Pietro, was a community leader and a successful grocery man, a descendant of one of the oldest established families in Castellamonte,[2] about thirty miles north of Turin in a secluded setting with the Italian Alps forming a magnificent backdrop.

Southern Europe was in political turmoil during Antonio's youth. After having been ruled by the Sardinian monarch, the Piedmont had been captured by Austria. Then Napoleon Bonaparte, in neighboring France, invaded the area in April 1796 and drove the Austrians from the region. To Napoleon's army, consisting of thirty thousand starving soldiers, came Napoleon's famous proclamation: "You are badly fed and all but naked. . . . I am about to lead you into the most fertile plains in the world. Before you are great cities and rich provinces; there we shall find honour, glory, and riches."[3]

Amidst this political unrest Antonio married Maria Pollino

Marchetto the next year, in 1797. He was sixteen at the time, and Maria was twenty-one. Napoleon had no intention of driving the Austrians from the region and returning the rule to the Sardinian monarchy. (He incorporated it into the French Republic in 1802.) France's Piedmontese subjects could either cooperate with their powerful, ambitious conqueror or face the consequences. Lebolo chose to cooperate, and in 1799, at age eighteen, he volunteered to serve as a soldier under the French flag. The next year he was made a *brigadiere* (sergeant). On March 22, 1801, Lebolo was injured at the rebellion of San Agostino; the nature and extent of his injury is unknown, but it was sufficiently serious that he was discharged from the service. At the time he was a quartermaster.

Antonio appears to have been employed in police work after his release from the military. The records on his personal life are sketchy except that he and Maria had a son, Pietro Giovanni Enrici, who was born July 17, 1800, and died thirteen days later.[4] Ten years later the couple had a second son, whom they named Michael Pietro Antonio.

Antonio's whereabouts between 1802 and March 1808 and between January 1811 and July 1814 are unknown. He was in Castellamonte between March 1808 and December 1810, as he signed numerous legal documents during that period, records that are still intact in the archives at Turin. One author, Stanley Mayes, refers to him as "a former gendarme of Milan," which may account for his absence from Castellamonte in that period, although that statement is unconfirmed thus far in military or police records.[5]

Napoleon's Further Conquests

Napoleon Bonaparte was not content with capturing just Italy. His unbridled passion to be a powerful world ruler remained unchecked, and his interest now turned to Egypt. While Europe was entering a new age of political and industrial awakening, Egypt had remained dormant. The only formidable threat to Napoleon's ambition was England. He knew that if he conquered Egypt, he could seriously jeopardize Britain's lucrative overland trade routes to India. Besides, the French vividly remembered that the British had driven them from India about fifty years earlier and laid claim to their conquest.

With a force of 38,000 men, along with their animals, Napoleon's fleet of 328 ships crossed the Mediterranean Sea, anchoring at Abukir Bay near Alexandria, Egypt, July 1, 1798. The invaders also took with them to Egypt a select body of skilled scientists and artisans commissioned by Napoleon to document their findings in this ancient land of mystery. Among these 167 specialists were physicians, chemists, mineralogists, artists, cartographers, orientalists, zoologists, geographers, gunpowder experts, and mathematicians.⁶

The artists and scientists were in Egypt for only three years, but their impact on the Western world remains to this day. In July 1799 a large black basalt stone with engravings in three scripts—Egyptian hieroglyphic, demotic (a late, popular cursive Egyptian writing), and Greek—had been discovered at the Egyptian city of Rosetta, near the shores of the Mediterranean Sea. The French scholars could quickly see the potential value of this large stone, which became known as the Rosetta Stone. The Greek inscriptions, which were read at once, contained an Egyptian decree issued in 196 B.C. by the pharaoh Ptolemy V Epiphanes. Neither the hieroglyphic script nor the demotic was decipherable. But it was reasoned that all three writings contained the same information, which could provide a possible key to its decipherment. This proved to be the case.

Napoleon's group of scholars did a commendable work of translation, resulting in a twenty-four–volume publication printed between 1809 and 1813 titled *Déscription de l'êgypte.* This detailed encyclopedic work with its magnificent paintings and inscriptions caused a great sensation in Europe. It opened the eyes and aroused the interest of the Western world to this once great civilization, many of whose ancient monuments still existed, including pyramids, temples, obelisks, tombs, innumer-

A contempory view of Napoleon, surrounded by the savants, inspecting a mummy

able mummies, and numerous other artifacts. The easy accessibility of the antiquities was also a major factor.

Under Napoleon's military genius, the French army captured Cairo and within three weeks had essentially subdued the whole of Egypt. Napoleon, always conscious of himself and his desired impact on world history, told his men at Giza, "Soldiers, from these pyramids forty centuries look down on you."[7]

Soon the army marched to Upper Egypt to subdue the people there, while the accompanying artisans documented and recorded the spectacular sites as they proceeded. The distinguished French artist Vivant Denon, who was allowed to spend a day painting the ruins of the great temple at Dendereh, recorded, "Pencil in hand I passed from object to object, drawn away from one thing by the interest of another. . . . I felt ashamed of the inadequacy of the drawings I made of such sublime things."[8]

When the French military division rounded a bend of the Nile, and the ancient temples of Luxor and Karnak came into full view, a strange occurrence took place. On January 27, 1799, the French division came to "a spontaneous halt and burst into applause." A lieutenant recorded that "without an order being given, the men formed their ranks and presented arms, to the accompaniment of the drums and bands." The grandeur of the moment came when "an entire army paid a spontaneous tribute to antiquity."[9] The superb site was Karnak and ancient Thebes, the area from which the writings of Abraham and Joseph would be exhumed a few years later.

The French Are Expelled from Egypt

Napoleon's invasion of Egypt and its potential military ramifications did not go unnoticed by the British. On August 1, 1798, a month to the day after the French had landed, Admiral Horatio Nelson located and destroyed the French fleet anchored at Abukir. The British navy had no foot soldiers aboard to drive the French from Egyptian soil, but they effectively shut off their means of returning to Europe, severed their supply lines, and crippled their overall effectiveness. Without an adequate navy, the French could never effectively rule Egypt nor challenge England's dominance of the high seas.

A year later, on August 19, 1799, Napoleon abandoned his army and fled from Egypt. Shortly thereafter a British army landed at Alexandria, led by General Hutchinson, to whom the French General Menon surrendered. The French savants were allowed to keep their scientific and artistic collections with one exception. The highly acclaimed Rosetta Stone was surrendered to the British and shipped to London, where it is still prominently displayed in the British Museum. Fortunately the French had made wax copies of the trilingual stone, and these were shipped to France. Twenty-three years later a brilliant young French linguist, Jean Francois Champollion, working with the Rosetta Stone, would discover the key that would unlock the mysterious hieroglyphic writings of the ancient Egyptians.[10]

When Napoleon returned to Europe, his political and military career continued to flourish. At the height of his brilliant career, he controlled most of Europe. But after some disastrous setbacks, including an ill-fated attempt to invade Russia, he abdicated on April 1, 1814, and went into exile at Elba, a small French-owned island off the west coast of Italy.

Napoleon escaped from Elba in March 1815 and returned to France, where he organized his loyalists for one last burst of glory. But on June 18, 1815, at Waterloo, Belgium, Napoleon's final dreams of a world conquest were shattered. He was exiled by the British to the tiny isolated island of Saint Helena, in the south Atlantic, where he died May 5, 1821. In his will he stated, "I am dying before my time, murdered by the English oligarchy and its hired assassin," a reference to General Hudson Lowe, Great Britain's governor of Saint Helena.[11]

Lebolo Becomes an Exile

With Napoleon gone, the Sardinian monarchy was once again reenthroned. The king of Sardinia recovered his ancestral dominions of Savoy, Nice, and Piedmont and also acquired the Genoese Republic. Those who had been loyal to Napoleon were disliked by the reemerging monarchy, which labeled them "Bonapartists."

Antonio Lebolo, who had been involved in French law enforcement and in the military, would be offensive to the king, and so, like many other Bonapartists, he looked to Egypt as a new frontier far away from the problems of Europe. He had a friend of prominence in Egypt, Bernardino Drovetti, who had been France's consul general in Egypt between 1803 and 1814.

Drovetti was born and raised in Barbania, an alpine city in the Piedmont just seven or eight miles from Lebolo's hometown. He had served as a colonel in the French military in the Piedmont, where Lebolo served, and later served under General Joachim Murat, Napoleon's brother-in-law, in the Egyptian campaign. While protecting Murat in battle, Drovetti was badly wounded and his hand mutilated. Upon his release, he was honored for heroism by Napoleon, who assigned him to be France's diplomatic representative in Egypt in 1803.

When the French royal family returned to power in 1814,

Bernardino Drovetti and his agents

Drovetti was discharged because he was an avowed Bonapartist. Because he would be unwelcome if he returned to his native Piedmont, he remained behind in Egypt, where over the years he had established a close friendship with Mohamed Ali, the pasha of Egypt. Ali respected Drovetti's judgment and business acumen and welcomed his advice in commercial matters.

Thus, Antonio Lebolo left his wife, Maria, and his young son, Michael Pietro Antonio, to begin a new life in Egypt and an association with Bernardino Drovetti in archaeological excavations.

5

LEBOLO: EXCAVATOR AND ARTIFACTS DEALER IN EGYPT

Between 1815 and 1830, Egypt became a popular tourist attraction for Europe's well-to-do as well as a place of refuge and exploitation for many adventurers who were escaping the problems of the post-Napoleonic period. Antonio Lebolo arrived in Egypt early in this period. The exact date of his arrival is unknown, but certainly he was there by 1817. In the Registry Office's secret register in Turin in 1817 is a reference to correspondence from a Lebolo in Alexandria, Egypt, to "Most Illustrious Secretary."[1] The letter has not been located to confirm that this is Antonio, but it seems almost certain that it is. A letter from the Consulate General of the Sardinian Government to his "Eccellencae" at Livorno, dated July 3, 1817, states, "The letter you sent for Mr. Lebolo will be delivered into the hands of the first captain who will leave to Alexandria." It is signed "Spagnolini."[2]

In August or September 1817, Giovanni Battista Belzoni from Padua, a former European circus strong man who worked in the Egyptian archaeological excavations for Britain's Consul General Henry Salt, spoke disparagingly of two of Bernardino Drovetti's agents:

> At Gournou I found two more agents of Mr. Drovetti busied in digging the ground in all directions, and who had been tolerably successful in their researches for mummies. These agents were of a different cast from the two Copts who had been there before. Both of them were Piedmontese; one a rene-

*Giovanni
Belzoni, who
worked in
Egyptian
archaelogical
excavations*

gade who had deserted from the French army when in Egypt,
and entered the service of the Bashaw; the other had left
Piedmont after the fall of the late government. I did not like to
begin my work in any place near these people, and therefore
gave up the idea of prosecuting my researches in Gournou.[3]

Lebolo is undoubtedly the person Belzoni referred to who
had left Piedmont after the fall of the Napoleonic government.
Lebolo had several other encounters with this giant-sized rival,
"the Great Belzoni," that attest to this conclusion. Belzoni
referred to the other agent, named Rosignani, as a renegade.[4]

M. D. Brine, an English hosteler and merchant who had
established both a sugar factory and a rum factory along the
Nile at Radamone, referred to Lebolo in a March 1818 letter to
Drovetti. Lebolo was apparently involved in a controversy with
a peasant over some gold coins, and Brine was persuaded that
he was not guilty of any crime, explaining: "When the Casciff

was going to beat the peasant, he [Lebolo] went to another room saying that he would rather lose all the antiquities of this world, provided that none would be beaten."[5] Brine also mentioned that Lebolo gave the peasant and his wife gifts in behalf of "Mr. Drovetti, former General Consul of France."[6] This letter confirms that by March 1818 Lebolo was in Drovetti's employ, working with antiquities.

After Napoleon's defeat, the European exiles who chose Egypt as their new domicile had to adjust to a radically different lifestyle. Many former officers and men of means and prominence found themselves unemployed in a world economically, socially, religiously, linguistically, and culturally foreign to their own. While visiting at Brine's hotel, Colonel Fitzclarence, a former British military officer, observed that about forty Europeans, mostly Italians, worked in his sugar factory.[7]

At dinnertime, the former British officer met "a French officer of the late emperor's [Napoleon] imperial guard."[8]

> His name was Balle, and he had fled from France after the battle of Waterloo. He was a very handsome man, and had been in the Spanish War, so that we fought our battles over again. . . . He was anxious to go to America; the further the better, he said from France. I could not but pity the cruel dilemma in which he appeared to be. He told me he was of the legion d'honneur, and had hoped to have risen high in the service. His is a sad fall, from basking in the beam of imperial favour to becoming almost an object of charity to a sugar manufacturer.[9]

To make matters worse, one might add that a former French officer was now subservient to an Englishman as well. Such was the lot of numerous "Bonapartists."

Lebolo's Activities in Egypt

Most visitors to Egypt confirmed in their published works that the magnitude of the antiquities of Egypt were even more than they had pictured and anticipated. Ancient Thebes was undoubtedly the most magnificent city of ancient Egypt that was still somewhat intact. With the marvelous ruins of the city

Italian Count
Carlo Vidua, who
visited Antonio
Lebolo in Thebes

"of a hundred gates" on the east bank of the Nile, and additional ruins and the pit tombs of between sixty and eighty pharaohs, their wives, and their courtiers on the west bank, Thebes was a focal point for tourists, adventurers, and excavators. With the exception of the pyramids of Giza in the north and a few other marvels, most of the impressive antiquities of Egypt are located up the Nile River in southern Egypt.

Many European travelers, no matter how enthusiastic they were about the remarkable antiquities, also referred in their journals to the inconveniences and primitive conditions so alien to their own. The fascinating stories, treasures, engravings, and paintings that had enticed them to visit Egypt did not prepare them for the ever-present mosquitos, flies, disease, lice, fleas, poverty, cruelty, slavery, barking dogs, and thievery that they encountered in their day-to-day world. This was a wild, new frontier. But even these problems, more nuisances than deterrents, only temporarily dampened their zeal for exploring this exciting new world—a setting that had preserved the wonders of the past under layer upon layer of rubble and debris.

Antonio Lebolo worked for Bernardino Drovetti in Upper

Egypt in the years between 1817 or 1818 and 1821 or 1822. Drovetti lived in Cairo, about four hundred miles downstream from Thebes, close to the pasha whom he served as an adviser in many commercial enterprises. Mohamed Ali used Drovetti's expertise to help him upgrade his lagging economy. Drovetti did not personally oversee the excavations in Thebes, and, in fact, it appears that he seldom visited there. That was Lebolo's job. Count Carlo Vidua, a man of title, influence, and means from Turin, visited Thebes in 1820. In a letter to his father, he spoke of Lebolo's graciousness and his broad authority over the excavators in Thebes:

> But, among so many marvelous things, that are possible to be admired at Thebes, the most curious one of all is the valley where the kings' sepulchers lay. It is rather a lonely valley, arid, horrible, in which some holes like caverns are seen. Entering these caverns, long galleries, halls, chambers, and cabinets are found, in short, they are underground palaces, all covered with painted bas-relieves; and it is very marvelous. It is wonderful the preservation of the colors, the amount of the works, the scrupulous attention used to make them. Lately, a new one was discovered which surpasses all the others in beauty, in the perfection of the work, and in execution. I visited it two times. The second time I spent the whole day there, examining everything; it was already late evening, and I couldn't move myself away from there.
>
> I dined inside there in a beautiful hall, much more elegant than our ballrooms. Also, I believe that, considering all, this sepulcher of the king of Thebes is a much more sumptuous dwelling than the dwellings of our living European kings. Who, do you think, gave me the honor of those sepulchers, and who reigns in Thebes in exchange of the dead king? A Piedmontese, Mr. Lebolo from Canavese, formerly a police officer in service of France, came to Egypt and was employed by Mr. Drovetti in the excavations, which he does continuously in Thebes. Our Piedmonteses really have a ready spirit, and are capable of succeeding in everything; from police work to antiquities is a big jump. In those ten days that I lived in Thebes, Mr. Lebolo accompanied me, took me everywhere, had me come to dinner at his house, which is among monu-

ments and half embedded in tombs, all filled with mummies, papyruses, and little statues. An Egyptian bas-relief was the top of the door; we made fire with pieces of mummies' coffins. Mr. Lebolo commands those Arabs; sometimes he has about 200 or 300 at his command; the Turkish commander respects him for fear of Mr. Drovetti. Oh, if Sesostri had lifted his head up, and had seen a Piedmontese commanding in the city with one hundred doors! When you see count Lodi, tell him that we drank to his health among the ruins of Thebes. Mr. Lebolo served for some time in Piedmont with the carabineers and spoke very highly of his leader. He was also under count of Agliano in Savoy. To show my gratitude to such courtesy of this Canavese-Theban man, I took the task of sending a letter to his family; which I include here, praying you to make sure that it will reach its destination.[10]

In addition to acting as superintendent of the archeological digs for Drovetti, Lebolo was also involved in buying and selling antiquities. Giovanni ("Yanni") D'Athanasi, who was employed in Thebes by Henry Salt, the British consul general, wrote:

> Not many days after they left, Mr. Salt was taken dangerously ill and his recovery was tedious, and attended with some hazard. As soon as he found himself well re-established in health, his thoughts again reverted to his darling objects of research and he desired me to go and occupy the place which Mr. Belzoni had lately filled at the excavations which were being carved out at Thebes. Upon this gratifying mission I set out without loss of time, and immediately on my arrival arranged the order of the excavations; I also made some purchases of antiquities, not withstanding all the difficulties which I experienced through means of a certain Antonio Lebolo, a countryman of Mr. Drouetti, who had just been buying up all the antiquities the Arabs had to sell. Singularly enough, however, he had left in their hands, for what reason I know not, the finest specimen of all; namely, a Greek mummy, that of the wife of a governor of Thebes, named Soter Corneliou, which I immediately purchased.[11]

Not only did Lebolo supervise Drovetti's excavations in Luxor and purchased antiquities in his behalf, but he was also

*Henry Salt, the
British consul
general in Egypt*

his representative in hosting visiting dignitaries. Vidua's Theban entries in his journal read as follows:

May 7, 1820 - . . . to Luxor or Thebes

May 8, 1820 - Gave a quick glance at Luxor and visited Canak [Karnak] all day, all alone (first visit).

May 9, 1820 - Rest. Conversed with Mr. Lebolo and Rifaud. In the evening at the temple of Luxor.

May 10, 1820 - Morning at Madamad—second short visit to Canak [Karnak].

May 11, 1820 - Morning. Third visit to Canak [Karnak] with Mr. Rifaud and Lebolo.

May 12, 1820 - Passed on to Gurna—at Lebolo's house—walked to Memnonio. In the morning I saw Medine Abu—evening at small temple of Isis and at Memnonio.

May 13, 1820 - Morning first visit to tomb of a king discovered by Belzoni—evening at the second great statue.

May 14, 1820 - Rested in a boat. Evening at the temple of Gurna.

The Colossi of Memnon

May 15, 1820 - After having measured the temple of Gurna and the granite doors, spent all day in the Belzoni Tomb—there I ate lunch.

May 16, 1820 - at Lebolo's house at Memnonio, at the statues of Medine Abu, there measured an isolated temple, then to the temple of Der Scelued—finally at Luxor, in the evening on the pillars of Luxor.

May 17, 1820 - Last visit to Luxor with Mr. Rifaud. Traveled to Gurna. Visited three tombs of the Kings. The evening with Lebolo.[12]

Notice that on May 12 Vidua mentions that he visited Lebolo's "house." Lebolo actually occupied one of the numerous caverns that dotted the hillside above the Arab village of Gournah. The magnificent ruins of the Rameseum (the mortuary temple of Ramses II), called in 1820 "the Memnonio," was about a mile from Lebolo's "house." He and Vidua walked from the cave dwelling to the Memnonio. On May 16 Carlo Vidua again referred to Lebolo's "house" at Memnonio.

It was the custom in that day for important visitors to have

El Gournah, where Lebolo resided while in Egypt

their names carved on the ruins of antiquities by experienced craftsmen. When Dr. Brian L. Smith and I visited the Theban area in February and early March 1992, we specifically looked for graffiti on the temple walls and ceilings, obelisks, and tombs, searching for Vidua's name. We located it in several conspicuous places on monuments on both sides of the Nile. I later contacted a Belgian scholar, Roger O. De Keersmaecker, who has spent considerable time in collecting and cataloging non-Egyptian graffiti from the monuments of Egypt. He reported that he had located Vidua's name twenty-seven times, chiseled on some of the most famous monuments in Egypt.[13]

Dr. Smith and I found Lebolo's name chiseled on the west side of a large pillar on the east side of the Rameseum. The carving reads "Lebolo 1820." Many other European dignitaries' names were observed nearby, chiseled on the pillars and walls. Asked whether he had located Lebolo's name carved elsewhere in Egypt, De Keersmaecker confirmed that we had located the only such carving he has thus far located.

In Drovetti's correspondence file in Turin are letters from

Vidua "graffiti" on Egyptian tomb

several other persons who wrote to Drovetti and thanked him for Lebolo's graciousness. One man, John Hyde, told Drovetti, "When you next write to Mr. Lobilau [Lebolo] may I . . . obtrude upon your indulgence as to request you will remember me kindly to him, and reiterate my thanks for the kindly hospitalities I received from him during my stay at Gourna."[14]

F. Brouzet, a retired senior officer of the Royal Gendarme, wrote, "If the good Mr. Lebolo is still with you in Alessandria, please give him our regards, we wish him all the best in the world in his work."[15]

F. Cailliaud, a French writer and mineralogist, mentioned the tomb where Lebolo stored his collection of antiquities: "When we arrived in Gourna Mr. Lebolo brought me to his house where together we opened the tomb where he had collected the antiquities, I, having personally broken off the seal of the trunk containing the papyri and one after the other one I inspected them."[16]

Linant De Bellefonds wrote to Drovetti: "At 9 o'clock we arrived in Gourna . . . [and] had dinner at Libollo's [Lebolo]

Lebolo's name carved into the Rameseum

house; we went to his house to see two very pretty young ostriches."[17]

William John Bankes, a scholar and traveler, who served for a time as secretary to Henry Salt, wrote of Lebolo:

"Saturday June 19, 1819. Had the first visit to Mr. Lobau [Lebolo]. Visited the large statues of Memmon and his wife.

"Monday 21st June 1819 Dined with Mr. Loblau [Lebolo] at Gournae.

"Sunday 18th July 1819 dined with Mr. R. Lopped and with Mr. Lobelauu [Lebolo]."[18]

Valley of the Nobles and Pit Tomb 33

The burial grounds on the west bank of the Nile at Thebes are divided into three sections: the Valley of the Kings, the Valley of the Queens, and the Valley of the Nobles. The most splendorous tombs belonged to the kings, the wealthy pharaohs, who spared little in preparing for eternity. Leading excavators such as Bernardino Drovetti and Henry Salt were interested in excavating in the Valley of the Kings, where the richest treasures of the past would logically be unearthed. In theory, one who is grave robbing shouldn't waste time digging in paupers' graves. Since Lebolo served as Drovetti's foreman in Thebes, what he and his crews discovered belonged to his employer. Because Drovetti had lost his position as consul general after 1815, he did not have an adequate income until he sold some artifacts, so he could not pay Lebolo and the work crews regularly. In order for the excavators to survive, both Drovetti and Salt allowed them to collect artifacts on their own after they had met their commitments to their employers.

It appears that Lebolo was allowed to personally excavate in the Valley of the Nobles—the burial site of prominent men, such as scribes, artisans, mayors, advisers, administrators, and astronomers, who aided the pharaohs. Their tombs, carefully hewn, were adorned with murals, personal effects, and considerable wealth, but visibly pale in comparison with most of the tombs of the pharaohs. Count Carlo Vidua, Lebolo's affluent guest, wrote: "Mr. Lebolo works successfully in his new career; he found beautiful pieces for the Drovetti museum; and since he was allowed by him to do some excavations of his own, he gathered for himself a small collection, which will bring him a moderate fortune."[19]

Since Lebolo was superintending many archeological digs and directing the labors of hundreds of workers over a period of several years, it is impossible, with the available facts, to determine where he exhumed the eleven mummies that were later shipped to the United States, the last four of which were purchased by Joseph Smith. Many LDS tour groups traveling in the Middle East stop at Pit Tomb 33 in the Valley of the Nobles, supposing this to be the site where Lebolo discovered the writings of Abraham. It is important to review how this pit tomb came to be selected and to see if such a conclusion is warranted.

Oliver Cowdery, Joseph Smith's scribe, told Michael H. Chandler's story as follows:

> The records were obtained from one of the catacombs in Egypt, near a place where once stood the renowned city of

Thebes, by the celebrated French traveler, Antonio Lebolo, in the year 1831. He procured license from Mehemet Ali, then viceroy of Egypt, under the protection of Chevalier Drovetti, the French Consul, in the year 1828, and employed four hundred and thirty-three men, four months and two days (if I understand correctly)—Egyptian or Turkish soldiers, at from four to six cents per diem, each man. He entered the catacomb June 7, 1831, and obtained eleven mummies. There were several hundred mummies in the same catacomb; about one hundred embalmed after the first order, and placed in niches, and two or three hundred after the second and third orders, and laid upon the floor or bottom of the grand cavity. The two last orders of embalmed were so decayed, that they could not be removed, and only eleven of the first, found in the niches.[20]

In *Who Was Who in Egyptology*, a biographical index of influential people in Egypt, Warren R. Dawson mentions that Lebolo was excavating in a pit tomb in Thebes at Gurneh. Dr. Ross T. Christensen, a former associate professor of anthropology and archaeology at Brigham Young University, couples that statement with Oliver Cowdery's statement quoted above to hypothesize that Pit Tomb 33 was possibly the tomb whence came the writings of Abraham.[21] Dr. Christensen explained his rationale for this hypothesis:

> As I recall, I was doing research in 1960 and 1961 on Thebes for a paper I was to present at the 13th Annual Symposium of Archaeology of the Scriptures. In my work, I came across a book titled *Topographical Bibliography of Ancient Egyptian Hieroglyphic Texts, Reliefs, and Paintings*. The volumes were by two British female scholars, both highly reputed, who were named Bertha Porter and Rosalind L. B. Moss. They in turn had taken their information on the matter from Duemichen, a nineteenth century German Egyptologist of note. Volume one, titled *The Theban Necropolis*, was a storehouse of information. The book had the ground plans of what we call the private tombs of noblemen. From the information given by Dawson, that Lebolo's discovery was a pit-tomb—one under the surface of the ground—and that it had some Ptolemaic mummies in it, I thought that the tomb in which Lebolo found the mummies would have been a private tomb, not a tomb of a Pharaoh, and would be presented by the authors.

So of all those presented, I simply picked out the largest tomb to study. It was the tomb of Petamenopet, a nobleman of the twenty-sixth or Sait dynasty, and called by Egyptians today, Tomb 33. I also noticed that it seemed to have a number of recesses in it, which I figured could be the "niches" Oliver Cowdery referred to. As I counted the niches, there seemed to be sufficient to hold the 100 embalmed mummies that Oliver reported were in these niches. Then as I began to compare this ground plan with other ground plans, it appeared to me that Tomb 33 could be the tomb Lebolo discovered. It certainly was at Gurneh, it was right in the area of the pit-tombs, and it seemed to be the only one with a "grand cavity" big enough to hold a total of three or four hundred mummies, two or three hundred of which were in the second and third order. Also, the presence of the recesses or "niches" in the side, sufficient and big enough to house about 100 mummies of the first order, was another factor. Tomb 33 seemed to be the only one that fit the description. A great number of the ground plans had no "niches" at all, and some of the ground plans did not seem big enough to house three or four hundred mummies. Thus, it was by a process of elimination that I concluded with my hypothesis that Tomb 33 could be the tomb in which Lebolo found his mummies.

Question: Would not the Egyptian government have records of all the original excavations?

One must remember that Egypt was not controlling her own land during much of the nineteenth century, and during much of the period of excavations, the governments of Turkey, France, and Britain were involved. I strongly doubt that one could learn from the Egyptian records information that would not be available to him in any large library.

Now, I suppose I have been recognized by some as the discoverer of Lebolo's tomb, but let me assure all interested parties that this conclusion is based only from a study of published sources, a study accomplished far away from the actual site of the tomb. The conclusion is only a possibility, albeit a rather good one at present. This assumption does not depend upon any personal field work.[22]

Dr. Christensen's tentative conclusion raises several questions and problems:

1. Did the excavators dig down or destroy the brick walls of

the pit tomb where the eleven mummies were exhumed? Often the excavators destroyed the adobe brick walls as they dug, looking for anything that might have been buried outside the walls of the tomb. Therefore, the pit tomb that housed the eleven mummies may no longer exist in its pristine condition as it was prior to its excavation.

2. Warren Dawson mentioned that Lebolo excavated a tomb in Gurneh without any attempt to designate its location. It was a tomb that contained a cache of twelve or thirteen Ptolemaic mummies and papyri that have subsequently been shipped to several prominent museums in Europe. The find has received some notoriety because of Greek inscriptions on some of the sarcophagi. This pit tomb, if it contained only the Soter collection, as it is called, could not be the same tomb in which the eleven mummies were found as described in the Oliver Cowdery account, since all eleven mummies were received intact by Chandler in New York City. No doubt Lebolo was the superintendent who excavated the Soter family tomb, but it was not the tomb that contained the eleven mummies that were shipped to the United States.

Dr. Christensen was cautious in suggesting Pit Tomb 33. He merely selected the largest pit tomb in Gurneh in the Porter and Moss bibliography and supposed that it must logically fit the description. This tentative conclusion was made from the Porter and Moss publication and description, as he said, and not from any archaeological fieldwork.

3. What is a niche? By definition, a niche is "a recess in a wall esp. for a statue."[23] If one follows this definition exactly, Pit Tomb 33 does not have niches in the walls. If small anterooms that adjoin the larger cavity are called niches, then this definition would apply to Pit Tomb 33 and many other tombs in the Valley of the Nobles as well.

4. Several statements from Michael H. Chandler's account in the *History of the Church* are incorrect. For example, Lebolo's name is incorrectly spelled Sebolo.[24] The year of the excavation is given as 1831, but this is inaccurate since Lebolo died in

Piedmont in 1830. Lebolo did not procure a license from Mehemut Ali in 1828, since he was living in Castellamonte, Piedmont, at that time. It is more likely that he received a license in 1818. He did not enter the catacomb on June 7, 1831, as reported, because he died the year before. Who wrote the account that Chandler quoted to the Church leaders in Kirtland? Because of several incorrect dates, including some after Lebolo's death, it is obvious that this explanation was not written by Lebolo but by a relative or a friend after his death, or perhaps by the shipping agent. There may have also been problems translating the document into English from French, Italian, German, or even Arabic. Certainly the information did not originate with Chandler, since he would lack the necessary details to produce such a document.

Early Excavations of Pit Tomb 33

In *Der Grabpalast des Patuamenap,* a book on the Theban tomb of Pedamenopet (Pit Tomb 33), German Egyptologist Johannes Duemichen drew a scale model of Pit Tomb 33. He stated that it had been first sketched by Richard Pococke, an English minister, some 150 years earlier. Pococke's works, published in London in 1743, describe Pit Tomb 33 as follows:

> I went into two very extensive apartments cut in the rock, on the south side of those hills we went to the day before. . . . To one of them A. in the thirty-fourth plate, is a descent of ten steps to an area cut in the rock, which leads to a room in which are square pillars cut out of the rock: Beyond that there is a long room with pillars on each side in like manner; all the apartments are adorn'd with hieroglyphics; but the stone is scaled in such a manner, and is so black in some of the first apartments, that there is great reason to think the place has been damaged by fire. Beyond these rooms, the apartments extend to the right, there being several steps down; one part leads to a gallery cut round the rock, which has some apartments on one side; and in this, as well as in the apartments of the other grotto mark'd B. are holes cut perpendicularly down to other apartments below, where I saw doors and openings, and where probably might be cut under the palaces of the

Kings of Thebes, if they were not the very palaces themselves, to retire to when they pleased, from their tents or other places more exposed to the wind or heat.[25]

Pococke explored Pit Tomb 33 in 1737–38, which means that Pit Tomb 33 was accessible to visitors at least by 1738. He and his hired men either dug down to the tomb or the tomb had already been exploited before his arrival, since most grave robbers were searching for coins and other objects, and the coffins and the mummies were often desecrated in their quest for wealth. This being the case, Lebolo did not need 433 men to dig for four months and two days to enter this tomb, as the account in the *History of the Church* states.

Lise Mannicke, a Danish Egyptologist, wrote:

It is possible to identify two of the tombs Pococke saw, for in his publication he gave very neat plans of them. They are the two Saite tombs which now have the numbers 33 and 37. He includes a page of description of the architecture, the walls much damaged by fire and the bones lying about, but he takes the tombs to be the "apartments" of the living, dug under the palaces of the kings (by which he meant the mortuary temples). However, it is of great interest to find here the first mention of a decorated private tomb.[26]

The enmity that existed between the French and the English did not remain behind in Europe nor did it end at the Battle of Waterloo. Giovanni Finati, a native of Ferrara, Italy, and an interpreter for European travelers in Egypt, explained how excavation sites were staked out and protected:

Excavations and researches were almost immediately resumed upon Mr. Salt's account, under the direction of his secretary, Mr. Beechey and of Mr. Belzoni; and I found that some curious discoveries had been already made by them previous to their departure for the upper country, and especially in what seem to have been the principal private sepulchers of the city. But the rivalry of the French consul, Drovetti, in the same pursuit and speculation, had become very inconvenient, and soon led to violent and continued altercations between the adherents of the two factions; so that all the site of ancient Thebes was subsequently, either by the direction or the tacit consent of the government, (administered at that time in Upper Egypt by the Defterdar Bey,) portioned out and allotted into two great divisions, as French and English ground, each party being only entitled to dig within his own limits, and only authorized to appropriate what should be found there, an expedient which, however, very imperfectly allayed their jealousies and contentions.[27]

Has Any Site Excavated by Lebolo Been Found?

A few years ago a colleague of mine at Brigham Young University, Dr. S. Kent Brown, was sitting next to Dr. Laszlo Kakosy, a renowned Egyptologist from Budapest, Hungary. Both were en route to a Coptic convention in Poland. During their conversation, Dr. Kakosy asked Dr. Brown if he recognized the name Antonio Lebolo. Lebolo's name, he reported, is carved over a passageway in Pit Tomb 32 in the Valley of the Nobles, where Dr. Kakosy and his crew were excavating in behalf of the Hungarian government. Dr. Brown told Dr. Kakosy that I had been pursuing this research for several years, and we subsequently began to correspond in 1986. The following statement is an excerpt Dr. Kakosy shared with me from one of his many publications:

> Many valuable objects were removed from the tomb about 1818–1820 when it was visited by Antonio LEBOLO an Italian adventurer who acted as a dealer in antiquities. He mentioned a tomb in Gurna from which he took away numerous mummies and coffins. There are serious indications that the shaft-tomb, hitherto not identified, was no other than the tomb of DJEHUTIMES. We can adduce the following evidence to support this assumption:
>
> 1. There is no doubt that LEBOLO had visited tomb 32 since he wrote his name on the ceiling of the tunnel-passage.
>
> 2. He speaks of a shaft-tomb lined with mud brick. Tomb 32 has a large and a smaller shaft; many mud bricks have been found inside the tomb. There are mud brick constructions in Rooms I, and III and in the tunnel. Many stamped bricks bear the name of DJEHUTIMES.
>
> 3. There are two lids of granite sarcophagi in the Museo Egizio in Turin. One of them bears the name of Overseer (of

Dr. Laszlo Kakosy and H. Donl Peterson in front of Pit Tomb 32

Amun) DJEHUTIMES. The style is that of the nineteenth Dynasty; the sarcophagus found in tomb 32 bears the same name and title. No trace of a lid has been discovered in the burial chamber by our Mission.

The other object in Turin is the upper part (head and trunk up to the hips) of a lid of granite sarcophagus belonging to a woman. This displays the same style and features as that of DJEHUTIMES. Although the inscriptions containing the name are lost, there is little doubt that it can be attributed to ISIS, wife of DJEHUTIMES. This is additionally confirmed by the presence of the fragments of the missing lower part in the tomb. A check of the measurements of these fragments still remains to be done; if these are in accord, it will be verified that the unbroken part had been taken, probably by Lebolo, while the fragments lying scattered here and there in the rubble had been left in situ.

4. A lid of a Ptolemaic stone sarcophagus, again in Turin, was made for the scribe SHEP-MENU, son of NES-MENU. We know the names of both from tomb 32, where they are written on mummy-wrappings. So this is one more object found in the tomb of DJEHUTIMES in the last century.

5. The best documented of LEBOLO's plundering were the coffins and the mummies of the SOTER family, now scattered in a number of museums (Berlin, British Museum, Leiden, Louvre, Turin). This was a noble family in Thebes in the second century A.D., probably of Greek origin, the members of which adopted Egyptian funerary beliefs and rites. Some of them had Greek, others Egyptian names. This find became famous through the representations of the zodiac on the coffins.

During our excavation a mummy of the Roman Period has been discovered which displays similarities to those of the SOTER family. In this case there is no doubt that it was LEBOLO who took the finds from the tomb. As to the origin of the three lids of stone sarcophagi there is no information in the files of the museum in Turin. However, their arrival to Turin makes it probable that they too had been transported by LEBOLO.

Thus, one is left with the impression that in the early last century, after a number of plunderings in Antiquity and later, numerous complete coffins with mummies in them were still left in the tomb. Earlier intruders had searched primarily for metal objects.[28]

The early nineteenth-century explorers and tourists left their graffiti behind in the tombs, on the walls, and on any other possible surface to immortalize their presence there. Speaking of Egypt, one nineteenth-century visitor stated: "This country is a palimpsest in which the Bible is written over by Herodotus, and the Koran over that."[29] The excavators laid claim to their tombs by engraving their names on the walls and other obvious places.

Lebolo's name has been found in only one tomb: Pit Tomb 32. Dr. Kakosy states that several hundred mummies could be stored in this large tomb. Could Pit Tomb 32 be the site from which the sacred writings were removed? It is a possibility, but it is only one of several sites where Lebolo had laborers digging. His name will probably be found engraved in other pit tombs and caves by future students interested in this research.

6

LEBOLO RETURNS TO EUROPE

Once antiquities were exhumed in Thebes, if they were not soon sold near the excavation sites, the dealers frequently shipped them down the Nile to the more accessible market-places at Alexandria on the Mediterranean, where they were either sold or stored in warehouses pending future sales. In 1821 and 1822 Lebolo is frequently mentioned conducting business in Cairo and Alexandria. From the known documents he is not mentioned excavating anyplace after 1820; rather, he seems to have spent his time buying and selling artifacts and exotic animals. While Lebolo was excavating for Drovetti in upper Egypt he was also acquiring antiquities. Recall that Giovanni D'Athanasi, who worked for Henry Salt in the Theban digs, wrote in 1819 that he had purchased some antiquities "notwithstanding all the difficulties" he had experienced "through means of a certain Antonio Lebolo, a countryman of M. Drouetti, who had just been buying up all the antiquities the Arabs had to sell."[1]

Lebolo left Egypt for Europe sometime in 1822. Whether this is the first time he left Egypt is uncertain, but it appears to be the first time he is mentioned arriving in Trieste. In the Trieste newspaper *Dell' Osservatore Triestino* dated October 12, 1822, his name appeared in a column listing recent arrivals and departures of prominent people. Two entries are relevant: "Ant. Lebolo pos. per Venezia," translated as "Antonio Lebolo, land owner, departing for Venice"; and "Bern. Drovetti neg. per Treviso," translated as "Bernardino Drovetti, merchant, departing for

63

THE ITALIAN PENINSULA IN THE EARLY 19TH CENTURY

Trentino

Lombardy

Venetia

Venice[3]

Trieste[4]

Trieste

Castellamonte[1]
Turin[2]

Piedmont

Parma

Modena

Tuscany

Papal
States

Sardinia

Kingdom
of the
Two Sicilies

1. Castellamonte: Lebolo's birth place and place of death
2. Turin: Capital of Piedmont
3. Venice: The city where Lebolo dealt in Egyptian artifacts
4. Trieste: Port of quarantine for Central Europe

Treviso." This Bernardino Drovetti is almost certainly not the consul general, but his nephew by the same name. A Giuseppi (Joseph) Lebollo is listed as traveling to Treviso the same day as this Mr. Drovetti.

There appeared to be more on Lebolo's mind than antiquities when he left Egypt in 1822. For one thing, Maria, his wife of twenty-four years, had died in Castellamonte on November 7, 1821, at the age of forty-five. Particulars about her death are unknown. The only reference from Lebolo that may allude to her health or death—or perhaps only his prolonged isolation from his family—is in a letter dated November 25, 1821, that he wrote from Alexandria to a Mr. Segato in Cairo. He concluded with these words: "In the meantime please take care of my family."[2] He had not been home to his native Piedmont for several years and probably felt that he couldn't return without facing possible incarceration.

Lebolo Remarries

The story takes a strange turn when we learn that on October 10, 1822, two days before the newspaper notice of Lebolo's departure from Trieste to Venice, an unmarried black woman about nineteen years of age named Anna Mora (which means Negress), who is referred to as Anna Mora Darfour and also as "Donna Affricana" (African lady), and her two young daughters were accepted at the Institute of the Catecumena at Venice, to be indoctrinated in Christian teachings. Apparently Lebolo accompanied Anna and her two daughters on the ship from Egypt to Trieste. At the Catecumena, Anna Mora Darfour was given the Christian name of Anna Maria.

On June 12, 1824, Anna Maria and her older daughter, Rosina, who was about four at the time, were baptized, and Rosina was renamed Rosa Maria. The younger daughter, who was about two, had been baptized previously in Trieste and given the name Maria Catherina. It appears that she was ill when she arrived in Trieste, and as a precaution she had been baptized because of her illness. On her mother's baptism day, this child was given the full church baptismal rites. According to the church records, the godmothers and witnesses at the June 1824 baptisms and confirmations were there at the request of Bernardino Drovetti.[3]

Following the baptisms that day, Antonio married Anna Maria Darfour. One historian, A. Bertolotti, explained that Lebolo "married a black woman, whom Drovetti gave him as a gift, after he provided her with civil and religious education."[4] The parish entry reads:

Venice

Parish of St. Mary of the Rosary, commonly called St. Dominic alle Zattere.

Year 1824, 12 June, Sig. Antonio, the son of Pietro Lebolo, married first to the late Maria Marchetti born in Castellamonte (Diocesis of Ivrea) in Piedmont, presently domiciled in Alexandria, Egypt and Anna Maria Darfour, daughter [guest] of this reverend house of future christians, having acted in accordance with the three canonical laws and applied for marriage, were united in matrimony by Rev. Agostino Kvijungich the Prior of the above Institute and in the presence of those attending the ceremony at the Church of St. Giobatta of Catecumena at the altar of the Blessed Virgin.[5]

It is assumed that Anna Maria was a former slave taken from Darfour in western Sudan, south of Egypt, where blacks were frequently captured, marched in chains to Egypt, and sold there on the auction block. Slavery, both black and white, was still practiced by both Europeans and Americans at that time, and many prominent Europeans living in Egypt had black mistresses. It is not known if Anna Maria's two young daughters were Lebolo's children born to him in Egypt, or if she had been Lebolo's mistress in the land of the pharoahs, or if the children were hers by another man.

The day after Antonio married Anna Maria, another interesting account appeared in the Catecumeni church records:

Venice at the Catecumen
June 13, 1824
Giovanni Antonio Lebolo, formerly Said moro Affricano [black African], was accepted into this pious house of the Catecumena on the 27th of March 1823, at about 11 years of age, to become a Christian.

He was baptized today in the church of this pious institution of the Catecumen by me, Prior Agostino Kvijungich.

Godfather at the sacred baptismal font was Sig. Antonio Lebolo, a merchant and landowner and son of Pietro from Castellamonte, in Piedmont, and Marianna Meuta.

Who was this black African boy to whom Lebolo gave his Christian name and for whom Lebolo was listed as godfather? Because he was baptized the day after the marriage, he may have been Anna Maria's relative, such as a younger brother, or a personal acquaintance.

We have no evidence that the young boy ever lived with Antonio and Anna Maria, and he is never mentioned in the family parish records in Castellamonte. This brief account is included here because someday his name may appear in some newly discovered records, and this information may assist some historians who are otherwise baffled.

Between Trieste and Egypt

Notice that Lebolo's place of residence in June 1824 was recorded on the marriage record as Alexandria, Egypt. There are several documents in which Lebolo was mentioned as doing business in Europe and Egypt between 1822 and 1825. He was not only recognized as Drovetti's agent in Egypt, but he was also called upon to do favors for various people even after he left the Theban digs. This record is meager, but the records that we have found are listed here.

On April 22, 1823, Antonio Lebolo and Bernardino Drovetti, the consul general's nephew, arrived in Trieste from Venice.[6] At that time Venice was about eleven hours by sailing vessel from Trieste, the Austrian port where much international trade was carried out.

On June 16, 1823, Antonio Lebolo, "a merchant from Venice," arrived in Trieste.[7]

On January 28, 1824, J. Rifaud wrote to Baron Drovetti from Du Fayoum about a grievance he had with Lebolo:

> Since Mr. Lebolo has returned to Egypt, he should think of the amount of 1,000 piastres he owes me. I have documents and notes of the goods that I gave him. I hope that you, being the General Consul of the nation, would like to take in consideration this fact and do justice to me.
>
> I took the liberty to write to you many times during his absence and also before Mr. Lebolo's departure; now that he's back I hope he won't rob me of what I have the lawful right to possess.[8]

At one time Rifaud and Lebolo were co-agents under Drovetti. Rifaud correctly refers to Drovetti as France's consul general again in 1824; Drovetti served as France's consul general in Egypt between 1803 and 1814 and was reinstated under the restoration there between 1820 and 1829.

The Trieste newspaper dated June 12, 1824, indicated that Antonio Lebolo had departed from Trieste to Venice on June 10, just two days before his wedding to Anna Maria.

On August 16, 1824, Lebolo departed from Trieste inland to Udine, according to the August 28 newspaper listing.

The general aide-de-camp and great-master of horses of the king of Wurttenberg wrote to Drovetti from Stuttgart in October 1824 and thanked him for the successful arrival of some horses from Nubia. He also requested another shipment of horses, sheep, and livestock. In the letter he states: "Mr. Lebolo, who will have the honor of handing you this letter, is interested to present one [a letter] from me to His Royal Highness Le Bassa."[9]

A man named Filiberto Maruchi wrote to Drovetti from Cairo on February 8, 1825, about some financial misfortunes he was having in Egypt and added this statement: "Mr. Lebolo saw the white horse and he says that it's beautiful; he says that another, the black one, is for him, a gift from Abdin Bey of Gondola, and they say it is very beautiful."[10] Several Europeans who had moved to Egypt in the Lebolo years were also involved in the exotic-animals trade along with the buying and selling of antiquities.

A traveler named G. B. Brocchi sent a letter, dated February 25, 1825, to his brother, concerning which the editor of his published journal wrote: "The above-mentioned Mr. Lebolo coming from Cairo, was passing through Bassano toward the end of 1824, and then went to Monaco, commissioned by the viceroy of Egypt to present to the sovereign two ostriches of extraordinary beauty."[11]

Several major European archeological collections are beholden to Lebolo for his excavations and sales. The Kunsthistoriches Museum in Vienna is indebted in part to Lebolo's efforts. In a book by Egon Komorzynski, written in 1965, we read:

> In every instance, the further additions of that collection are considered old Egyptian memorials that the Austrian doctor, Ernst August Burghart, under the director of the emperor, king, court and state council, collected in Egypt during 1821. The largest share was bought by Burghart from a collector by the name of Antonio Lebolo in Alexandria, and the remainder was probably purchased from art dealers. He did not undertake to do his own archaeological digging. Sad to say, it was not then nor later undertaken to make up an exact listing of his acquisitions. From several summary listings it is known only that the amount consisted of 9696 pieces of money, 30 knightly antiquities that were meant for the Emperor's collection, 60 small statues, 27 papyri, statues out of bronze or glazed pottery, amulets (13 of which were of gold), canopies and other assembled vessels, which came from three mummies that were in double enclosed coffins.[12]

The Vatican museum in Rome is the beneficiary of some of Lebolo's efforts. Dr. Giovanni Marro, in summarizing a letter from French architect Francois Gau, dated May 10, 1820, said that "Lebolo has sold for 10,000 Roman Scudi to the pontifical government a rich collection of Egyptian antiquities displayed in Rome in the Vatican Museum."[13] Included in this collection were ten large granite statues.

The Soter collection, divided among several prominent museums in Europe and Egypt, was unearthed by Lebolo's men in Thebes. Of a late period, the collection contained Greek inscriptions that were warmly received by Western scholars, who could personalize the mummies, coffins, and artifacts because the language could be read. The Soters were prominent Greeks in upper Egypt who adopted some Egyptian ways, and Cornelius Soter was archon (mayor) of Thebes. B. H. Stricker lists portions of the Soter collection in Turin, the British Museum in London, the Bibliothèque Nationale and the Louvre in Paris, the Berlin Museum, and museums in Leipzig, Florence, Leyden, and Cairo.[14]

Home to Castellamonte

After being away from home for about nine years, Antonio Lebolo returned to Castellamonte in late 1825 or early 1826. When he left, he was in exile and facing an uncertain future in Egypt, having had to leave behind his wife Maria and their young son, Pietro, his extended family, friends, and career. When he returned to the Piedmont, Lebolo was fairly prosperous. His new family consisted of his wife Anna Maria, her two daughters, and Joseph, a son born to Antonio and Anna probably in Trieste. A second son, Joannes, was born in Castellamonte February 4, 1826, and a third son and their last child, Joannes Thomas, was born in Castellamonte November 24, 1827. Pietro, Antonio's sixteen-year-old white son by his first wife, suddenly had his father back, a new stepmother about seven years older than he, and several new siblings.

One biography referred to Lebolo's lifestyle in Castellamonte as "oriental pomp."[15] A recent historian wrote that the small, isolated community never forgave Antonio for bringing a black wife and his somewhat eccentric lifestyle into that cloistered alpine setting.[16]

In Castellamonte, Lebolo became involved in sundry business transactions between 1826 and 1829, including the grocery business and the purchasing and selling of a considerable amount of real estate. He was generous, perhaps to a fault, in lending money to many borrowers. One biographer stated that because of his flamboyant lifestyle, he was soon reduced to poverty. A review of his inventory and financial affairs at his death indicates that this conclusion is not accurate. He loaned a considerable amount of money, but if most of these debtors had paid their obligations, his family would probably have fared quite well.

THE WILL AND DEATH
OF ANTONIO LEBOLO

When Michael H. Chandler sold the mummies and the accompanying papyri to the Latter-day Saints at Kirtland, he gave the Church leaders a somewhat detailed account about the discovery of the mummies and the illness, death, and will of Antonio Lebolo. According to Oliver Cowdery's record of Chandler's statement, "on his way from Alexandria to Paris, [Lebolo] put in at Trieste, and, after ten days' illness, expired. This was in the year 1832. Previous to his decease, he made a will of the whole, to Mr. Michael H. Chandler, (then in Philadelphia, Pa.,) his nephew, whom he supposed to be in Ireland. Accordingly, the whole were sent to Dublin, and Mr. Chandler's friends ordered them to New York, where they were received at the Custom House, in the winter or spring of 1833."[1]

Once again there are several statements in Chandler's account that are inaccurate. He said that Lebolo entered the catacombs in 1831. However, Lebolo was probably not involved in digging after 1822, and he died in 1830. The account also mentioned that in 1832 Lebolo was in Trieste, on his way to Paris, when he became ill; and that after a ten-day illness, during which time he made out his will,[2] he died in Trieste, leaving the eleven mummies to his Irish nephew, Michael H. Chandler, who he supposed was living in Dublin, Ireland. There appears to have been no will legally recorded by Lebolo in Trieste. The state archives do not list such a document. The date when Lebolo supposedly willed the antiquities could not have been 1832, since he died in Castellamonte, not Trieste, in 1830.

Antonio did draw up a will in Castellamonte, Piedmont, three months before his death.[3] In the will, dated November 17, 1829, he explained:

> I have decided, while I am able to and am sound of mind, and in perfect control of my senses, although ill in my body, to take care of my temporal possessions by means of this present will and testament.
>
> I give and I leave to my wife Anna, because of her chaste and honest condition of a widow, the usufruct of my goods and real estates, but in such usufruct living together with my universal heirs and with my parents Pietro and Marianna Lebolo.[4]

The will indicated that there was an estrangement in the family, for Lebolo continued:

> And if my aforementioned wife would not or could not live with them [her in-laws and her children], in such a circumstance, I give and leave to her for her alimony and clothing, the yearly amount of 240 lire, which will be paid by my heirs or for them by their guardian, otherwise in advance, and I want that my mentioned wife be satisfied and content for such yearly amount, without requiring anything else from my heirs, under the law of the "quarta uxoria" [fourth wife], that she might want to claim.[5]

After providing for his faithful nurse, Luigia, who cared for him during his illness, and giving a generous contribution to the Catholic church, Lebolo continued:

> And as for the remainder of my possessions, real estates, credits, personal properties, interests in shops, bonds and stocks, wherever they are and can be found, I proclaim and nominate as universal heirs Pietro, my only child from my first wife, and also Giuseppe, Giovanni, and Tomaso, other legitimate and natural children of mine from my aforementioned second wife, all four in equal part and portion; and in the case that one or more of them might die in their youth, in this case I substitute for the dead one the other living children, always in equal parts.[6]

No Irish nephew is mentioned in Lebolo's will.

Lebolo nominated his cousin Giovanni Meuta to serve as guardian for his three youngest sons, who were "still of tender age to be assisted by Antonio's younger brother Giuseppe."[7]

Apparently Lebolo's oldest son, Pietro, was having a difficult time accepting either his younger half-brothers on equal terms or the circumstances under which he anticipated that he would have to live with them in the future. Lebolo specifically stipulated in his will that he was "particularly forbidding my said first born son Pietro to divide my possessions which I want to remain undivided until my youngest son reaches his legal age." He also made provision for Pietro to be independent of the remaining family in Castellamonte if he chose to leave, by promising him title to seven parcels of land amounting to over 615 *tavole* (38.1039 square acres).[8] This provision was allowed "not to force him [Pietro] against his will to live with his other brothers, my universal coheirs, and with the already aforementioned usufructuaries, already since now to keep in place of the interest of my inheritance, that could belong to him in his adulthood."[9]

Lebolo gave to his father all the dowry of his first wife, Maria (Pietro's mother).[10] However, shortly after the ink had dried, he had second thoughts about the restrictions he had placed upon Pietro. Eighteen days later he recalled the notary, Giacomo Buffa, and the witnesses and issued the following addendum relative to Pietro's inheritance:

> Said Mr. Lebolo, who writes the addendum has revoked and revocates the prohibition and obligation to his first born son both for the division of his possessions and for the dowry of his late mother Maria Pollino Marchetto; he [Mr. Lebolo] wants that his mentioned son Pietro Lebolo can, as he pleases, determine the division of the inheritance, even without his brothers and coheirs having yet reached their legal age, provided that said first born son will take care of all the expenses that will be necessary to such division, and if the division will be postponed until the legal age of the aforementioned heirs, the expenses will be equally divided among the coheirs. And as for the said dowry of his mother, said Mr. Lebolo, who is

writing this addendum, wants that his aforementioned son Pietro can dispose of it as he pleases, and use as he will see fit.[11]

Events Following Lebolo's Death

During the night of February 18–19, 1830, Antonio Lebolo died at the age of forty-nine at his home in Castellamonte. In his will, he requested that after his death, the following men would assist in taking an inventory of his possessions: his cousin, Giovanni Meuta; the three younger boys' guardian, Lebolo's brother Giuseppe; the notary Giacomo Buffa; and Lebolo's friend Francesco Bertola.

Surely the eleven mummies germane to our story were listed among Lebolo's personal belongings—or were they? To inventory all of his effects took several men nine days to com-

Home of Antonio Lebolo in Castellamonte, Italy

plete, since his grocery business contained a large inventory that prolonged the procedure.

On February 27, 1830, in the room where Lebolo died, the designated auditors found some promissory notes.[12] On March 3, a book with a blue cover was located, containing 104 sheets listing the names and amounts owed by those who were apparently extended credit at Lebolo's store.[13] On March 4, a book of ninety-two pages was found, listing some names of others who were indebted to Lebolo.[14] On March 5, Lebolo's considerable real estate holdings were catalogued. He had previously listed the names of those to whom he was indebted and had given to the auditors their names and the amounts he owed.

Toward the end of the eighty-eight–page inventory is this statement: "Finally it has been verified by the heirs that nothing more is possessed by the dead Mr. Antonio Lebolo."[15]

Are we off on a tangent, or do we have the right Lebolo? If a picture of Drovetti had not been listed among Lebolo's personal possessions in the room where he died, one might wonder if we had traced the wrong man. Where were the eleven mummies that he exhumed in Egypt and that he reportedly willed at his death? No mummies were listed in the inventory nor mentioned in the will, an amazing fact when the market value of antiquities was so very high. No Irish relatives were mentioned in the will. Anna Maria and his four sons were Antonio's sole heirs.

Mr. and Mrs. Francesco Morozzo have lived in the Antonio Lebolo house in Castellamonte for many years. It has changed but little since Lebolo lived there more than 160 years ago except for the addition of water and electricity.

In an interview conducted by Dan C. Jorgensen, who was serving in Italy as an LDS mission president, Mr. Morozzo remembered playing as a little boy in the attic of Lebolo's house, "an attic filled with boxes of old letters, keepsakes, etc." He also remembered "much foreign correspondence with strange non-Italian stamps." Unfortunately, as time passed and he inherited the home, the attics were cleaned out and all of the "junk was burned."[16]

The Lost Mummies Are Found

An explanation is necessary to clarify how Lebolo's will was located.

In the fall of 1984, I was in Italy on a professional development leave from Brigham Young University to pursue this research. Several predecessors had searched unsuccessfully for Lebolo's will in various Piedmont archives, and I too had previously spent time at the county courthouses in Ivrea, Castellamonte, and Turin, also without success.

One Sunday that October I attended a branch meeting of the LDS church in Turin, where I met a sister who might be able to assist me and my research assistant as an interpreter and translator in the local libraries, museums, and archives. Patrizia Pianea, a convert to the Church of one year, was very proficient in English, French, and her native Italian. As we were discussing my project, a little boy about two years of age, closely pursued by his watchful mother, walked into the empty classroom where Patrizia and I were visiting. The mother, Jerrilyn Comollo, was formerly from Arizona. She heard me mention to Patrizia the name Antonio Lebolo and told me that her husband, Adriano, had at one time looked in vain for any documents about Lebolo. Needless to say I was anxious to meet Adriano, a district high councilor who would be speaking in the branch sacrament meeting that morning.

At the conclusion of the services, we visited for a time and Jerrilyn and Adriano invited my assistant and me to dinner later that week. During the dinner, Adriano mentioned that he had seen a legal document with Antonio Lebolo's signature on it in the state archives in Turin. I was scheduled to fly to Egypt within a day or two, so I asked Adriano to send me a photocopy. I also asked if he would check other documents issued by the same notary to see if he had worked with Lebolo on any other legal matters, and emphasized how important it was to this research to locate Lebolo's will.

In Cairo a week later I received a phone call at four in the morning from my wife, Mary Lou. The Comollos had phoned my home in Orem, Utah, and excitedly announced that they had found Lebolo's will, a lengthy inventory, and another document that mentioned eleven mummies. Even though I had hopes of finding some excellent material in Egypt relative to Lebolo's sojourn there, this breakthrough took precedence, so I canceled my commitments in Egypt and arranged to return to Italy.

We spent the next week in the state archives in Turin, photographing the will and inventory and looking for any new information that may be found there. One document that pointed our attention in a new direction was the legal paper that mentioned the eleven mummies. It too had been prepared by Giacomo Buffa, the notary who had drawn up Lebolo's will and who had helped to inventory his holdings. The paper, dated July 30, 1831, read as follows:

> Special power of attorney from Mr. Giovanni Meuta, guardian of the children Giuseppe, Giovanni and Tomaso Lebolo to the head of Mr. Pietro Lebolo from Castellamonte.
>
> [Giovanni Meuta] desiring to award, as it depends on him, all the interests of his said administered children Lebolo, and procured for them the liquidation of the following belongings left them by the said late Antonio Lebolo, their common father, that is 1) *Eleven mummies given by him to Mr. Albano Oblassa, so that he [Mr. Oblassa] would arrange to sell them.* [Emphasis added.] 2) As of Mr. Gustavo Bourlet, debtor of 1800 fiorini, to be exchanged with said Mr. Lebolo, with also a woman's large scarf, referred to as the Turkish scarf, worth 300 fiorini also given to said Mr. Bourlet, so that he [Mr. Bourlet] would arrange to sell it. 3) And finally as of Mr. Giovan Batista Gauttier and Rosa Gauttier, without a fixed residence, owners of a menagerie of foreign animals, both debtors to said Mr. Lebolo for 2,150 fiorini [recorded] in six promissory notes written in favor of [Mr. Lebolo] himself, in order to take care of the accounts concerning the above mentioned matters and credits and to obtain the cash from them, [Mr. Meuta] has decided and has been nominated as guardian of said Lebolo children, as he determines and nominates in this present document, Mr. Pietro Lebolo, first born son of said Antonio, born and residing in Castellamonte, and presently living in the aforementioned city of Trieste, here I, the under-

signing notary, am accepting for him, as functioning "ex offi-
cio publico," so that said Mr. Meuta, according to his position,
has given and gives to Mr. Pietro Lebolo all and complete
power to summon to any court or Magistrate said Oblassa,
Bourlet and Gauttier, and propose against them all the reasons
he might believe as necessary, in order to receive said credits,
to deal with them and receive any amount of which they
might be in debt, either [if they pay] spontaneously or by ver-
dict, in favor of the [people] mentioned for any amount until
final and general satisfaction is reached. Also with authority
given to said Mr. Lebolo to delegate, in the name of the principal and for the interest of said Lebolo children in relation to
the above specified credits, one or more proxies to whom he
would also give all necessary and opportune authority, with
maximum power to said Mr. Pietro Lebolo to do, for the above
specified credits, all that the principal could do, with the
clause *cum libera et ut alter ego.*[17]

It would appear that the family located a ledger book of
Lebolo's business transactions in Trieste of which they were
unaware when the will was initially read and the inventory was
concluded nearly a year and a half before. The newly found documents not only listed four people still indebted to Lebolo, possibly with the accompanying contracts, but it also contained six
promissory notes.

Some writers have questioned if Lebolo had more than
eleven mummies in this collection. This legal document should
finally answer the question. Eleven mummies were mentioned
in this particular collection—no more, no less. The twelve or
thirteen mummies with Greek inscriptions, referred to as the
Soter collection, were from another dig and another collection
organized by Lebolo.[18] Some writers have confused the Soter
mummies, which were divided among several European museums, with the eleven sent to New York City. This collection of
Lebolo's mummies in Trieste totaled eleven in 1831, and eleven
mummies were acquired by Michael H. Chandler in New York
City in 1833.

Since Antonio Lebolo was in Trieste in October 1822 and
perhaps earlier, and subsequently made several more trips to

Egypt, it is uncertain when these particular mummies arrived in Trieste from Egypt. They could have been stored in Egypt and/or Trieste for several years. The Albano Oblasser Shipping Company, which transported goods between the two areas and other parts of the world, had been in business for several years prior to 1822 and remained in business several years after 1831.

It is difficult, if not impossible, to trace the mummies aboard the ships that freighted them from Egypt to Trieste and from Trieste to New York City. Since antiquities were in demand and brought a high price, the shippers, leery of the unscrupulous, were not anxious or willing to broadcast the nature of their merchandise aboard ship. Consequently, shipping manifests nearly always had such generic listings as "25 boxes" or "40 crates" or "merchandise" and did not specify the particular contents.

It is regrettable that we do not know if Pietro Lebolo was successful in his legal endeavors in Trieste, but he apparently had some personal obstacles to overcome. In the court docket in Trieste dated September 12, 1831, Pietro Lebolo was charged with "truffa" (fraud). The case was dismissed, and the existing documents do not tell us who pressed the charges. The actual proceedings of the court cases are missing from the state archives in Trieste and are reportedly unavailable elsewhere. No 1831 court cases have been located in Trieste with the names mentioned either as plaintiffs or defendants. Gustavo Bourlet was found guilty of fraud, a felony, in a Trieste court case in 1828, and he was found guilty of several infractions. But none of his fraudulent acts in 1828 appear to be tied with any dealings he had with Lebolo.[19]

Postscript from Castellamonte and the Lebolos

We are about to leave Italy and focus our attention on the mummies in the United States; but before we do this, a short note on the Lebolo family seems appropriate to partially complete the story. On October 10, 1831, over a year and a half after Lebolo's death, his widow, Anna Maria, returned to Castellamonte in company with Giuseppe Brogliatti to try to claim some personal property she had left behind. According to a legal document, she was then living in Turin, about thirty miles away. Her children were not living with their mother but still resided in Castellamonte. The document states:

> He [Antonio Lebolo] has given the usufruct of all his goods, real estate, and personal property, to his wife Anna and to all sole heirs who are: Pietro, Giuseppe, Tommaso and Giovanni, all brothers and all his sons. If by chance, his wife Anna cannot or will not live with them he has provided for her for food and clothes 240 lire per year without claiming anything more.
>
> Since that Anna, Lebolo's widow, does not want to live with her sons and having already a new residence in Torino, after having made known her decision to Mr. Giovanni late Bernardino Meuta attorney and guardian of Lebolo's heirs, she asks of the same guardian to give her some personal property to be determined and systematically pay the sum due.[20]

Those entrusted to judge such matters granted to Anna the following personal belongings: "The gold ring with the inscription "amour" listed as number 211 valued at seven lire; the "gold collier" valued at 70 lire listed as number 213 and also the cornel trimmed in gold listed as number 216." [Number 216 in the inventory reads "a broken gold and a gold cornel all valued at 19 lire.] . . . "[21]

The assets and the liabilities of the inheritance were explained to Anna, as well as the fact that there were many financial uncertainties because of the many debtors. Arrangements were made for her to be paid quarterly. Since she was illiterate, she consented to the agreement by signing a cross on the document.[22] One might wonder if she was living in a Catholic convent in Turin as she had done in Venice, since her whereabouts are not known thereafter. Convents were required only to provide the numbers of residents and not to disclose their names.

Lebolo's children died relatively young.

• Maria Lebolo, Anna Maria's youngest daughter, passed away on April 29, 1832, at age twelve "from an unexpected disease." She was buried in Castellamonte.[23]

• Rosa Lebolo died less than three months later, on July 18, 1832, at age sixteen and was buried in Castellamonte.[24]

• Joseph Lebolo, Antonio and Anna's oldest son, died at age nine on March 17, 1835.[25]

• Pietro Lebolo, Lebolo's oldest and only white son, died November 21, 1843, at thirty-three. (His death notice lists his age at death as thirty-five.) He had been a wax dealer.[26]

• Tomaso Lebolo, Antonio and Anna's youngest son, a steward on the bark *Mimosa,* fell overboard and drowned in Boston harbor December 26, 1857, when he was thirty.[27] His death certificate lists both of his parents, Antonio and Anna, as deceased.

The fate of Antonio and Anna's second son, Giovanni, is unknown. He probably left Castellamonte; otherwise his death certificate should have been located in the local parish records, which have been fairly well scrutinized by several researchers.

Are These Mummies the Right Mummies?

I returned home from Italy in late November 1984 with photocopies of the will, the inventory, and the legal authorization for Pietro to check on the eleven mummies in Trieste that had been entrusted to Albano Oblasser and were to be sold in behalf of Lebolo's four sons. One link was missing in the story. How could we know that these mummies were the eleven that Michael Chandler received, the ones with which the writings of Abraham and Joseph were found? In early March 1985, frustrated about this missing piece of the puzzle, I wrote to the Comollos. Adriano reported what happened:

> At the beginning of March '85 we received a letter from Professor Peterson: ". . . we need to find . . ." It struck me as a divine order, so back to work.
> At first Jerri and I conjectured that any other news concerning the destiny of those mummies could only be found in Trieste. However, just for thoroughness, we decided to cast one last glance in the Archives of Torino. I felt an inspiration, after I had expressly prayed for that problem, to seek among the notaries of Torino, not among those of Ivrea, and there we found the line connecting Italy with America.
> All this has been a wonderful experience and we have felt

to be in some way connected with Joseph Smith and have felt nearer to him.[28]

The document they found, which proved that the eleven Lebolo mummies that Albano Oblasser was authorized to sell were indeed the mummies sent to New York City, was a notarial document issued by F. Clemente Cleonzo in Turin on October 5, 1833, in behalf of Pietro Lebolo. It states:

Special Power of Attorney from Pietro Lebolo in favor of Francesco Bertola, Professor of Veterinary Medicine.

Year of the Lord 1833, Oct. 5, in Torino in my office on the 3rd floor of S. Albano's House, No. 18 S. Tomaso Street, in front of me, Royal Notary Clemente Cleonzo. In the presence of Mr. Antonio Bruno of Bra and Mr. Vincenzo Cuire of Vigone, him too living in this capital, witnesses requested and found fit, known by me and by my constituent Mr. Pietro Lebolo.

Here assembled in front of me Royal Notary and in the presence of the above mentioned witnesses, Mr. Pietro Lebolo of the late Antonio, born in Castellamonte and living in this capital (Torino) who acts in his own behalf and acts in his capacity as special and general procurator with the ability to designate other special power of attorney for Giuseppe, Giovanni and Tomaso, Lebolo brothers dependent upon their tutor Sig. Meuta Giovanni, as instilled with the act of July 30, 1831 received Buffa, instilled in Castellamonte on the same day, paid 3.87 lire as from receipt Buffa properly stamped by the Department of Foreign Affairs, all of the universal heirs of their late father. Pietro Lebolo has called and calls as his special procurator Francesco Bertola son of the living Francesco also born in Castellamonte—Piedmont and living in Philadelphia, Professor of Veterinary Medicine who accepts me here, myself Notary undersigned, acting as public official accepting for him, therefore he receives the authority to claim the 11 mummies and other antique objects located in various boxes belonging to the deceased Antonio Lebolo who sent them to Albano Oblasser of Trieste. Albano Oblasser sent them to New York to the house of Mr. M'Led and Quellerspie of Meetland and Kennedy. Mr. Bertola has authority to sell them to whoever he thinks will fulfill the conditions, pay the amount that the procurator will decide and he will send the same through quittance, and in case of dispute he will protect the interests of the Misters constituents and he will take care of all of the problems that might come up in order to obtain a quick liquidation of such objects. In other words he will do whatever the constituents would do if they were to conduct the transaction themselves.

Mr. Bertola will do everything under the *cum libera ut alter ego* stipulation with promise to ratify everything he will do as it is ratified at once and will account for his actions. Of this request I have received public witness and I have read and pronounced the present act and pronounced the content of the present act for the clear understanding of the parties involved and the witnesses undersigned.[29]

The veterinarian who had left Castellemante and moved to Philadelphia, Pennsylvania, was Francesco Bertola Jr. His father, the senior Francesco Bertola, was the man to whom Lebolo referred in his will as "my friend" and whom he asked to assist in inventorying his personal holdings. Young Francesco was authorized to legally pursue the combined shipping firms of Maitland & Kennedy and McLeod & Gillespie in New York City in behalf of the Lebolos to receive their money for the sale of the eleven mummies and some other boxes of antiquities.

It is probable that Albano Oblasser still had the mummies stored in Trieste when Pietro Lebolo checked on them in the summer of 1831. Why they were sent to New York City and not to Rome, Vienna, London, Paris, or some other European city is not known; possibly mummies were a greater curiosity in the United States than in Europe in 1833 and would bring a higher return.

There are some unsolved problems as to why the Lebolo family had not received the quittance from the sale of the mummies, since Michael H. Chandler had them in his possession at least six months before the Lebolos sent the letter authorizing Francesco Bertola Jr. to follow through on the shipping costs, customs, and other charges relative to the eleven mummies arriving in the United States, and paying the Lebolos for their sale.

How does Michael H. Chandler, an Irish immigrant, figure

into the story as Lebolo's heir when all of Lebolo's possessions were willed to his wife Anna and his four sons?

How do we reconcile Chandler's story that he inherited the eleven mummies with the legal document that clearly states that two New York maritime companies were authorized to sell them for the Lebolos for the highest price, and no heir is mentioned?

How do we explain that Bertola was not informed of any Irish nephew by the Lebolo family, but only to contact the New York maritime merchants to acquire the funds from the sale of the mummies?

MICHAEL H. CHANDLER
AND THE MUMMIES

The eleven mummies were shipped from Trieste to New York to the combined maritime firms of Maitland & Kennedy and McLeod & Gillespie, prominent businesses that dealt in international trade. These companies were commissioned by Pietro Lebolo through the Oblasser Shipping Company to sell the antiquities and then send the proceeds to Antonio Lebolo's heirs in Castellamonte. Unfortunately some important details are missing in this part of the story. If the merchants were offering the antiquities for the best possible price, they would probably publicize them for auction in the New York newspapers. However, no notices have been found that mention the arrival of the mummies or advertise an auction for their sale.

The newspapers were checked for the period of January 1830 to March 1833, since it is not known when the mummies arrived in New York City. Did Pietro Lebolo insist that Oblasser ship the mummies to the maritime merchants in New York in an attempt to sell them after July 30, 1831, or had Oblasser previously shipped them? If they were sent to New York before July 30, 1831, and if the merchants' lists in the newspapers are complete and our research has been thorough, the receivers made no attempt to advertise their availability. I found shipping records that indicated Oblasser previously worked with the four New York merchants mentioned, but no evidence of the shipment of the mummies.[1]

I wrote to the National Archives in Washington, D.C., relative to the shipment of the mummies from Trieste to New York City and received the following reply, dated June 20, 1988:

> I have made a careful survey of dispatches from the U.S. Consul in Trieste, 1831–1833, and of miscellaneous correspondence received by that consul during this period. I found no reference to the shipment of Egyptian mummies from Trieste to New York in these years. It is possible that no reference was made to the mummies because the shippers were afraid some obscure law or regulation might forbid the importation of human remains into the United States.[2]

I had previously written to the National Archives and Records Service relative to my research and had been reminded that "most records of the Treasury Department were destroyed by a fire in 1833."[3]

Michael H. Chandler had the eleven mummies in his possession in Philadelphia and was displaying them by April 3, 1833. To make arrangements to ship them from New York to Philadelphia and to pay the custom fees and shipping costs could have been accomplished in less than a week, since a ship sailed from New York to Philadelphia in less than a day in the early 1830s. In addition to allowing sufficient time for shipping and port arrangements, it would also have taken one to three weeks to schedule a hall in Philadelphia, have the owners prepare any props necessary for the exhibition, and correlate the displays with newspaper and handbill advertising. This, of course, is conjecture, but it seems logical to assume that the mummies arrived in New York no later than March 1833.

Who Was Michael H. Chandler?

Several genealogists and historians have attempted to resolve whether or not Lebolo and Chandler were related, but without success. Lebolo's ancestry has been traced for several generations prior to his birth, since the family was primarily centered in Castellamonte. But genealogists have not been able to locate Chandler or his wife in any Irish records. We know only that the couple both called themselves Irish in several legal documents and census records in the United States. Therefore the research is at a stalemate until Chandler's roots can be traced to finally affirm or deny any family relationships with Lebolo. There were some Lebolos living in England in the mid-1800s, including one named Antonio, but the records are insufficient to correlate the families.[4]

Relying on public records from Ohio, we find that Michael H. Chandler was born in Ireland around 1797. His wife, Frances F. Ludlow, also of Irish descent, was born about 1798. They were married in Ireland, and four children were born to them between 1820 and 1827 while they were living there: Thomas, Ann, William H., and George W. A fifth child, Catherine, was listed in various censuses as being born in either Ohio, Pennsylvania, or Canada in 1829. The last seven of the Chandlers' twelve children were born in Pennsylvania or Ohio.

How Chandler first learned of the existence of the Lebolo mummies is also unknown. The account in the *Messenger and Advocate* continues:

> On opening the coffins he discovered that in connection with two of the bodies, were something rolled up with the same kind of linen, saturated with the same bitumen, which, when examined, proved to be two rolls of papyrus, previously mentioned. I may add that two or three other small pieces of papyrus, with astronomical calculations, epitaphs, &c. were found with others of the Mummies.
>
> When Mr. Chandler discovered that there was something with the Mummies, he supposed, or hoped it might be some diamonds or other valuable metal, and was no little chagrined when he saw his disappointment. He was immediately told, while yet in the Custom House, that there was no man in that city, who could translate his roll; but was referred by the same gentleman, (a stranger,) to Mr. Joseph Smith, jr. who, continued he, possesses some kind of power or gifts by which he had previously translated similar characters.[5] Bro. Smith was then unknown to Mr. Chandler, neither did he know that such a book or work as the record of the Nephites had been brought before the public. From New York [Chandler] took his collection to Philadelphia, where he exhibited them for a compensation.
>
> While Mr. Chandler was in Philadelphia, he used every

exertion to find some one who could give him the translation of his papyrus, but could not, satisfactorily, though from some few men of the first eminence, he obtained in a small degree, the translation of a few characters. Here he was referred to bro. Smith. From Philadelphia he visited Harrisburgh, and other places east of the mountains, and was frequently referred to bro. Smith for a translation of his Egyptian Relic. It would be beyond my purpose to follow this gentleman in his different circuits to the time he visited this place the last of June, or first of July, at which time he presented bro. Smith with his papyrus.[6]

Chandler or his wife apparently had close ties with one or more of the New York merchants or another contact, either through blood ties or close friendship. Someone who purchased the mummies was willing to pay the customs fees and freight expenses and help Chandler leave his job and go about the country displaying the mummies and papyri for profit. Through the occasional sale of a mummy and profits made by charging entrance fees, Chandler hoped to make a living and also repay his underwriters. More evidence will be presented in chapter 13 to support this theory.

Mummies Are Displayed in Philadelphia

In April 1833 several Philadelphia newspapers and other publications announced in advertisements and articles news about a new exhibit at the Masonic Hall. An ad in the *U.S. Gazette* appeared fifteen times between April 3 and 23 and read:

> The largest collection of EGYPTIAN MUMMIES ever exhibited in this city, is now to be seen at the Masonic Hall, in the Chesnut Street above Seventh.
>
> They were found in the vicinity of Thebes, by the celebrated traveler Antonio Lebolo and Chevalier Drovetti, General Consul of France in Egypt.
>
> Some writings on Papirus found with the Mummies, can also be seen, and will afford, no doubt, much satisfaction to Amateurs of Antiquities.
>
> Admittance 25 cents, children half price. Open from 9 A.M. till 2 P.M., and from 3 P.M. to 6.

Masonic Hall in Philadelphia, where the Egyptian mummies were displayed

Readers of the *Philadelphia Daily Chronicle* would have seen the following ad, which was published on April 3, 6, 9, 11, 13, 16, 18, and 22:

> Now Exhibiting at the
> MASONIC HALL
> Chesnut Street above Seventh,
> A large collection of Egyptian Mummies and
> other Antiquities, found in the vicinity
> of Thebes, by the celebrated traveller
> Antonio Lebalo, under the protection
> of Mahomet Ali, Viceroy of Egypt

Brief articles appeared in several publications, including the following.

U.S. Gazette for the Country (April 8 and 10): "We must ask

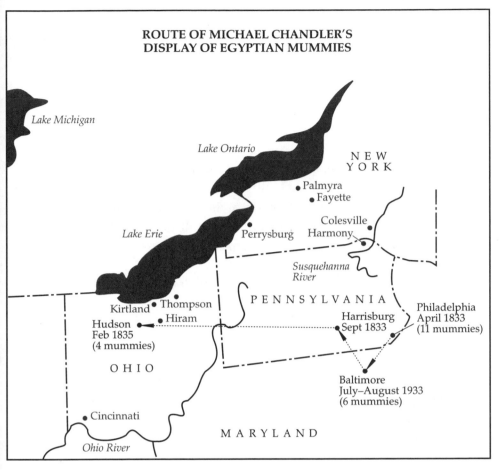

ROUTE OF MICHAEL CHANDLER'S
DISPLAY OF EGYPTIAN MUMMIES

Lake Michigan

Lake Ontario

NEW YORK

• Palmyra
• Fayette

Colesville •
Perrysburg Harmony

Lake Erie

Susquehanna
River

Kirtland • Thompson   PENNSYLVANIA   Philadelphia
         • Hiram   April 1833
Hudson •   Harrisburg   (11 mummies)
Feb 1835   Sept 1833
(4 mummies)

OHIO
                                          Baltimore
                                          July–August 1933
• Cincinnati   (6 mummies)

                   MARYLAND
Ohio River

attention to the exhibition of Mummies at the Masonic Hall. These old folks who flourished perhaps when Moses and Aaron were little boys, deserve some public attention. The rolls of papyrus, the hieroglyphics, the wrappers and other appliances, are all exceedingly interesting."

Daily Intelligencer (April 9): "A collection of nine bodies, said to have been found in the vicinity of Thebes, by the celebrated traveller Antonio Lebolo, and the Chevalier Drovetti, the General Consul of France in Egypt, is now to be seen at the Masonic Hall, in Chestnut Street, above Seventh. Besides these, several rolls of Papyrus, obtained at the same time, are also exhibited. From the appearance of the mummies they must be of considerable antiquity."[7]

Atkinson's Saturday Evening Post (April 13), under the heading "Epitome of the Times": "We must ask attention to the exhibition of Mummies at the Masonic Hall. These old folks who flourished pdrhaps [*sic*] when Moses and Aaron were little boys, deserve public attention. The rolls of papyrus, the hieroglyphics, the wrappers, and other appliances, are all exceedingly interesting."

The Pennsylvanian (April 16, 1833): "The Mummies, now exhibiting at the Masonic Hall, are said by competent critics, to be veritable. They are well worth a visit. One of them was, while in New York, stripped of its envelopes, it being supposed that valuable ornaments might be upon it. The search ended in disappointment of course."

Note that this article confirms that one mummy had been unwrapped while it was still in New York. The *Messenger and Advocate* account stated that Chandler found two rolls of papyrus with two of the bodies, and that the coffins had not been opened before they arrived in New York City.

The *Philadelphia Saturday Courier* dated Saturday, April 20, 1833, reported: "The ten Egyptian Mummies now exhibited at the Masonic Hall, have been inspected by several gentlemen competent to judge them; and are pronounced to be genuine specimens of the relics of those who, 'walked about in Thebes' streets, three thousand years ago.'"

Within the next few weeks Chandler had a placard made of the unsolicited endorsement of the seven doctors. The placard, called "The Certificate of the Learned," reads as follows:

> Having examined with considerable attention and deep interest, a number of Mummies from the catacombs, near Thebes, in Egypt, and now exhibited in the Arcade, we beg leave to recommend them to the observation of the curious inquirer on subjects of a period so long elapsed; probably not less than three thousand years ago. The features of some of these Mummies are in perfect expression.—The papyrus, covered with black or red ink, or paint, in excellent preservation, are very interesting. The undersigned, unsolicited by any per-

son connected by interest with this exhibition, have voluntarily set their names hereunto, for the simple purpose of calling the attention of the public to an interesting collection, not sufficiently known in this city.

> JOHN REDMAN COXE, M.D.
> RICHARD HARLAN, M.D.
> J. PANCOAST, M.D.
> WILLIAM P.C. BARTON, M.D.
> E.F. RIVINUS, M.D.
> SAMUEL G. MORGAN [Morton], M.D.

I concur in the above sentiments, concerning the collection of Mummies in the Philadelphia Arcade, and consider them highly deserving the attention of the curious.

> W.E. HORNER, M.D.[8]

This same placard was used more than two years later when it was circulated in Kirtland at the time Chandler first met the Prophet Joseph Smith.

An advertisement that appeared daily in the *Philadelphia Gazette* between May 10 and June 3 explained that the collection of antiquities had been moved to the Arcade, a new location, "at No. 9, east avenue, downstairs, opposite Mr. Ker's china store." The *U.S. Gazette* ran the same ad between May 11 and May 31.

The following article appeared in both the *Daily Chronicle* (May 20) and the *Saturday Courier* (May 25): "Nine mummies, found not long since in the vicinity of Thebes in Egypt, are being exhibited in Philadelphia. The reservoirs of this species of curiosity seem to grow more abundant the more they are drawn upon. Seven years ago, Mr. Peale of the New York Museum gave $1800 for one of these specimens, which may now be obtained for less than a fourth part of the sum. A strange market, indeed, for the proud land of the pyramids to come to! Its mummies would seem to be more worth than its men."

The Mummies Diminish in Numbers

Michael Chandler told leaders of the Church in Kirtland that eleven mummies of the first order of burial had been unearthed by Lebolo in the Theban tomb. Pietro Lebolo went to Trieste to check on the eleven mummies that were entrusted to Oblasser,

*The Philadelphia
Museum/Philadelphia
Arcade, site of
exhibit of mummies
(see note 8, chapter 8)*

the shipping company owner. Chandler had a placard printed to announce his exhibit, and the placard confirmed that the original shipment consisted of eleven mummies. Over the months either some of the Philadelphia newspaper reporters were careless mummy counters or Chandler's collection began to diminish in number. I have concluded that both possibilities were plausible: some reporters occasionally were careless in counting the number of mummies on display, and at the same time the collection was diminishing in number.

After Chandler concluded his display at the Philadelphia Arcade, he began touring. The next exhibit of the mummies of which we are aware was in Baltimore in July and August 1833. By then the number of mummies had dwindled to *six.*

The exhibit was very popular in Baltimore. The mummies were displayed at the Baltimore Museum, which had recently been remodeled for a Fourth of July reopening less than three weeks before. A newspaper advertisement placed by J. E.

Walker, manager of the museum, was published July 20 and read as follows:

> The citizens are respectfully informed that the Manager has received from the vicinity of Thebes, that celebrated city of Ancient Egypt, six strangers, illustrious from their antiquity, count, probably an existence of at least one thousand years anterior to the advent of our blessed Saviour, and contemporaries; if so, of the first Sovereigns of Israel, viz: Saul and David. They are by no means insignificant aspirants to public patronage. In the present day, in a country unknown, and where transatlantic ancestors, at that period wrapt in the gloom of Idolatry and Paganism, what singular and interesting points of history could they not unfold, connected with those early periods of the world, were the vital spark, so long at rest, permitted to resuscitate their slumbering remains. But surely none could view these truly singular remnants of *Auld Lang Syne*, without being carried retrospectively to these far distant periods of Antiquity.[9]

Admission to the exhibit was twenty-five cents.

A lengthy article in the *Baltimore American and Commercial Daily Advertiser* on July 22 had been copied from the *Philadelphia Daily Chronicle*. It was sober and reflective in tone. The writer, writing under the pseudonym "Pythagorus," began, "I had yesterday, a solemn, silent intercourse with eight or ten foreigners from the vicinity of Thebes." He concluded:

> I cannot but hope that curiosity may lead all who can spare 25 cents to see these fragments of mortality. How far, 3,000 years hence, any remnant of those, who may look upon these Egyptian Mummies, may exist to call into notice the curious speculations of the living, it may be well to think of. The pouting lip, the bright and scornful eye, the panting bosom of the present beauty, will probably be more fleeting than the actual remains I now exhort my fellow citizens to contemplate and think upon.

A Baltimore Museum ad in the *Gazette* announced on August 10, 1833, "The exhibition of the Egyptian Mummies will close on Wednesday Evening, the 14th instant." Apparently the exhibit was extended, for the same newspaper bade the mummies a final farewell two days later by announcing, "The Egyptian Mummies will positively close on Friday Evening, 16th inst."

The placard Michael Chandler distributed as he continued to exhibit his mummies referred to this success in Baltimore: "They [the mummies] have been exhibited in Philadelphia and Baltimore, to crowded audiences; in the latter place, although only engaged for two weeks, the exhibition was prolonged to five weeks, with attraction."[10]

Whether the six mummies Chandler exhibited in Baltimore were displayed elsewhere after he left that city is not known. The next documented exhibition was in Harrisburg, Pennsylvania, where a duplicate of the Baltimore ad was printed in the weekly *Harrisburg Chronicle* on September 9, 1833.

Apparently five of the original eleven mummies were sold in the Philadelphia and Baltimore areas within the first four months after Chandler obtained them. Between September 1833, when he left Harrisburg, and February 1835, he sold two others, for that is the number he had when we next pick up his trail in Hudson, Ohio. Those four remaining mummies were the ones the Saints in Kirtland purchased in early July 1835.

The Search for the Missing Mummies

My search for clues on Chandler's whereabouts between September 9, 1833, and February 16, 1835, was unsuccessful. If he displayed the mummies in small communities during that time, his arrivals and departures could have gone unrecorded in local newspapers, which were usually published either weekly or biweekly. This means he could have arrived in a town, circulated some handbills advertising his exhibit, displayed them for a few days, and then gone on his way with no newspaper account of his visit if he arrived and left between editions.

In our search in communities between Baltimore and Kirtland, particularly those along the Erie Canal, Dr. Brian L. Smith and I happened to stumble across the following account in Hudson, Ohio. There was no newspaper mention of a visit by Chandler there, but we did locate a journal of events of interest in Hudson that the city founder's son, David Hudson Jr., had kept. Entry number 124, dated February 1835, stated: "Mr. Edgerly's Sign.—At Baldwin's Store today, I saw a handbill, giving notice that there was to be an exhibition of mummies at the Mansion House of L. Edgerly. I went out, looked on the sign, and saw the words 'Mansion House' on it. It was not in my mind that that was on the sign."[11]

In an entry dated Thursday, February 19, Hudson wrote: "Exhibition of Mummies.—There was an exhibition of four Mummies at Mr. Edgerly's tavern on Monday, Tuesday and Wednesday. I went in to see them yesterday. [T]hey were ghastly looking objects, and the sight of them was not desirable."[12]

No doubt these were the four remaining mummies exhibited by Michael Chandler, who in early 1835 listed his hometown as Stow, Ohio, a town just a few miles from Hudson.

Oliver Cowdery's report in the *Messenger and Advocate* indicated that according to Chandler, the seven missing mummies had been "purchased by gentlemen for private museums," making it next to impossible to trace their whereabouts.[13] Two mummies had been bought on behalf of Philadelphia's Academy of Natural Sciences by Dr. Samuel George Morton, one of the medical doctors who signed the "Certificate of the Learned" encouraging the public to see Chandler's exhibit at the Arcade in Philadelphia. (Dr. Morton's name was incorrectly given as "Morgan" on the certificate.)

The minutes of the academy for May 21, 1833, read: "Dr. Morton called the attention of the members to some mummies now in the city—the remarkable development of the cranium in one." The minutes for June 4 state that the "head of a Mummy from Thebes" was deposited at the academy by Dr. Morton. This was followed by another cranium on June 18.

On December 10 and 17, 1833, Dr. Morton, who was vice president of the academy, dissected the two Egyptian mummies before academy members. It can be determined that these two were originally from the Chandler collection, for in a work entitled *Catalogue of Skulls of Man and the Inferior Animals in the*

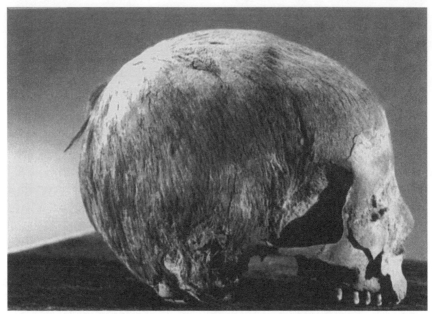

Photograph of mummy head number 60, "Princess," one of two mummies from the
Chandler collection at the Philadelphia Academy of Natural Sciences

Collection of Samuel George Morton M.D., Penn. and Edinb., Dr.
Morton gave the following information:

> [Entry Number 48] Embalmed head of an EGYPTIAN girl
> eight years of age, from the Theban catacombs. Egyptian form,
> with a single lock of long fine hair. Dissected by me before the
> Academy of Natural Sciences of Philadelphia, December 10,
> 1833.

> [Entry Number 60] Embalmed head of an EGYPTIAN lady
> about 16 years of age, brought from the Catacombs of El
> Gourna, near Thebes, by the late Antonio Lebolo, of whose
> heirs I purchased it, together with the entire body: the latter I
> dissected before the Academy of Natural Sciences, on the 10th
> and 17th of December, 1833, in presence of eighty members
> and others. Egyptian form, with long, fine hair. Crania
> Aegyptiaca, plate 10, fig. 6.[14]

Note that Dr. Morton said he purchased the mummy from
Lebolo's heirs—the story that Chandler maintained two years
later when he claimed to be Lebolo's nephew.

Dr. Samuel George Morton, from a portrait by Paul Weber, 1851 (Courtesy Library, The Academy of Natural Sciences, Philadelphia)

Note also that Dr. Morton was apparently more interested in the mummies' skulls than their bodies. He was testing the popular theory of that day that a larger cranial cavity indicated that a person had superior intelligence. Dr. Morton would fill with buckshot the skulls he procured and then weigh them to determine the respective size of the cavity. The skulls in such experiments were separated from the bodies.

In a paper entitled "Observations on Egyptian Ethnography, Derived from Anatomy, History, and the Monuments," delivered nearly ten years after he purchased the two mummies from Chandler, Dr. Morton reported: "In the year 1833, I purchased of the heirs of the late Senior Le'Bolo, a dilapidated mummy from Thebes, of which I prepared the skeleton, now preserved in the Anatomical Museum of the University of Pennsylvania. It measures about five feet ten inches, and is in every respect beautifully developed excepting the cranium, which is small in proportion and of indifferent conformation." In a footnote Dr.

Morton explained: "I have reason to believe that this cranium, which I obtained separate from the rest of the mummy, belonged to another Egyptian skeleton subsequently procured from the same source."[15]

Thus, we learn that Dr. Morton bought two Theban skulls, numbered 48 and 60, at approximately the same time, and that he identified number 60 as coming from Antonio Lebolo's heirs. He dissected both bodies in December 1833. The next Egyptian mummies, whose numbering begins with 759, were presented to Dr. Morton by "G. R. Gliddon, Esq., later United States Consul for the City of Cairo" seven years later, in 1840. There is little doubt that number 48, as well as number 60, was purchased by Dr. Morton from Michael H. Chandler.

Dr. Morton's crania collection is now located in the University of Pennsylvania. The cranium of the sixteen-year-old girl was displayed at Brigham Young University between 1979 and 1983 through the courtesy of the University of Pennsylvania[16] and has since been returned to the university's Egyptian Museum. The location of the five mummies that were in Michael Chandler's possession before he sold the last four to Joseph Smith is unknown.

Francesco Bertola Jr. in America

In chapter 7, I cited a letter written in behalf of the Lebolo family in which Pietro Lebolo commissioned Francesco Bertola Jr., who had moved from Castellamonte to Philadelphia, to see why the New York City merchants to whom the mummies had been sent had not sent to the family the money from their sale. Since Michael H. Chandler had the mummies in his possession by early April 1833, it seems logical to assume that financial arrangements had already been concluded with the purchaser and the New York shipping companies of Maitland & Kennedy and McLeod & Gillespie. In an attempt to learn about the sale, I tried to trace the activities of Bertola, Lebolo's former Castellamonte neighbor, in the United States.

There is no listing of a Francesco Bertola Jr. in the

Philadelphia city directory for the years 1833, 1834, 1835, 1836, or 1837. The closest name is Frank Bertole, who is listed as a baker. This could be the anglicized spelling of Francesco Bertola, but the different occupation is puzzling.

An exchange of letters between the Sardinian consul in New York City and the Sardinian government in northern Italy sheds a little light on the story. The Province of Ivrea (near Castellamonte) sent a brief inquiry to the Sardinian consulate in New York on February 1, 1837, which was received on February 11, 1837. Referring to "Francesco Bertola, Master of Horses," the message stated: "He left New York sometime ago to go to Buffalo. We desire to hear from him, since he has not written to his family resident in Castellamonte for about a year."[17]

In a return letter dated June 28, 1837, to his "Excellency" in Sardinia, the Sardinian consul in New York City explained: "Mr. Francesco Bertola left Philadelphia towards the beginning of last November [1836] and he established his residence in this city. But last March he found the opportunity to give lessons in the Italian language in a pensione in nearby New York, and he told some of his friends that he wanted to go there. However, he did not want to tell them, by any means, neither the name nor the location of the above mentioned boarding-house. It will be my duty to make further inquiries about him. Then, I'll be solicitous to inform you of my findings."[18]

In a final letter to Sardinia, dated December 23, 1837, the consul in New York City gave the following update on the matter: "Mr. Francesco Bertola whose case has been registered under #26 on June 28, after the ministerial record #8 last February 11, now lives in Bloomingdale, a village three miles distance from this city. He gives Physical Science lessons in a little college [boarding-school]. He receives from what he told me and from what I heard from other people a salary of $300.00 plus room and board."[19]

The Lebolos did not continue to pursue the matter of seeking closure on the sale of the mummies after October 1833, as far as has been determined, so the payment may have arrived shortly after Francesco Bertola Jr. was granted power of attorney to bring matters to a conclusion. Since correspondence ceased, unless a new notary was hired, Bertola probably had no dealings with the sale of the mummies; or if he did, it was only to find that the transaction had been completed.

When Bertola told the representative from the Sardinian Consulate that he did not want his friends to know the name or the location "by any means" of the boardinghouse where he was living and teaching, one has to wonder why the secrecy. Either he had severed ties with his family in the Piedmont or he was a very poor letter writer, since he had not written home for about a year. It is assumed that his detachment from his friends and family is unrelated to the sale of the mummies.

Nothing more is known about Francesco Bertola Jr. in the United States. His father, Francesco Bertola Sr., the confidant of Antonio Lebolo who assisted in inventorying Lebolo's possessions after his death, died December 27, 1842, in Castellamonte.[20] He did not mention his son in his will.[21]

EGYPTIAN MUMMIES IN AMERICA, 1823–1833

As we have seen, Michael H. Chandler's Egyptian antiquities displays attracted large crowds wherever he exhibited them. To appreciate better the novelty of Egyptian mummies being exhibited in the United States, it might be well to review the uniqueness of such displays at that time.

Though a few Egyptian mummies were being shipped to the major cities of Europe for exhibit in the early 1820s, they were nonetheless still a source of great curiosity. A London newspaper article quoted in the Palmyra, New York, *Herald* on Wednesday, July 24, 1822, reported:

> Thousands of persons have been within the last few days at the Custom House at Plymouth [England], to see an Egyptian Mummy which has lately been brought there, and must be sold for payment of the duties. It was announced to be seen three days before the sale, which took place on Friday last, and ever since Tuesday morning, the customhouse had been crowded by persons of all ranks, from the highest to the lowest, all eager to get a view of so great a curiosity. The exterior coffin is very highly decorated and very beautiful; it is supposed to be made of shittim wood, and is in high preservation.
>
> The exterior of the coffin has several figures painted round the sides, the colours of which are exceedingly bright. The body, which is that of a female, is placed in a shell, and wrapped up in an immense quantity of coarse linen cloth, a great part of which is in a perfect state. The body is in some parts much decayed, and had altered exceedingly since it was exposed to the air, but even now the skin and nails are to be

seen perfect on the hand, and the bones are quite entire, even to the toes and finger joints. The head appears to have been sawed open for the purpose of taking out the brain.

It is said to be upwards of 2000 years old, and is supposed to have been a person of quality.[1]

The First Egyptian Mummies in America

Egyptian mummies were rare indeed in the United States in the 1820s and early 1830s, and more especially on the sparsely settled frontier such as the Western Reserve. The first Egyptian mummy to be shipped to the United States, as far as is known, arrived in Boston harbor in 1823. Jacob Van Lennep of Smyrna, a Dutch merchant who served as the consul general of the Netherlands, sent a mummy to Boston "to be given to some public establishment as a mark of respect to that city."[2]

It is not known why Boston was held in such esteem, but Mr. Van Lennep went to considerable trouble to acquire this rare gift. When he asked Mr. Lee, the British consul in Alexandria, Egypt, to procure a mummy, the official replied that "having found no good ones, opened, in [Alexandria] or Cairo, [he had] commissioned a person going to Thebes to select one, and he succeeded in procuring the best that had been seen in a long time."[3] Unfortunately, the antiquities dealer from whom the mummy was purchased is not mentioned by name in the report.

Mr. Tilden and Captain Edes, who took charge of the mummy upon its arrival in this country, presented it, in Van Lennep's behalf, to the Massachusetts General Hospital, to be used in raising funds for that institution. The mummy arrived April 25, 1823, and was delivered on May 4 to the hospital.[4]

An article about the mummy stated: "Several of these Mummies are deposited in the British and French Museums, and other celebrated Cabinets in Europe, which some among us have seen. This Specimen, which was taken from a recently discovered Catacomb, at Thebes, is in the finest state of preservation, and is the only one ever brought to America."[5]

While confirming data about the Massachusetts General Hospital's acquisition of the first Egyptian mummy in 1823, I

The first mummy (left), nicknamed "Paddy." and the third mummy to be displayed in the United States

learned that it was found to be a man named Padihershef, now affectionately called "Paddy." An entry on a paper sent to me from the City Life Museums in Baltimore was labeled "Padihershef—Documentation, Boston newspaper in 1823." The article, headlined "More Mummies" and dated June 17, 1824, described the arrival of two additional mummies: "The brig Peregrine, Clark, from Gilbraltar, arrived on Tuesday, brought TWO MUMMIES, fresh from Thebes, and of un-doubted antiquity. At this rate the flesh of mummy will be as cheap as that of dogs. The market is already glutted; a few more of the Egyptian carcasses, with a mermaid or two, and the stock for our museums will be as cheap as the candidates for our presidency."[6]

As of this writing, nothing else is known about this second arrival of mummies. Unless the reporter knew something that we don't know, it hardly seems justified to conclude that the one mummy that arrived over a year before would have glutted the market.

In his book *Moravia and Its Past,* author Leslie L. Luther included an entry dated September 23, 1823, from Moravia, a village in central New York State:

> Walked up in the market square . . . and saw written over the door "A Live Ostrich" . . . went in and saw it. . . . Curious looking tent there went in and saw the Egyptian mummy, a young lady three thousand years old, lately to arrive from the City of Thebes, the city with its hundred gates. She was found enclosed in two coffins made of sycamore, and on top of each coffin her profile is carved out of the wood. The coffins smell very disagreeable indeed. She is said to be a real woman by the doctors who have examined her in Boston and no deception. She makes a ghastly and unlovely appearance. Has turned black. Said to be when alive, red, just the color of the likeness on the coffin.[7]

This "young lady three thousand years old" was probably one of the two mummies that arrived in Boston about three months before.

The third documented shipment of an Egyptian mummy to the United States was mentioned in the *New York Evening Post* on August 10, 1824. The newspaper article does not document where in Egypt it was exhumed, nor does it mention the excavator's name or the receivers in the United States. A detailed picture of the sarcophagus accompanies the article, and above the picture is this announcement: "Now exhibiting from 8 in the morning until 9 in the evening, at 328½ Broadway, nearly opposite the Hospital, a MUMMY, just arrived from Egypt. Admittance, 25 cents; children, half price."

Under the picture is this text:

New-York, August 1, 1824

SIR,—When you first announced to me the arrival of a human Mummy, from Egypt, I made an overture immediately for its particular and careful examination. At that time, the body was entirely covered by the cloth and bandages of embalming. These were opened in the presence of the most respectable witnesses, at the College of Physicians; and the disclosures afforded satisfactory evidence of genuineness.— My attending friends, and myself, were highly gratified by the fair opportunity we enjoyed of inspecting such a curious piece of antiquity;—and if I was to express an opinion to my fellow-citizens, it would be in the form of an exhortation, for them to view this rare and real production, without delay. Accept my thanks for the addition you have made to our stock of rational information.

SAMUEL L. MITCHILL,

Captain Larkin Lee.

We, the subscribers, think the Mummy, a real and interesting preparation, and worthy of being viewed as a fair specimen of Egyptian embalming.

VALENTINE MOTT,
J. D. JAQUES,
N. H. DERING,
WM. JS. MACNEVEN.

The Dr. Samuel L. Mitchill who examined the mummy and further exhorted the public to visit the mummy "without delay" appeared in LDS Church history five years later when Martin Harris took a transcript of some Book of Mormon Egyptian writings to him and to Dr. Charles Anthon hoping to have them authenticated.[8]

Other Shipments of Mummies

In 1826 two mummies were displayed at Peale's Museum and Gallery of the Fine Arts in New York. One writer explained:

Rubens Peale had two mummies exported directly from Cairo to New York by an Egyptian agent; these were placed on exhibition in Peale's Museum in 1826; and after sixteen days a special attraction announced for the edification of "the scientific and curious" was the partial unwrapping of the mummies "by several of the most respectable physicians of this city . . . in the Lecture Room of Peale's Museum," admission fee 25 cents; "N.B. On this occasion, children cannot be admitted."

One of these mummies seems to have suffered from too much handling, but the other, still on exhibition in 1827, might "be viewed by the most delicate female without exciting the smallest disagreeable feeling."[9]

The article listed several Egyptian antiquities displayed with the mummy, including "an Egyptian Papyrus, well preserved."

Peale's two mummies were probably the fourth shipment of mummies from Egypt. Sixteen years later they were listed in the collection of the great American showman P. T. Barnum. According to Dr. John Wilson of the Oriental Institute in Chicago, they were destroyed in an 1865 fire.[10]

The next known Egyptian mummy in the United States, the fifth shipment documented, was reported in American Museum advertisements that ran in New York's *Commercial Advertiser* between January 26, 1832, and February 13, 1832:

> AMERICAN MUSEUM, Broadway, opposite St. Paul's Church, and near the point of the Park. The public are respectfully informed, that This Evening, and every evening this week, the Grand Cosmorama will present the same pieces embraced in Sacred History, as exhibited on Christmas.
>
> Bones of the Mammoth.—These extraordinary remains will be removed shortly. Those who desire to see them must call instantly.
>
> This Museum is the largest in America—occupies four spacious halls, 100 feet each, besides the largest Cosmorama in the world. Admittance 25 cents.
>
> THIS DAY ADDED:
>
> The Egyptian Mummy, recently received from Thebes, in Egypt. It is a great curiosity and well worthy the attention of every man of science and discernment. This Mummy was taken from one of the most remarkable Catacombs, and is considered to be very old. It is enclosed in its Sarcophagus or Coffin, ornamented with numerous hieroglyphics.[11]

In the same column beginning February 24, 1832, under the heading "Amusements," the ad for Peale's Museum and Gallery of the Fine Arts also mentioned the mummy:

> PEALE'S MUSEUM–And Gallery of the Fine Arts, Broadway, opposite the Park.–This Museum is one of the

largest and most extensive in the union, containing the most valuable gallery of portraits of distinguished Americans, besides other valuable paintings by eminent artists. The collections in the departments of Natural History and Miscellaneous Curiosities, including rare works of art and ingenuity, is unrivalled. The Egyptian Mummy is decidedly the finest ever brought to this country, direct from Egypt, with its double coffin, and, without doubt, at least 3000 years old.[12]

Notice that only one mummy was mentioned in this 1832 advertisement, whereas two were mentioned in 1826.

To match Peale's ad, some five weeks later the American Museum enhanced its continuing ad and stated that its Egyptian mummy was "decidedly the most remarkable relic of the art of embalming ever brought to America":

CONTINUATION OF ATTRACTION.—AMERICAN MUSEUM, Broadway, opposite St. Paul's Church. The Egyptian Mummy, recently received from Thebes in Egypt, and upwards of three thousand years old, is decidedly the most remarkable relic of the art of embalming ever brought to America. It is enclosed in its sarcophagus or coffin, and nightly attracts crowds of visitors. The American Museum is by far the largest in America—occupies four large salons, each one hundred feet in length, besides the largest Cosmorama in the world, comprising 100 glasses. Among the wonders exhibiting at this Museum, are the Bones of the Mammoth, and numerous fossil remains recently received in Kentucky.[13]

As these creative showmen competed for bragging rights and additional revenue, the American Museum seems to have won the competition by announcing on March 12, 1832, a public dissection of its Egyptian mummy:

Public Dissection of the Egyptian Mummy
American Museum, opposite St. Paul's Church
Order and Rules to be observed.
1st. Every gentleman to procure tickets of the lower door keeper.
2d. No gentleman will be allowed to leave his seat on any account.

3d. All questions to be directed to the superintending operator.

4th. No ladies admitted.

After the dissection, the body will remain in state, for the gratification of the curious. Ample arrangements have been made.[14]

The American Museum had the dissected body "lying in state" for at least ten days, no doubt attracting many to see it. Meanwhile, Peale's Museum continued to advertise its mummy, with its double coffin, as "decidedly the finest ever brought to this country."[15]

Some who may accept the invitation to challenge the accuracy of this research (and I hope there will be some) will note that because of interest in Egyptian mummies, papyri, and other antiquities in the United States in the 1820s and 1830s, mummies were displayed frequently and in various cities. Initially, it is confusing, when we read of a mummy on display, to know whether it is part of a new collection of antiquities or ones previously mentioned. For example, "Paddy," the first Egyptian mummy in the U.S., was displayed in Boston in May 1823, and in Philadelphia as early as April 1824.[16]

A mummy was displayed in Springfield, Ohio, on May 1, 1830, according to a report in the *Western Pioneer* newspaper: "The Mummy which has attracted so much attention throughout the U.S. for many months past is about to be exhibited in this town. From what we have heard, it is well worth the attention of the curious and scientific." Under a picture of the female's sarcophagus, the report explained that "this mummy was brought to this country by captain Turner of Charlestown, Mass. from Trieste at which place it had been received from Thebes." This female is probably one of the two mummies shipped to Boston in the second shipment.

Michael Chandler's Mummy Collection

The eleven mummies in the Chandler collection were, as far as is known, the largest number shipped to the United States up until that time and comprised the sixth shipment of Egyptian mummies arriving in the country.

When Chandler displayed his Egyptian exhibit in Cleveland prior to his arrival in Kirtland, it received considerable publicity in area newspapers. The *Cleveland Daily Advertiser* published the following news release on March 26, 1835:

> EGYPTIAN MUMMIES.—Our limited room will not at present permit an extended description of these remarkable posthumous travellers who are now in this village; but we cannot forbear calling upon those of our citizens who have not seen these ancient specimens of humanity, to visit them before they are removed, which we understand will be in 3 or 4 days. The exhibitor permits as free an examination of them as is consistent with their preservation. Specimens of the ancient method of writing on papyrus, found with the mummies, are also shown by Mr. Chandler, whose intelligent conversation adds much to the interest of the exhibition. The collection is offered for sale by the proprietor.[17]

These points are significant to note: (1) the mummies and papyrus were freely examined by the patrons, which probably caused some damage to both the mummies and the papyrus; (2) Mr. Chandler seemed informed enough about his exhibit to have the reporter call his narrative "intelligent conversation"; and (3) he was anxious to sell the last four mummies and terminate the transient lifestyle he had been engaged in for the past two years.

A *Cleveland Whig* reporter who visited the exhibition at Chandler's request reported:

> We accepted the invitation of Mr. Chandler to visit last evening his exhibition, just opened at the Cleveland House, of *Four Egyptian Mummies*, purporting to have been obtained from Thebes, by the celebrated traveller Lobelo [sic]. The announcement of such an exhibition, is very apt to bring with it the suspicion of imposition; as much probably from its rarity in this "back-woods country," as from the state of advancement which has been attained in the arts of humbugery and deception. But we have no hesitation in saying, that a very slight examination of these relics, will convince any

one that there is no deception about them, and that there are in truth before him, the bones and sinews, if not the flesh and blood, of four ancient beings of his own race, whose frames have survived the decay of some two thousand years. The relic forms are those of *three males and one female* [emphasis added]— of mature age, and two of them at least, evidently far advanced in life at the period of their deaths. The first sight of them produces sensations by no means pleasant—but those feelings soon give way to others of a different character, and the more you contemplate them the more interested you become. Curiosity immediately becomes excited; a variety of queries rapidly passes through the mind—which are by no means solved by contemplation. What nation were they of? At what age and where did they live? What were their names? their circumstances? their occupation? Were they slain in battle—or died they a natural death by the "visitation of God?" What was the leading trait in the character of that old man, whose arms repose in a cross over his breast? Has he not truly what the phrenologists call an "intellectual head?" Imagination perhaps is better than science to solve the question. And that female too—the mother of Agamemnon, for aught that appears—her aged head still retains the hair that graced it in youth.—The peculiar features that distinguish the sex in our day, are distinctly preserved in this withered form. This train of thought becomes richer as it advances; and the visitor before he is aware of it, will become absorbed in meditation and awe. There will be no mirth in that hall—or if there is, it will be forced and unnatural. An involuntary feeling of solemnity and awe will reign in its stead. We speak from experience.

The exhibitor will relate and illustrate incidents which add much to the interest of the exhibition. *There was found deposited in the arms of the old man referred to above, a book of ancient form and construction, which, to us, was by far the most interesting part of the exhibition. Its leaves were of bark, in length some 10 or 12 inches, and 3 or 4 in width. The ends are somewhat decayed, but at the centre the leaves are in a state of perfect preservation. It is the writing of no ordinary penman, probably of the old man near whose heart it was deposited at the embalming. The characters are the Egyptian hyeroglyphics; but of what it discourses none can tell. That probably, like the name of the author, and of the figure before you, will never be unfolded. There is also another book, more decayed, and much less neatly written—its character and import involved in like mystery.* [Emphasis added]

There is no concealment about this exhibition; the spectator is allowed to examine as critically as he pleases; and in this respect it is much more satisfactory than any similar exhibition we ever witnessed. We are not apt to speak favorably of the thousand and one performances and exhibitions with which we are annually afflicted—which have a tendency to excite the worst passions of youth, and lead many into habits of profligacy. But that of which we have been speaking, we consider an exception to their usual character, and tendency. Mr. Chandler will remain at the Cleveland House a few days; and visitors to his interesting exhibition are taxed the moderate fee of 25 cents.

The following lines, ascribed to the poet Campbell, though not new to all our readers, contain some fine points of poetry and sentiment, and are apposite in this connexion:

ADDRESS TO THE MUMMY
In Belzoni's Exhibition, London.

And thou hast walked about, (how strange a story!)
In Thebes' streets, three thousand years ago,
When the Memnonium was in all its glory,
And time had not begun to overthrow
Those temples, palaces and piles stupendous
Of which the very ruins are tremendous.

Speak! for thou long enough hast acted Dummy.
Thou hast a tongue? come let us hear its tune.
Thou'rt standing on thy legs above ground, Mummy!
Revisiting the glimpses of the moon,
Not like thin ghosts or disembodied creatures,
But with thy bones and flesh, and limbs and features.

Tell us! for doubtless thou canst recollect,
To whom shall we assign the Sphinx's fame?
Was Cheops or Cephrenes architect
Of either pyramid that bear his name?
Is Pompey's pillar really a misnomer?
Had Thebes a hundred gates, as sung by Homer?

Perhaps thou art a Mason, and forbidden
By oath to tell the mysteries of thy trade:
Then say what secret melody was hidden

In Memnon's statue, which at sunrise played?
Perhaps thou were a Priest. If so, my struggles
Are vain—Egyptian priests ne'er owned their juggles.

Perchance that very hand now pinioned flat,
Has hob-a-nobbed with Pharaoh, glass for glass,
Or dropped a half-penny into Homer's hat,
Or doffed thine own to let Queen Dido pass,
Or held, by Solomon's own invitation,
A torch, at the great Temple's dedication.

I need not ask thee if that hand, when armed,
Has any Roman hero mauled and knuckled:
For thou wast dead and buried and embalmed,
Ere Romulus and Remus had been suckled.
Antiquity appears to have begun
Long after thy primeval race was run.

Since first thy form was in this box extended,
We above ground have seen some strange mutations:
The Roman empire has begun and ended;
New worlds have risen; we have lost old nations;
And countless kings have into dust been humbled,
While not a fragment of thy dust has crumbled.

Didst thou not hear the pother o'er thy head,
When the great Persian conqueror, Cambyses,
Marched armies o'er thy tomb with thundering tread;
O'erthrew Osiris, Osus, Apis, Isis,
And shook the Pyramids with fear and wonder,
When the gigantic Memnon fell asunder?

If the Tomb's secrets may not be confessed,
The nature of thy private life unfold.
A heart has throbbed beneath that leathern breast,
And tears adown that dusky cheek have rolled.
Have children climbed those knees, and kissed that face?
What was thy name and station, age and race?

Statue of flesh! Immortal of the dead!
Imperishable type of evanescence!
Posthumous man, who quittest thy native bed,
And standest undecayed within our presence,
Thou wilt hear nothing, till the judgment morning,
When the great trump shall thrill thee with its warning!

Why should this useless tegument endure,

If its undying guest be lost forever?
Oh let us keep the soul embalmed and pure
In living virtue, that when both must sever,
Although corruption may our frame consume,
The immortal spirit in the skies may bloom.[18]

Notice that the first record mentioned by the reporter was "a book of ancient form and construction," buried with the old man, and was "the most interesting part of the exhibition." The leaves were of "bark," a reasonable description of papyri, "in length some 10 or 12 inches, and 3 or 4 in width." It sounds as if the reporter were describing some unbound papyri approximately half the width of ordinary 8 1/2" x 11" paper that was stacked. A second book, also identified with the old man, is described as "more decayed" and less "neatly written" than the first. These records were in addition to the rolls that will be discussed later.

The best description known of the four mummies that the Church purchased about three months later comes from the March 27, 1835, edition of the *Telegraph* in Painesville, a town about thirty miles east of Cleveland. It reads:

Mr. Editor,—The history of the ancients is replete with grandeur & curiosity, and who is there so callous, as not to be excited with sufficient curiosity to traverse with interest, all the dark labyrinths of pagan lore and long gone by usages. History, indeed, calls to mind spirits which have long since been traversing the golden works of the celestial world; but, how much more are we reared to them, when we can commingle with bodies *spiritless,* who traversed this earth, thousands of years ago, as we now do, possessing passions and wants, ambition, avarice and superstition like ourselves. Could we but look forward beyond the dark curtain of time and see the mighty changes, which will transpire for thousands of years to come, we should be lost in amazement. The past is wonderful although very incomplete; yet we are daily obtaining new light from the researches of scientific antiquarians. The discoveries in the long buried cities of Herculaneum and Pompeii which have been hidden from the world about 1800 years are truly interesting. The habits, manners and customs of those once inhabited cities are plainly inferred from the appearances of the charred dwellings and other edifices for public purposes—their amphitheaters and temples of Isis, holy utensils and baths &c. &c.

But the most interesting of all antique subjects, is the opening of the catacombs of Egypt where human bodies are found in a complete state of preservation or nearly so. How, or by what agency these bodies were preserved, or for what object is wholly an enigma. Many have conjectured that the doctrine of the resurrection was embodied in the Egyptian religious faith, and others again suppose that the practice of embalming their dead originated in their abhorrence to decay—but all is speculation. Curiosity has frequently prompted us to visit and critically examine mummies which were found in the catacombs near Thebes; and to realize that I was viewing one of my own species who had lived like myself and been a member of a community three or four thousand years ago, produced a sensation like that of associating with people of another world.

I received a short description from a friend in Cleveland of four mummies that are now exhibiting in that place which may not be uninteresting to some of your readers. [signed] A Gardner

The reader apparently enclosed the following newspaper article, which his friend had sent him:

Dear Sir: I send you a description of *four Mummies,* now exhibiting in this place. They were found in June, 1832—three miles from Thebes, 236 feet deep in a catacomb or vault 94 by 18 feet in the clear. Some stone described by the finder 32 ft. long, 8 high and 5 feet wide, evidently belonging to Mount Lebyen, to which there are strong indications of a rail-road. The stone were put together with a cement and exhibited superior workmanship.

Some of the bodies stood in nitches of the wall; a row of bodies, however, laid on the bottom 8 feet deep (reversed,) more or less decayed. This statement of the owner is accompanied by good authority.

No. 1—4 feet 11 inches, *female*—supposed age 60; arms extended, hands side by side in front; the head indicating motherly goodness. *There was found with this person a roll or book, having a little resemblance to birch bark; language unknown.* Some linguists however say they can decipher 13–36, in what they term an epitaph; ink black and red; many female figures. [Emphasis added]

No. 2—Height 5 ft. 1 1–2 inch; *female;* supposed age 40. Arms suspended by the side; hands brought in contact; head damaged by accident; *found with roll as No. 1, filled with hieroglyphics, rudely executed.* [Emphasis added]

No. 3.—Heighth 4 ft. 4 1–2.—*Male,* very old, say 80; arms crossing on the breast, each hand on its opposite shoulder; *had a roll of writing as No. 1 & 2;* superior head, it will compare in the region of the sentiments with any in our land; passions mild. [Emphasis added]

No. 4.—Height 4 ft. 9; *female.* I am inclined to put her age at about 20 or 25, others call her an old woman; arms extended, hands by her side; auburn hair, short as girls at present in their new fashion. Found with her a braid of hair, three stran[d]s of the color of that on her head and 18 inches long. The head approximates to the form of the Orang Outang. The occipital and bazillar region very large; the head indicating a person of the lowest grade of human beings. Slander, fight, and devotion to the passions were undoubtedly peculiar traits in her character. They were enveloped in linnen saturated with gum, the qualities of which are not well understood. A thousand yards are supposed to be used on each body; 186 thicknesses have been counted on one of them. They are covered so as to preserve the exact form of the body and limbs. No. 3 and 4; the envelope is mostly stripped off; on 1 and 2 it is some broken. No. 1, fine linnen; No. 2, coarse; No. 3, very coarse; No. 4, very fine. The bodies evidently were reduced before winding. The man, No. 3, whose cerebral organization indicates a mind able to guide the destinies of a nation, is enveloped in the poorest and coarsest linnen, while the woman, No. 4, whose head indicates a disposition which may well be represented as the demon of society, was in the most careful manner enveloped in the finest of linnen and with a much greater proportion of gum. Is not this circumstance an intimation to us that rank was not according to merit—that superiority in station did not follow from superiority of mind, but from extraneous circumstances.

It is interesting to observe in these individuals the external indications of disposition which at this day build up and pull down society; that these relics of another and unknown age were once animated with life, and actuated by passions, hopes

and fears, as we now are. How pleasing to contemplate that
aged man, by rules that will not deceive, in the active exercise
of those sentimental powers of the mind from which the hope
of immortality springs. In such minds there is light—in such
minds a nation will find prosperity, and society an anchor. But
how sad to contemplate the history of that young female
(No. 4)—revenge and hate indignant frown upon her brow.

The love of property is not indicated on either of their heads
as being in any proportion as strong as with us. Did they not
hold property in common? and is not this remark applicable to
Indians? [signed] FARMER.[19]

Several points are significant in this long article.

1. Mr. Chandler states that the mummies were exhumed at
Thebes "in June 1832," as he reported to Oliver Cowdery a little
over three months later. Perhaps he was referring to a document
that so stated the date even though it is incorrect. Nonetheless,
his story is consistent.

2. The Theban tomb had niches in the wall, as was later mentioned to Church leaders. The reporter said, "This statement of
the owner is accompanied by good authority." This report may
indicate a document or documents from which Chandler
received his information.

3. This last article, which describes the four "Mormon"
mummies better than any other known to us, mentioned that
there were three females and one male. The quotation previously cited reversed the number and stated that there were three
males and one female mummy. This confusion persists throughout the entire story of the mummies.

4. Three of the four mummies had an accompanying "roll or
book" buried with them. No such record is mentioned in connection with the fourth mummy.

5. The reporter was a strong believer in phrenology, which is
"the study of the conformation of the skull based on the belief
that it is indicative of mental faculties and character."[20]
Phrenology was popular and widely accepted in the 1830s, a
belief that has since gone the way of other such theories of men.

JOSEPH SMITH AND THE SACRED PAPYRI

Shortly after the Latter-day Saints in Kirtland, Ohio, purchased the mummies and papyri the first week of July 1835 from Michael H. Chandler, Joseph Smith, assisted by scribes W. W. Phelps and Oliver Cowdery, "commenced the translation of some of the characters or hieroglyphics." He wrote: "Much to our joy found that one of the rolls contained the writings of Abraham, another the writings of Joseph of Egypt, etc.,—a more full account of which will appear in its place, as I proceed to examine or unfold them. Truly we can say, the Lord is beginning to reveal the abundance of peace and truth."[1]

The Egyptian records occupied much of Joseph's time during the rest of July 1835. His history states: "The remainder of this month, I was continually engaged in translating an alphabet to the Book of Abraham, and arranging a grammar of the Egyptian language as practiced by the ancients."[2]

Pressing Church matters, including a three-week visit to Michigan, prevented him from returning to the papyri for the next two months. His next journal entry relative to the translation reads: "October 1.—This afternoon I labored on the Egyptian alphabet, in company with Brothers Oliver Cowdery and W. W. Phelps, and during the research, the principles of astronomy as understood by Father Abraham and the ancients unfolded to our understanding, the particulars of which will appear hereafter."[3]

How much the Lord revealed to these brethren is, of course,

Joseph Smith translating the papyri (from a painting by William Whittaker)

unknown, but we can draw some tentative conclusions from this journal entry. From the text of the Book of Abraham we see that the principles of astronomy as understood by Abraham and some of his predecessors is alluded to in chapters three through five. Joseph and his scribes were being introduced to a new "Egyptian grammar." It appears that new words and meanings were being revealed that were not in the Egyptian writings comprising the text of the Book of Mormon, such as *Kolob, Shinehah, Kokob, Olea, Kokaubeam, Oliblish, Enish-go-on-dosh, Kae-e-vanrash, Kli-flos-is-es,* and *Hah Ko-kau-beam.*

The Prophet wrote during this study that two prophets, Methuselah and Abraham, had been invited by the Lord to see things relative to the planetary system that no other prophets had been allowed to know. An entry in the Egyptian Alphabet and Grammar under "Kolob in the first degree" reads: "It signifies the first great governing fixed star which is the fartherest that ever has been discovered by the fathers which was discovered by Methusela and also by Abraham."[4]

In the text of the Book of Abraham, Abraham recorded that

"the records of the fathers, even the patriarchs" had come into his possession. Therefore he had "a knowledge of the beginning of the creation, and also of the planets, and of the stars, as they were made known unto the fathers," and he would write about some of these things "for the benefit of my posterity that shall come after me." (Abraham 1:31.)

The source of Abraham's profound knowledge of astronomy was not solely confined to the records he inherited from previous prophets. In Abraham 3:1–2 he explained: "And I, Abraham, had the Urim and Thummim, which the Lord my God had given unto me, in Ur of the Chaldees; and I saw the stars, that they were very great, and that one of them was nearest unto the throne of God; and there were many great ones which were near unto it." Abraham's knowledge of the endless creations of God was broadened even more when the great Creator of heaven and earth himself appeared to him and personally showed and explained to him some of His magnificent handiwork. (See Abraham 3:11–5:21.)

That vision of October 1, 1835, had a great influence on Joseph Smith's understanding. Like Abraham, who said that he would share some of the truths that he knew of the creation (Abraham 1:31), Joseph referred to these Egyptian writings seven years later as he taught the Saints in Nauvoo: "The learning of the Egyptians, and their knowledge of astronomy was no doubt taught them by Abraham and Joseph, as their records testify, who received it from the Lord."[5] He did not share full particulars of what he learned of the planetary system from the papyri.

A question remains: Joseph Smith was the first prophet of this dispensation and foreordained to restore all the significant truths of the past. (See Acts 3:19–21.) Did he, like Abraham, also have a vision of the principles of astronomy?

On October 3, 1835, most of the Twelve Apostles were at Joseph's house when he "exhibited to them the ancient records, and gave explanations." "This day," he added, "passed off with the blessing of the Lord."[6] His scribe at the time, W. W. Phelps, a

gifted poet and writer, was inflamed with these new truths that
expanded his understanding of the planetary system and man's
eternal nature, and wrote his powerful poem "If You Could Hie
to Kolob" (*Hymns,* no. 284):

> If you could hie to Kolob
> In the twinkling of an eye,
> And then continue onward
> With that same speed to fly,
> Do you think that you could ever,
> Through all eternity,
> Find out the generation
> Where Gods began to be?
>
> Or see the grand beginning,
> Where space did not extend?
> Or view the last creation,
> Where Gods and matter end?
> Methinks the Spirit whispers,
> "No man has found 'pure space,'
> Nor seen the outside curtains,
> Where nothing has a place."
>
> The works of God continue,
> And worlds and lives abound;
> Improvement and progression
> Have one eternal round.
> There is no end to matter;
> There is no end to space;
> There is no end to spirit;
> There is no end to race.
>
> There is no end to virtue;
> There is no end to might;
> There is no end to wisdom;
> There is no end to light.
> There is no end to union;
> There is no end to youth;
> There is no end to priesthood;
> There is no end to truth.
>
> There is no end to glory;
> There is no end to love;
> There is no end to being;

There is no death above.
There is no end to glory;
There is no end to love;
There is no end to being;
There is no death above.

The Prophet Continues Translating

On the afternoon of October 7, 1835, Joseph Smith "re-commenced translating the ancient records."[7] The next journal entry that refers to the papyri is on October 29, 1835, when he hired Warren Parrish to serve as his secretary. In a revelation through Joseph to Warren Parrish, the Lord declared: "Inasmuch as he [Warren] will continue to hearken unto my voice, he shall be blessed with wisdom, and with a sound mind, even above his fellows. . . . He shall see great things show forth themselves unto my people; he shall see much of my ancient records, and shall know of hidden things, and shall be endowed with a knowledge of hidden languages; and if he desire and shall seek it at my hands, he shall be privileged with writing much of my word, as a scribe unto me for the benefit of my people."[8]

Joseph recorded in his journal many days spent in translating the records that fall and winter, including November 19, 20, 24, and 25. On November 26, he and his scribe continued working, though they were both "severely afflicted with a cold." The next day, they administered to each other and, according to the Prophet's journal, "we were both relieved."[9]

Three brethren—William E. McLellin, Brigham Young, and Jared Carter—called on the Prophet on December 16. "I exhibited and explained the Egyptian records to them," he wrote, "and explained many things concerning the dealing of God with the ancients, and the formation of the planetary system."[10]

All of these events transpired within the first six months that Joseph Smith had possession of the Egyptian records. Greater demands on his time apparently kept him from returning to the translation for more than six years.

The care of the mummies and papyri were turned over on February 17, 1836, to Joseph Coe, who made arrangements to

The Kirtland Tempole. The four mummies were kept in the upper far-left room, where Joseph Smith began translating the ancient Egyptian papyri

hire a room at John Johnson's inn where they might be exhibited for a fee so that "some benefit may be derived from them." The Prophet admonished him, however, to manage them "with prudence and care, especially the manuscripts."[11]

By August 1836 the papyri had been moved to the Kirtland Temple, where the west room on the top floor was designated by the Prophet as a room he intended to occupy for a translation room.[12] About fifteen months later, on November 2, 1837, "the Church in Kirtland voted to sanction the appointment of Brother Phinehas Richards and Reuben Hedlock, by the Presidency, to translate business for the Church in procuring means to translate and print the records taken from the Catacombs of Egypt, then in the Temple."[13] Joseph Smith at that time was in Far West, Missouri, on Church business. This is the last entry in the *History of the Church* about the writings of Abraham and Joseph while the Church was headquartered at Kirtland.

The Church Displays the Mummies

After Michael H. Chandler sold the mummies and papyri to the Church, both members and nonmembers alike continued to be attracted to this most unusual exhibit in the isolated frontier setting of Kirtland, Ohio.

The mummies and papyri were not always kept together. On October 24, 1835, a Mr. Goodrich and his wife called on Joseph Smith to see the "antient [sic] [Egyptian] Records also called at Doct. F. G. Williams to see the mummies."[14]

The *Cleveland Whig* confirmed that President Frederick G. Williams of the First Presidency had jurisdiction over the mummies:

> CLEVELAND. *July 31.—Another Humbug.*—We are credibly informed that the Mormons have purchased of Mr. Chandler, three of the mummies which he recently exhibited in this village; and that the prophet Joe has ascertained, by examining the papyrus through his spectacles, that they are the bodies of Joseph, (the son of Abraham,) and king Abimelech and his daughter. With this shallow and contemptible story, Williams has commenced travelling about the country, and will, no doubt, gull multitudes into a belief of its truth. Surely one half of the world are fools.—*Whig.*[15]

A Cincinnati paper also spoke of the exhibition of the mummies by "one of their apostles":

> Last summer a man came to Kirtland and brought [among] the Mormons four Egyptian mummies. The exhibition exactly struck their fancy. All the Mormons flocked to see the wonderful sight; and Joseph deciphered some of the hieroglyphics, and made known in writing the name and character and antiquity of some of the mummies;—this was an additional proof of his divine inspiration. The man continued with them a week; and then a command was given them to purchase the whole, which they did for $2400. The mummies were soon sent out for exhibition by one of their apostles, but being unsuccessful, he brought them back to Kirtland, and threw them aside. There is reason to believe, that many who come here with high expectations, have met with sore disappointment.[16]

COURTESY RLDS CHURCH

*The upper west room of the Kirtland Temple, where Joseph Smith
worked on translating the ancient Egyptian papyri*

Some Reactions to the Antiquities

A number of Latter-day Saints wrote about the Chandler collection in letters and diaries. Among them were the following.

W. W. Phelps, writing to his wife, stated that Joseph Smith said the rolls of papyrus "contained the sacred record kept of Joseph in Pharaoh's court in Egypt and the teachings of Father Abraham. God has so ordered it that these mummies and writings have been brought into the Church. . . . These records of old times . . . will make a good witness for the Book of Mormon. There is nothing secret or hidden that shall not be revealed, and they come to the Saints."[17]

Benjamin Johnson wrote in his life story: "And when the writings of Abraham upon papyrus, which accompanied them were taken from its ancient casket, it seemed marvelous indeed.

And all rejoiced when the Prophet told us these writings would be translated."[18]

Stephen Post reported in his journal: "Mon 4. This A.M. I saw the writings of Abraham & Joseph that came with the mummies."[19]

Caroline Crosby reported that her brother Horace Barnes visited Kirtland and saw "Father [Joseph] Smith, [Sr.] and Emma [Smith], who showed him the records of Abraham, that were found with the mummies."[20]

John Whitmer, one of the eight witnesses of the Book of Mormon, wrote in his journal: "After this [Chandler's] exhibition Joseph the Seer saw these records and by the revelations of Jesus Christ could translate these words which gave an account of our forefathers. Much of which was written by Joseph of Egypt who was sold by his brethren, which when all translated will be a pleasing history and of great value to the Saints."[21]

John Corrill, who published a history of the Church in 1839, wrote: "In the summer of 1835, they purchased three or four Egyptian Mummies, with an ancient Egyptian record, written on papyrus, a part of which Smith professed to translate, making it out to be the writing of Abraham."[22]

Wilford Woodruff, who had been away from Kirtland for several months, wrote about a visit to the temple: "We then visited the upper rooms & there viewed four Egyptian mummies & also the Book of Abram [Abraham] written by his own hand & not only the hieroglyphics but also many figures that this precious treasure contains are calculated to make a lasting impression upon the mind which is not to be erased. Many other important views I was privileged with in the upper story the school rooms, belfry &c. all indicating great architecture & wisdom."[23]

Other sources could be cited, but these quotations are sufficient to indicate that according to teachings of early Church leaders, the ancient Egyptian records contained the writings of the patriarchs Abraham and Joseph.

What Did the Papyrus Records Contain?

Within three months after the scrolls were purchased, Joseph Smith had translated, or at least was aware of, the contents of chapters 3, 4, and 5 of the Book of Abraham, which chapters contain information on the planetary system. The first two chapters contained an account of highlights of Abraham's life story in Ur of the Chaldees and in Haran and the beginning of his journey from Haran to Egypt. This is the entire Book of Abraham presently printed in our scriptures.

But the Book of Abraham contained much more material than is presently in the Pearl of Great Price, and the Book of Joseph was never published. Oliver Cowdery wrote about the Egyptian records in an 1835 letter to William Frye. In this letter, which was printed in the *Messenger and Advocate* in December 1835, we have Oliver's impression of some of the unpublished contents of the books of Joseph and Abraham:

> The language in which this record is written is very comprehensive, and many of the hieroglyphics exceedingly striking. The evidence is apparent upon the face, that they were written by persons acquainted with the history of the creation, the fall of man, and more or less of the correct ideas of notions of the Deity. The representation of the god-head—three, yet in one, is curiously drawn to give simply, though impressively, the writers views of that exalted personage. The serpent, represented as walking, or formed in a manner to be able to walk, standing in front of, and near a female figure, is to me, one of the greatest representations I have ever seen upon paper, or a writing substance; and must go so far towards convincing the rational mind of the correctness and divine authority of the holy scriptures, and especially that part which has ever been assailed by the infidel community, as being a fiction, as to carry away, with one mighty sweep, the whole atheistical fabric, without leaving a vestage sufficient for a foundation stone.
>
> Enoch's Pillar, as mentioned by Josephus, is upon the same roll.—True, our present version of the bible does not mention this fact, though it speaks of the righteousness of Abel and the holiness of Enoch,—one slain because his offering was accepted of the Lord, and the other taken to the regions of everlasting day without being confined to the narrow limits of the

tomb, or tasting death; but Josephus says that the descendants of Seth were virtuous, and possessed a great knowledge of the heavenly bodies, and, that, in consequence of the prophecy of Adam, that the world should be destroyed once by water and again by fire, Enoch wrote a history or an account of the same, and put into two pillars one of brick and the other of stone; and that the same were in being at his (Josephus') day.

The inner end of the same roll, (Joseph's record,) presents a representation of the judgment: At one view you behold the Savior seated upon his throne, crowned, and holding the sceptres of righteousness and power, before whom also, are assembled the twelve tribes of Israel, the nations, languages and tongues of the earth, the kingdoms of the world over which satan is represented as reigning. Michael the archangel, holding the key of the bottomless pit, and at the same time the devil as being chained and shut up *in* the bottomless pit. But upon this last scene, I am able only to give you a *shadow*, to the real picture. I am certain it cannot be viewed without filling the mind with awe, unless the mind is far estranged from God: and I sincerely hope, that mine may never go so far estray, nor wander from those rational principles of the doctrine of our Savior, so much, as to become darkened in the least, and thereby fail to have that, to us, the greatest of all days, and the most sublime of all transactions, so impressively fixed upon the heart, that I become not like the beast, not knowing whither I am going, nor what shall be my final end!

I might continue my communication to a great length upon the different figures and characters represented upon the two rolls, but I have no doubt my subject has already become sufficiently prolix for your patience: I will therefore soon cease for the present.—When the translation of these valuable documents will be completed, I am unable to say; neither can I give you a probable idea how large volumes they will make; but judging from their size, and the comprehensiveness of the language, one might reasonably expect to see a sufficient to develop much upon the mighty acts of the ancient men of God, and of his dealing with the children of men when they saw him face to face. Be there little or much, it must be an inestimable acquisition to our present scriptures, fulfilling, in a small degree, the word of the prophet: For the earth shall be full of the knowledge of the Lord as the waters cover the sea.[24]

From this report on the unpublished content of the ancient writings, several doctrinal themes emerge:

1. Deity—three persons, yet in one
2. The Creation
3. Satan's influence in the Garden of Eden
4. The fall of man
5. Enoch's pillar (specifically the planetary system)
6. Virtuous descendants of Seth
7. Mighty acts of the ancient men of God
8. Final judgment under Christ
9. Michael the archangel holding the key of the bottomless pit
10. The devil at judgment confined to the bottomless pit

The Egyptian Scrolls and the Temple Ceremony

Facsimile 2 in the Book of Abraham, together with Oliver Cowdery's explanation of the contents of the book of Joseph, seem to have relevance with regard to the temple ceremony, about which Elder James E. Talmage wrote as follows:

> The Temple Endowment, as administered in modern temples, comprises instruction relating to the significance and sequence of past dispensations, and the importance of the present as the greatest and grandest era in human history. This course of instruction includes a recital of the most prominent events of the creative period, the condition of our first parents in the Garden of Eden, their disobedience and consequent expulsion from that blissful abode, their condition in the lone and dreary world when doomed to live by labor and sweat, the plan of redemption by which the great transgression may be atoned, the period of the great apostasy, the restoration of the Gospel with all its ancient powers and privileges, the absolute and indispensable condition of personal purity and devotion to the right in present life, and a strict compliance with Gospel requirements.
>
> As will be shown, the temples erected by the Latter-day Saints provide for the giving of these instructions in separate rooms, each devoted to a particular part of the course; and by this provision it is possible to have several classes under instruction at one time.

The ordinances of the endowment embody certain obligations on the part of the individual, such as covenant and
promise to observe the law of strict virtue and chastity, to be
charitable, benevolent, tolerant and pure; to devote both talent
and material means to the spread of truth and the uplifting of
the race; to maintain devotion to the cause of truth; and to seek
in every way to contribute to the great preparation that the
earth may be made ready to receive her King,—the Lord Jesus
Christ. With the taking of each covenant and the assuming of
each obligation a promised blessing is pronounced, contingent
upon the faithful observance of the conditions.

No jot, iota, or tittle of the temple rites is otherwise than
uplifting and sanctifying. In every detail the endowment ceremony contributes to covenants of morality of life, consecration
of person to high ideals, devotion to truth, patriotism to
nation, and allegiance to God. The blessings of the House of
the Lord are restricted to no privileged class; every member of
the Church may have admission to the temple with the right
to participate in the ordinances thereof, if he comes duly
accredited as of worthy life and conduct.[25]

The writings of Abraham and Joseph were purchased by the
Church in July 1835 and the partial endowment was introduced
to the brethren by the Prophet Joseph Smith in January 1836. Is
this merely coincidental? Elder Bruce R. McConkie, referring to
temple ordinances, wrote, "They were given in modern times to
the prophet Joseph Smith by revelation, many things connected
with them being translated by the Prophet from the papyrus on
which the Book of Abraham was recorded."[26]

11

CHAOS IN KIRTLAND

It appears that the Lord smiled upon the Saints in Kirtland in their early years as they struggled and sacrificed to expand their growing city, establish a holy people, and build a temple unto the Most High. They were led by a prophet, to whom the Lord had frequently spoken to guide him in this new gospel dispensation. Sacred writings, older than any previously known, had been brought to the Church for their guidance and confirmed to them that the Lord was continuously mindful of his children.

The temple was dedicated March 27, 1836, and during that week the Savior himself appeared within its sacred walls, along with the ancient prophets Moses, Elias, and Elijah, to ratify its divine acceptance. Many faithful Latter-day Saints saw and heard glorious heavenly manifestations during that season of rejoicing. Temple ordinances were introduced to the leaders for the edification and learning of the faithful. The members must have identified with the Nephites during the first years of their mini-millennium when their prophet Nephi wrote: "They were in one, the children of Christ, and heirs to the kingdom of God. And how blessed were they! For the Lord did bless them in all their doings." (4 Nephi 1:17–18.)

Sadly, the jubilation was but momentary. Historian Milton V. Backman explained the dilemma:

> The year following the dedication of the Kirtland Temple saw a spirit of pride, selfishness, disaffection, and apostasy sweep through the quorums of the Church. In the summer of

The Prophet Joseph Smith, translator of the ancient Egyptian papyri

1837, members of the Quorum of the Twelve Apostles, witnesses to the Book of Mormon, and other priesthood leaders met in the upper room of the Kirtland Temple. Though the preceding year many of these same individuals had witnessed in that building some of the most remarkable spiritual manifestations in the history of the restoration movement, now they were meeting to oppose the leadership of Joseph Smith. At this assembly, some persons who had once been faithful supporters of the Prophet recommended that he be replaced as president of the Church by David Whitmer. Others vehemently opposed this motion, including Brigham Young, Heber C. Kimball, and John Smith. Brigham Young, "in a plain and forcible manner," said that he knew that Joseph was a spokesman for the Lord, and though others "might rail and slander him [the Prophet] as much as they pleased," they "could not destroy" his appointment as a "Prophet of God."

Their apostate actions, he declared, would destroy their authority, cut the thread that bound them to the Prophet and to God, and lead them to destruction. Many of the disgruntled members, enraged at Elder Young's efforts to thwart their recommendations, threatened to resolve the conflict with physical blows. The meeting finally ended without agreement on a course of action. According to Elder Young, "The knees of many of the strongest men in the Church faltered."

On another occasion during this turbulent period, Warren Parrish, John F. Boynton, and other dissidents entered the temple on a Sabbath morning armed with pistols and bowie knives and sat in the Aaronic Priesthood pulpits at the east end. Shortly after the morning service began, the men interrupted the meeting in what Eliza R. Snow, who witnessed the interruption, called a "fearful scene." Drawing their pistols and knives, the dissidents rushed from the stand into the congregation and attempted to gain control of the building. Amid great confusion and with screams of alarm, some persons tried to escape by jumping out the windows. Local officials were summoned, and finally, with the assistance of the police, members of the congregation succeeded in removing the belligerents from the temple. Though no one was injured, the incident was another in a disrupting chain of events leading to the expulsion of the Saints from Kirtland just a few months later.[1]

Space does not permit a detailed account of all the problems facing the Kirtland Saints, as it takes us away from the central theme of this work, but it does appear to have been the "worst of times" for those leaders who had dared to hope and dream of what might have been.

Dr. Backman named some of the prominent leaders who stumbled and fell and the great impact that had on the few thousand Kirtland Saints. To keep things in perspective, one is reminded that today there are many stakes in the Church that are numerically larger than the entire membership of the Church in Kirtland in 1837 and 1838. Dr. Backman reported:

> Between November 1837 and June 1838, possibly two or three hundred Kirtland Saints withdrew from the Church, representing from 10 to 15 percent of the membership there.

Many of the apostates had served in major positions of responsibility. During a nine-month period, almost one-third of the General Authorities were excommunicated, disfellowshipped, or removed from their Church callings. Among those who left the Church during this stormy period were the three witnesses to the Book of Mormon (Oliver Cowdery, David Whitmer, and Martin Harris), four apostles (John F. Boynton, Lyman E. Johnson, Luke S. Johnson, and William E. McLellin), three of the original presidents of the First Quorum of Seventies (Hazen Aldrich, Leonard Rich, and Sylvester Smith), and two of the presidents of the seventies who were serving in 1837 (John Gould and John Gaylord). One president of the seventies (Salmon Gee) was disfellowshipped, and one member of the First Presidency (Frederick G. Williams) was released from his calling. Although some of these leaders were not excommunicated until after they had moved to Missouri, the roots of their apostasy stem back to transgressions that occurred in Kirtland. (Almost half of those who were excommunicated, disfellowshipped, or dropped from their positions of responsibility in 1837 or 1838 later repented and returned to the Church.)[2]

The Mummies Are in Danger

Joseph Smith, Hyrum Smith, and Sidney Rigdon fled from Kirtland the night of January 12, 1838, and moved to Missouri to escape the violence of the apostates. A faithful member reported that "immediately upon their departure persecution commenced with an iron hand. It was the life and glory of the apostates to hatch up vexatious lawsuits and strip the brethren of their property and means of removing. It seemed as though all power was given them to torment the saints."[3]

On January 15, 1838, John Smith wrote to his son George A. Smith about the fanatacism of some of the apostates: "I mentioned to you in my last [letter] that many had deserted from the Church and they are striving to destroy with a great deal more zeal than they did ever to build up."[4]

Nearly two millennia earlier, the prophet Mormon had observed the same degree of intensity of hatred among some apostates once they had forfeited the Spirit of the Lord: "And thus we can plainly discern that after a people have been once enlightened by the Spirit of God, and have had great knowledge of things pertaining to righteousness, and then have fallen away into sin and transgression, they become more hardened, and thus their state becomes worse than though they had never known these things." (Alma 24:30.)

Once apostates have forsaken the fountain of truth that brought peace and understanding to their souls, they seem to be unable to find solace and peace in any man-made organization. As a result, they can either repent and return to God or they remain embittered and openly rebel against the Lord, his gospel, and his people.

The Prophet's mother, Lucy Mack Smith, reported: "Their first movement was to sue Joseph for debt, and, with this pretense, seize upon every piece of property belonging to any of the family. Joseph then had in his possession four Egyptian mummies, with some ancient records that accompanied them. These the mob swore they would take, and then burn every one of them. Accordingly, they obtained an execution upon them for an unjust debt of fifty dollars; but, by various stratagems, we succeeded in keeping them out of their hands."[5]

The enemies of the Church had the antiquities in their possession for a short time. Hepzibah Richards, writing from Kirtland on January 18, 1838, to her brother Willard, serving his second mission for the Church in England, confirmed that "the mummies and records have been attacked. Mummies sold—Records missing."[6]

Warren Parrish, formerly the Prophet's personal secretary, was one of the apostate instigators who seized the mummies and the papyrus. The *Western Reserve Chronicle* reported on January 30, 1838, the following:

> TROUBLE AMONG THE MORMONS.—We learn from a source to be relied on, that the Mormon Society at Kirtland is breaking up. Smith and Rigdon, after prophecying the destruction of the town, left with their families in the night, and others of the faithful are following. The Reformers' are in possession of the Temple, and have excluded the Smith and

Rigdon party. An exposure of the proceedings of the Society is
in course of preparation by one [Warren] Parish, the former
confidential secretary of the prophet Smith. He has the
records, &c., in his possession.—*Cleveland Herald and Gazette.*

Jay Todd mentioned in his book *The Saga of the Book of
Abraham* that a legal "execution" had been made upon the
papyri. Part of the document that was missing was discovered
in 1968 by the Reverend Wesley P. Walters in Marissa, Illinois. It
reads: "I convey the two undivided thirds of records of and box
Exclusive of the mummies." The document, dated January 4,
1838, was signed by Joseph Smith Jr. and attested to by John P.
Markele and Nicholas Markele.

The next page of the document states: "I do hereby relin-
quish on the box and records which James Markell has Levied in
my favor as the property of J. Smith Jr. and my claim on the
same. Kirtland Jan. 4th 1838." It was signed Nicholas Markele
and attested to by John P. Markele.[7]

On the front of the document are the words "Article of
Agreement Between Joseph Smith Jun. and Joseph Smith Sr."

Todd's book prompted a reader to write and clarify how the
Church leaders, as Lucy Mack Smith said, "by various stratagems . . . succeeded in keeping them out of [the apostates']
hands." Mrs. Hazel B. Roese, writing from Ferndale, Michigan,
explained that there "were three brothers, John P. Markell was
my g. grandfather, [and] Nicholas and James were his younger
brothers. My beloved g. grandfather was 'Judge John Phillip
Markell.' The Markell family including their father Peter
Markell were very close friends of Joseph Smith. Knowing the
story as I have read it and remember my grandfather P. Henry
Booth relating it to me. Some one, if I remember correctly, related to Joseph Coe got the Records (Papyrus) and these
Markells of mine were foxey enough to conn this fellow out of
them. It seems he owed Judge Markell some money and Uncle
James was deputized to help retrieve the records. It was quite a
joke in the family."[8]

Removing the Mummies and Manuscripts from Kirtland

Though the antiquities had been wrested from the hands of the apostates, they obviously were not safe in Kirtland. William Huntington wrote of those perilous times:

> Many of the leading Elders apostatized and turned against the Prophet seeking to take his life, but God warned him to rise up by night and depart for Missouri which he did and as fast as possible all the faithful followed, and those who could not do so but were forced to stay another winter were hunted, harassed, robbed and mobbed by apostates and among that number I was one although at the same time my house was a hiding place for old father Joseph Smith his sons Carlos and Samuel and many others. In my house the mummies and Egyptian Records were hid to keep from sworn destruction by apostates."[9]

The Huntington family found a unique hiding place for the four mummies. Zina, William Huntington's teenage daughter, had some very unusual roommates:

> Candle in hand, Zina opened the door of her dark bedroom. In the dim light, she could see the four black shapes protruding from under the big, hand-carved wooden bed. They were the sarcophagi, each containing the mummified body of an ancient Egyptian—enough to frighten the sleep out of any teenage youngster.
>
> But Zina was not to be frightened by a few mummies, Egyptian or otherwise. She set her candlestick down on the chest of drawers, matter-of-factly dressed for bed and went to sleep wondering if the permanent sleepers beneath her had been nobles or kings or just ordinary folk like herself.
>
> The four sarcophagi had been placed in the Huntington home for safekeeping. Apostates and other enemies of the Church in Kirtland, Ohio were attempting to attach all Church property.
>
> To protect the mummies from seizure, they were removed from the temple and stored under Zina's bed. These were the mummies purchased by the Church along with the hieroglyphic manuscript of the Book of Abraham.[10]

William Huntington soon found that he could neither live in

his home nor sell his farm "because of the dishonesty of Mr. Bump who was one of the dissenters." Through the loan of a yoke of cattle from one friend and another loan of thirty-two dollars, the family fled Kirtland to go to Missouri. The father, William, walked and drove the ox team the distance of nearly one thousand miles. Before the Huntingtons left Kirtland, the mummies and the papyrus scrolls were turned over to another family.

Members of the Edwin Woolley family, who lived in Rochester, Ohio, had heard missionaries preach, and several were persuaded of the truthfulness of their message. In late 1837, in order to satisfy himself about Mormonism, Edwin traveled to Kirtland, eighty-five miles from Rochester, to meet Joseph Smith. At the time Kirtland was in chaos, and for his safety, the Prophet had left town. However, Edwin did learn the whereabouts of the Prophet's father, Joseph Smith Sr., who was then staying with the Huntingtons in New Portage, Ohio. Lucy Mack Smith recalled what happened:

> A man by the name of Edward [sic] Woolley came to Kirtland to see Mr. Smith; not finding him there, he went to New Portage, and persuaded my husband to accompany him home.
>
> After Mr. Smith had been at this gentleman's residence about two weeks, we became very uneasy about him; and, as we did not know at that time whither he had gone, William [Lucy's son] set out in pursuit of him, in order to learn, if possible, whether he had met with friends, and was well provided for, or had fallen into the hands of his enemies, and been murdered, for we had as much reason to apprehend the latter calamity, as to hope for the former good fortune.
>
> It was some time after William arrived at New Portage, before he could ascertain where my husband had gone. But as soon as he did receive the desired information he proceeded to Edward Woolley's, where he found his father in good health, but extremely anxious about the family.[11]

When Joseph Smith Sr. left for Edwin Woolley's home in Rochester, Edwin's brother recorded, he "hired a wagon to bring the mummies and the Record of Abraham, etc."[12] He stayed with the Woolleys for part of the winter before returning home.

Were the Mummies and Records Taken to Missouri?

The location of the Egyptian antiquities for the next year or two is uncertain. William I. Appleby stated in his journal that the mummies and papyrus were purchased in Kirtland for $2,400, and then "from Kirtland they were removed to Nauvoo."[13] However, all other references located contradict this statement, including the following experience told about Anson Call:

> After settling his family on his farm at Three Forks and prior to September, 1838, Anson made a business trip to Far West, Missouri, where he had an opportunity to visit with the Prophet Joseph Smith and receive information concerning the translations of the Book of Abraham and the work the Prophet was doing in revising the Bible. Anson writes:
> "While at Far West I happened in John Corl's [Corrill's] or the church store and my attention was called by Vincent Knights who was opening some boxes of goods. Says he, 'Joseph will be much pleased with these. ['] He had been very uneasy about the translation of the Bible and the Egyptian Records. Here they are, placing them on the table. Said he to me, 'If you will take one of these, I will the other and we will carry them over to Joseph's office.' There we found Joseph and six or seven other brethren. Joseph was much pleased with the arrival of the books, and said to us 'Sit down and we will read to you from the translations of the Book of Abraham.' Oliver Cowdery then read until he was tired when Thomas Marsh read making altogether about two hours. I was much interested in the work."[14]

This entry contains several valuable insights except for one problem: Oliver Cowdery was not in good standing in the Church in 1838 and would not have been in such a gathering by September 1838. Apparently Anson Call confused Oliver Cowdery's name with that of another person when he recorded this episode.

Samuel Woolley, in a diary entry in 1838, claims the distinction of helping to transport the mummies and papyrus from Kirtland to Far West, Missouri, when the Church's headquarters were moved there.[15] He was the last person to care for the antiquities while they remained in Ohio.

William Swartzell, the author of an anti-Mormon pamphlet, made the following entry on May 24, 1838, as he traveled about the state of Missouri: "Stayed at Richmond Landing this evening. This is the place where the Mormons land their goods for transportation across the country. I saw there Joseph Smith's box of mummys."[16]

Exactly what he meant is unknown. Was there only one box? And did it contain one mummy or all four mummies? And/or did it contain the papyrus and other antiquities?

On July 26, 1838, the same critic wrote: "Doing nothing today, except looking at the hands employed in getting out logs for brother Joseph Smith's house, in which he intends translating the hieroglyphics of the Egyptian mummies."[17]

The Missouri period in Church history was not a time to meditate and ponder the scriptures and translate the words of the prophets. Sadly, it was a time of combating corrupt politicians, irate neighbors, rapine, murder, a governmental "extermination order," false arrests and imprisonments, and general unrest. Whether all four mummies and the entire papyrus collection were in Missouri or not is difficult to determine, since very few records exist that mention them at all. The Nauvoo period would provide that necessary but temporary respite to allow the Prophet to return to the scrolls and prepare some for publication.

12

THE BOOK OF ABRAHAM
IS PUBLISHED

When the penniless Latter-day Saints were forced to leave Missouri during the winter of 1838–39, they found sanctuary in Commerce, Illinois, which William E. Berrett described as "a swampy terrain . . . covered with underbrush and scattered trees." He continued: "The land was practically deserted. Save for a half dozen stone and log houses squatting near the river bank and mockingly designated as 'Commerce' one might have counted the dwellings for miles around upon the fingers of his two hands. Swarms of mosquitoes, the then-unknown carriers of malaria fever, were everywhere. The place was unhealthy, shunned by settler and wayfarer."[1]

The Saints, living in squalid temporary encampments on both sides of the Mississippi River, were waiting to build their new homes. There were many places to live that were more inviting, but the impoverished Saints could not pay the price. Commerce was purchased through the Church leaders' signing long-term promissory notes totaling fourteen thousand dollars.

The Prophet renamed the swampy site Nauvoo, a Hebrew word meaning beautiful. With renewed hope and with great effort, the Saints went to work and transformed their marshy inheritance into "the City Beautiful."

Dr. Berrett described the transformation that took place in Nauvoo on the shores of the Mississippi between 1839 and 1844:

> Those people on the banks of the Mississippi, who like Jesus of Nazareth had nowhere to lay their heads, were

nearer to Zion than they had ever been before. Their heartrending troubles had swept them clean of all sordid desires. Those who were not pure in heart unconsciously remained behind. For the first time it began to dawn upon the Church that a "Zion People" was infinitely more important than a "Zion Place," for without a "Zion People" no spot in all the world could remain holy.

While the Church seemed at its lowest ebb to the casual observer, the strength within was greater than before. The faith of these people, their loyalty to the Prophet, and the missionary zeal which swept over them has never been paralleled in history. That deep and abiding strength was to change a swamp into a great city; miserable shelters into splendid houses; penniless people into the most prosperous citizens of Illinois. That missionary zeal was to carry the gospel into many lands and double the membership of the Church. . . . A people stripped of all earthly possessions, money, homes, factories, lands, rebuilt in five short years a city-state which was the envy of long-settled communities.[2]

The leaders in Nauvoo once again felt it was time to turn their attention to those sacred records they had been forced to shelve in Kirtland. In one of the last meetings of the Kirtland high council, held on November 5, 1837, the brethren considered soliciting funds to assist in the publication and further translation of the Abrahamic text: "The Church was called upon to know if they would sanction the appointment of the Presidents in authorizing Brother Richards and Brother Hadlock, to transact the business of the Church in procuring means to translate and print those records taken from the chatocombs [sic] of Egypt, now in the temple, the vote was full and prompt to confirm the same."[3]

Because Joseph Smith was absent from their midst, having gone to Missouri to conduct Church business, further printing and translating of the papyri was not possible at that time.

After an interruption of two and a half years, the Prophet had a statement prepared to be read to the high council in Nauvoo. At a council in his office on June 20, 1840, his clerk, Robert B. Thompson, presented the proposition that the Prophet be freed from all temporal duties to enable him to concentrate on the spiritual needs of the Church. A portion of the document read: ". . . he felt it his duty to engage more particularly in the spiritual welfare of the saints and also, to the translation of the Egyptian Records—the Bible—and wait upon the Lord for such revelations as may be suited to the condition and circumstances of the Church."[4]

On July 3, 1840, members the high council sustained the Prophet's request and entered the following statement in their minute book: "We feel perfectly satisfied with the course taken by Joseph Smith Jr. and feel a disposition as far as it is in our power to assist him so as to relieve him from the temporalities of the church in order that he may devote his time more particularly to the spiritualities of the same, believing by so doing we shall promote the good of the whole Church."[5]

To emphasize that they were in earnest about publishing, the First Presidency released a statement dated August 31, 1840, and addressed "To the Saints Scattered Abroad." The message included these passages:

> Having through the kindness of our God been delivered from destruction, and having secured a location upon which we have again commenced operations for the good of His people, we feel disposed to go forward and unite our energies for the upbuilding of the Kingdom, and establishing the Priesthood in their fullness and glory. The work which has to be accomplished in the last days is one of vast importance, and will call into action the energy, skill, talent, and ability of the Saints, so that it may roll forth with that glory and majesty described by the prophet; and will consequently require the concentration of the Saints, to accomplish works of such magnitude and grandeur. . . .
>
> Dear brethren, feeling desirous to carry out the purposes of God to which work we have been called; and to be co-workers with Him in this last dispensation; we feel the necessity of having the hearty cooperation of the Saints throughout this land, and upon the islands of the sea. It will be necessary for the Saints to hearken to counsel and turn their attention to the Church, the establishment of the Kingdom, and lay aside every selfish principle, everything low and groveling; and stand forward in the cause of truth, and assist to the utmost of

their power, those to whom has been given the pattern and design. . . .

Believing the time has now come, when it is necessary to erect a house of prayer, a house of order, a house for the worship of our God, where the ordinances can be attended to agreeably to His divine will, in this region of country—to accomplish which, considerable exertion must be made, and means will be required—and as the work must be hastened in righteousness, it behooves the Saints to weigh the importance of these things, in their minds, in all their bearings, and then take such steps as are necessary to carry them into operation; and arming themselves with courage, resolve to do all they can, and feel themselves as much interested as though the whole labor depended on themselves alone. . . .

Connected with the building up of the Kingdom, is the printing and circulation of the Book of Mormon, Doctrine and Covenants, hymnbook, and the new translation of the Scriptures. It is unnecessary to say anything respecting these works; those who have read them, and who have drunk of the stream of knowledge which they convey, know how to appreciate them; and although fools may have them in derision, yet they are calculated to make men wise unto salvation, and sweep away the cobwebs of superstition of ages, throw a light on the proceedings of Jehovah which have already been accomplished, and mark out the future in all its dreadful and glorious realities. Those who have tasted the benefit derived from a study of those works, will undoubtedly vie with each other in their zeal for sending them abroad throughout the world, that every son of Adam may enjoy the same privileges, and rejoice in the same truths.[6]

Some may wonder if this statement includes the Book of Abraham, since it is not specifically mentioned. There should be no question that it does, since the original subheading for the statement read "Printing the New Translation and Abraham's Record."

Approximately a year later, on August 16, 1841, Brigham Young presided over a special conference of the Church in the absence of Joseph Smith, who was at home "on account of the death of his child." The Prophet arrived at the afternoon session and explained the purpose of the conference, stating that "the time had come when the Twelve should be called upon to stand in their place next to the First Presidency, and attend to the settling of emigrants and the business of the Church at the stakes, and assist to bear off the Kingdom victoriously to the nations, . . . and at the same time relieve him, so that he might attend to the business of translating." The motion was "moved, seconded and carried, that the conference approve of the instructions of President Smith in relation to the Twelve, and that they proceed accordingly to attend to the duties of their office."⁷

The Times and Seasons

On January 28, 1842, the Lord gave to Joseph Smith the following revelation for the Twelve concerning the *Times and Seasons,* the Church's bimonthly newspaper: "Verily thus saith

Wilford Woodruff, who was the business manager for the Times and Seasons

the Lord unto you, my servant Joseph, go and say unto the Twelve, that it is my will to have them take in hand the editorial department of the *Times and Seasons,* according to that manifestation which shall be given unto them by the power of my Holy Spirit in the midst of their counsel."[8]

Six days later Wilford Woodruff was named business manager of the printing office, and John Taylor was called to work alongside Joseph Smith in the editorial department. Apparently the Lord had important matters at hand, with two of the Twelve assigned to directly oversee the affairs of the Church newspaper under the Prophet's direction.

In the issue of the *Times and Seasons* dated February 15, 1842, the retiring editor, Ebenezer Robinson, wrote his last editorial. After reviewing the difficulties he had had in protecting the printing press in Missouri—by burying it in the earth—and relating other personal privations he had endured, he announced an exciting new era in printing in the Church:

> The Times and Seasons is now placed on a permanent basis, with a liberal patronage, and its circulation daily increasing. The building in which it is published was erected expressly for a printing establishment; with spacious rooms, where each branch can be carried on in its own department, without interfering with the other. The church, also, is in a flourishing and prosperous condition—more so than at any previous period since its rise; naught but joy and gladness seems to pervade the bosoms of the saints, and peace and happiness attend all their footsteps.
>
> Under these circumstances I now take leave of the editorial department of the Times and Seasons, having disposed of my entire interest in the printing establishment, book-bindery, and stereotype foundery, and they are transferred into other hands. The Editorial chair will be filled by our esteemed brother, President Joseph Smith, assisted by Elder John Taylor, of the Quorum of the Twelve, under whose able and talented guidance, this will become the most interesting and useful religious journal of the day.
>
> With these considerations, I feel confident that the agents and friends of the Times and Seasons will exert themselves to support the press; knowing that while it is under the supervi-

sion of him whom God has chosen to lead his people in the last days, all things will go right.[9]

In the same edition, Joseph Smith explained why he had undertaken this new role as editor of the Church newspaper:

As it regards ourselves we have very little to say, but shall leave it for the future to unfold; and for a discerning public to judge. The important events that are daily transpiring around us; the rapid advance of truth; the many communications that we are receiving, daily, from elders abroad; both in this country, in England, from the continent of Europe, and other parts of the world; the convulsed state of the nations; the epistles and teachings of the Twelve; and the revelations which we are receiving from the most High, will [no] doubt furnish us with material to make this paper interesting to all who read it, and whilst we solicit the patronage, and support of our friends, we pray that the God of Israel may inspire our hearts with understanding and direct our pen in truth.[10]

At that time, Joseph Smith was preparing the Abrahamic translation for publication in the paper. Elder Woodruff recorded in his journal:

Truly the Lord has raised up Joseph the Seer of the seed of Abraham out of the loins of ancient Joseph, & is now clothing him with mighty power & wisdom & knowledge which is more clearly manifest & felt in the midst of his intimate friends than any other class of mankind. The Lord is Blessing Joseph with power to reveal the mysteries of the kingdom of God; to translate through the Urim & Thummim Ancient records & Hieroglyphics as old as Abraham or Adam which causes our hearts to burn within us while we behold their glorious truths opened unto us. Joseph the Seer has presented us some of the Book of Abraham which was written by his own hand but hid from the knowledge of many for the last four thousand years but has now come to light through the mercy of God. Joseph has had those records in his possession for several years but has never presented them before the world in the english language untill now. But he is now about to publish it to the world or parts of it by publishing it in the Times & Seasons for Joseph the Seer is now the Editor of that paper & Elder Taylor assists him in writing while it has fallen to my lot to take charge of the Business part of the establishment. I have had the privilege this day of assisting in setting the [type] *for printing* the first [piece] of the *BOOK OF ABRAHAM* that is to be presented to the inhabitants of the *EARTH* in the *LAST DAYS*. My soul has been much edifyed of late from time to time in hearing Joseph the Seer converse about the mysteries of the Kingdom of God, truly God is with him & is making him mighty in wisdom & knowledge & I am convinced for myself that none of the Prophets Seers or Revelators of the Earth have ever accomplished a greater work than will be accomplished in the Last days through the mercy of God by JOSEPH THE SEER.[11]

On February 20, Elder Woodruff recorded in his diary that during the week the newspaper staff had "prepared a plate for making a cut at the commencement of the Book of Abraham which is to be published in the 9 No of the 3 vol of the Times & Seasons which will be interesting to many of the inhabitants of the earth."

The next day Joseph Smith sent an announcement to the Saints relative to the building of the temple in Nauvoo. At the conclusion of this announcement was an addendum that read in part:

> We would also say to all the churches, that inasmuch as they want the blessings of God and angels, as also of the Church of Jesus Christ, and wish to see it spread and prosper through the world, and Zion built up and truth and righteousness prevail,—let all the different branches of the Church of Jesus Christ of Latter-day Saints in all the world, call meetings in their respective places and tithe themselves and send up to this place to the Trustee in Trust, so that his hands may be loosed, and the Temple go on, and other works be done, such as the new translation of the Bible, and the record of Father Abraham published to the world.[12]

The Prophet dictated a statement to Willard Richards to be included in the March 1, 1842, edition of the *Times and Seasons*, outlining his objectives as editor. He planned to publish various documents in serial form, including the Book of Abraham, for the benefit of the Church. This is his statement:

A considerable quantity of the matter in the last paper was in type before the establishment came into my hands.—Some of which went to press without my review or knowledge and a multiplicitty of business while entering on the additional care of the editorial department of the Times and Seasons must be my apology for what is past.—

In future I design to furnish much original matter which will be found of inestimable advantage to the saints,—& all who desire a knowledge of the kingdom of God,—and as it is not practicable to bring forth the new translation of the Scriptures & various records of ancient date & great worth to this generation in the usual form by books I shall permit specimens of the same in the Times & Seasons as fast as time and space will admit,—so that the honest in heart may be cheered and comforted and go on their way rejoicing,—as their souls become exposed.—& their understanding enlightened by a knowledge of God's work through the fathers in former days as well as what He is about to do in latter days to fulfill the words of the fathers.—

In the present no. will be found the commencement of the Records discovered in Egypt some time since as penned by the hand of Father Abraham which I shall outline to translate & publish as fast as possible till the whole is completed and as the saints have long been anxious to obtain a copy of these records those [who] are now taking this Times & Seasons will confer a special favor on their brethren who do not take the paper by informing them that they can now obtain their hearts.[13]

However, that statement was not published. Rather, the following brief statement addressed "to Subscribers" and signed by Joseph Smith appeared in the March 1 edition of the paper: "This paper commences my editorial career, I alone stand responsible for it, and shall do for all papers having my signature henceforward. I am not responsible for the publication, or arrangement of the former paper: the matter did not come under my supervision."[14]

Only that disclaimer for any previous responsibility for the editor's chair was printed. One may conjecture that the demands on the Prophet's time kept him from finishing the Inspired Version of the Bible (JST) and translating more of the Book of Abraham, which he had hoped to publish "till the whole is completed."

The first segment of the Book of Abraham was published in the *Times and Seasons* under the date of March 1, 1842. It included Facsimile 1 and the text that is now found in Abraham 1:1–2:18. The paper was apparently not printed March 1, since an entry in the Prophet's journal on that date reads: "During the forenoon I was at my office and the printing office, correcting the first plate or cut of the records of Father Abraham, prepared by Reuben Hedlock, for the *Times and Seasons*, and in council in my office, in the afternoon; and in the evening with the Twelve and their wives at Elder Woodruff's."[15] The occasion was Elder Woodruff's thirty-fifth birthday.

The next day the Prophet recorded, "I read the proof of the *Times and Seasons*, as editor for the first time, No. 9, Vol. III, in which is the commencement of the Book of Abraham."[16] On March 4 he was in the printing office "exhibiting the Book of Abraham in the original to Brother Reuben Hedlock, so that he might take the size of the several plates or cuts, and prepare the blocks for the *Times and Seasons*; and also gave instruction concerning the arrangement of the writing on the large cut, illustrating the principles of astronomy, with other general business."[17]

The "large cut" Joseph referred to was Facsimile 2, which was published in the next edition of the newspaper in double-page size. Reuben Hedlock's name, as the engraver, still appears on Facsimiles 2 and 3 in the present edition of the Pearl of Great Price.

On March 8, Joseph Smith wrote in his journal, "Recommenced translating from the records of Abraham for the tenth number of the *Times and Seasons*, and was engaged at [my] office day and evening."[18] The next day he noted: "Examining copy for the *Times and Seasons*, presented by Messrs. Taylor and Bennett, and a variety of other business in my office, in the morning; in the afternoon continued the translation of the Book of Abraham, called at Bishop Knight's and Mr. Davis', with the recorder, and continued translating and revising, and reading letters in the evening, Sister Emma being present in the office."[19]

The history is not clear about whether Joseph was further translating new material or proofreading the text he had translated seven years before in Kirtland. The handwritten text for the second installment that was published in the *Times and Seasons* had been completed in Kirtland, and very few changes were made in the printed copy.

The second installment of the Book of Abraham, which included the rest of the text of the present Book of Abraham, Abraham 2:19–5:21, and Facsimile 2 in an oversized double-page hypocephalus, appeared in an issue of *Times and Seasons* dated March 15, 1842. However, it was actually printed March 19, according to Wilford Woodruff's journal entry for that date: "Spent the day in the printing Office we struck off about 500 No of the 10 No 3 vol of Times & Seasons which contained the portion of the Book of Abraham that gave his account of Kolob, Oliblish, God sitting upon his Throne The Earth, other planets & many great & glorious things as revealed to Abraham through the power of the priesthood. The truths of the Book of Abraham are truly edifying great & glorious which are among the rich treasures that are revealed unto us in the last days."

Facsimile 3 was published May 16, 1842, without any explanation as to why it was detached from the text printed two months earlier. It is assumed the woodcut was not ready to be included in the previous edition. The Prophet simply stated in his journal on May 16, 1842: "I published in this day's *Times and Seasons* the following *fac-simile* from the Book of Abraham."[20]

More of the Book of Abraham Is Promised

The two short March 1842 entries in the *Times and Seasons* are not the entire text of the Book of Abraham. For the introduction to the Book of Abraham Joseph Smith wrote: "A Translation of some Ancient Records that have fallen into our hands, from the Catacombs of Egypt, purporting to be the writings of Abraham, while he was in Egypt, called the Book of Abraham, written by his own hand upon papyrus."[21] The present text of the Book of Abraham does not deal with Abraham while he was Egypt, but only some preliminary experiences he had prior to going there. He was on his way to Egypt from Ur, by way of Haran, with a stop in Shechem, when the story ends. Does this mean that the five chapters presently printed in the Pearl of Great Price are not the complete Abrahamic text Joseph Smith purchased from Michael H. Chandler?

The *Times and Seasons* dated February 1, 1843, has the following notice, written by John Taylor, who succeeded the Prophet as editor:

> We would respectfully announce to those of our subscribers, (and there are a good many of them) who commenced their subscriptions for the Times and Seasons at the time when brother Joseph took the editorial department, that the term for which they subscribed for is nearly at a close: most of those commenced at the seventh and eighth numbers; at the time when the translations from the Book of Abraham commenced. This is the sixth number, which only leaves four weeks until the time that they subscribed for, will be fulfilled.
>
> We have given this timely notice that our friends may prepare themselves. We would further state that we had the promise of Br. Joseph, to furnish us with further extracts from the Book of Abraham. These with other articles that we expect from his pen, the continuation of his history, and the resources that we have of obtaining interesting matter; together with our humble endeavors, we trust will make the paper sufficiently interesting.[22]

A month later, on March 1, the Twelve Apostles wrote to the branches of the Church "in and around Ramus" and asked the Saints to assist the Prophet and his family by being generous with their means to allow him to devote his time to bringing forth "the revelations, translation, and history." The statement reads:

> BELOVED BRETHREN:–As our beloved President Joseph Smith is now relieved from his bondage and his business, temporarily, and his property, too, he has but one thing to hinder his devoting his time to the spiritual interests of the Church, to

*John Taylor, who
succeeded Joseph
Smith as editor of
the* Times and
Seasons

the bringing forth of the revelations, translation, and history. And what is that? He has not provisions for himself and family, and obliged to spend his time in providing therefor. His family is large and his company great, and it requires much to furnish his table. And now, brethren, we call on you for immediate relief in this matter; and we invite you to bring our President as many loads of wheat, corn, beef, pork, lard, tallow, eggs, poultry, venison, and everything eatable at your command, (not exepting unfrozen potatoes and vegetables, as soon as the weather will admit,) flour, etc., and thus give him the privilege of attending to your spiritual interest.

The measure you mete shall be measured to you again. If you give liberally to your President in temporal things, God will return to you liberally in spiritual and temporal things too. One or two good new milch cows are much needed also.

Brethren, will you do your work, and let the President do his for you before God: We wish an immediate answer by loaded teams or letter.

Your brethren in Christ, in behalf of the quorum,

Brigham Young, President.

Willard Richards, Clerk

P.S. Brethren, we are not unmindful of the favors our President has received from you in former days. But a man will not cease to be hungry this year because he ate last year.[23]

As far as is known, the Prophet, with many demands on his time, was unable to return to translating the Book of Abraham after March 1843.

A nonmember, in a sixteen-page pamphlet recalling his visit to the Church headquarters at Kirtland, stated:

> The Mormons have four mummies, and a quantity of records, written on papyrus, in Egyptian hierogliphics, which were brought from the catacombs near Thebes, in Egypt. They say that the mummies were Egyptian, but the records are those of Abraham and Joseph, and contain important information respecting the creation, the fall of man, the deluge, the patriarchs, the book of Mormon, the lost tribe, the gathering, the end of the world, the judgment, &c. &c. This is as near as I can recollect; if there is an error I hope some of the Mormons will point it out, and I will recall it. These records were torn by being taken from the roll of embalming salve which contained them, and some parts entirely lost but Smith is to translate the whole by divine inspiration, and that which is lost, like Nebuchadnezzar's dream, can be interpreted as well as that which is preserved; *and a larger volume than the Bible will be required to contain them."* [Emphasis added.][24]

Papyri Fragments Pasted on Paper

The fragments of papyrus that the Church received from New York's Metropolitan Museum of Art in 1967 had been cut into smaller pieces and mounted on irregular-sized sheets of paper, apparently to make it more convenient to work with the Egyptian manuscripts. The smallest piece of backing (fragment number 11) is $4^7/_8$ inches by $6^3/_4$ inches, while the largest piece (fragment number 9) is $7^5/_8$ inches by $12^1/_2$ inches. All twelve fragments were glued on stiff backing paper to preserve them from further disintegration.

It is a fair assumption that much of the papyri was glued to backing paper. Whether this was done in Kirtland, Missouri, or Nauvoo is not known. In an article published in the May 1968 issue of the *Improvement Era,* Dr. T. Edgar Lyon explained that the backing paper contained parts of maps of Ohio's Western Reserve; floor and building plans assumed to be for the Kirtland Temple; sketches probably of the proposed temple in Jackson County, Missouri; and a piece labeled "House of the Lord for the Presidency," which Dr. Lyon said "resembles papyri sketches."[25] To further protect them, some of the fragments were placed between panes of clear glass.

How many fragments were in the collection that Joseph Smith purchased is unknown, but we may conclude from the following incident that there were many. In 1906 historian Preston Nibley accompanied President Joseph F. Smith, a nephew of the Prophet and the sixth president of the Church, on a visit to the Nauvoo House. Brother Nibley reported that President Smith "recalled with tears the familiar sight of 'Uncle Joseph' kneeling on the floor of the front room with Egyptian manuscripts spread out all around him, weighted down by rocks and books, as with intense concentration he would study a line of characters, jotting down his impressions in a little notebook as he went."[26]

If there were only twelve or fifteen pieces of papyri in the entire collection, as some writers have concluded, they could easily be studied while a person was comfortably seated at a desk or table. The fragments Joseph Smith was studying apparently were not all under glass, nor were they all mounted; had they been so, it would have been unnecessary to weight them down. The twelve fragments from this collection now in the hands of the Church, I can personally attest, can be placed on an average-sized desk for convenience in working with them.

Translating the Papyrus

Students of the Book of Abraham have wondered how long it took Joseph Smith to translate the record. The *History of the*

Church does not provide us with a definitive answer. Journal entries in the *History of the Church* provide documention of when the translation was done, but one quickly notices that the history does not mention every day, and those days that are mentioned give very little detail.

When the Prophet did mention he worked on the translation, was he engaged in this activity several hours a day or only for short times here and there? If we list all of the entries in the *History of the Church* in which the Prophet, either alone or in company with his scribes, worked with the scrolls, we find a total of twenty-four days mentioned. Did he spend all twenty-four days, and possibly others not reported, in academically learning—that is, "studying out in his mind"—what he could about the unknown text and in translating only the five chapters contained in the present Pearl of Great Price?

If Anson Call's account is accurate that some brethren in Missouri read from the writings of Abraham for nearly two hours, the Prophet translated considerably more of the papyri than is currently printed in the *Pearl of Great Price.* An average reader can read aloud the published Book of Abraham account in approximately thirty to thirty-five minutes. And how does one separate inspired truth that someone has learned through honest scholastic study from direct revelation? Believing as we do that the Lord can and does speak to his children in various ways, such as through dreams, visions, theophanies, inspiration, and stupor of thought, this is a difficult question to attempt to answer.

By way of comparison, students of the Book of Mormon estimate that Joseph Smith, aided by the Urim and Thummim, spent approximately sixty working days in translating the gold plates, producing a double-columned text of 531 pages.

Of the approximately twenty-four days when Joseph was reported working with the papyri, about two-thirds of his time was spent "continually engaged in translating an alphabet to the Book of Abraham, and arranging a grammar of the Egyptian language."[27] Since there was no dictionary of Egyptian hiero-

JOSEPH SMITH AND THE TRANSLATION OF THE BOOK OF ABRAHAM

Location	Dates	No. of Days	Nature of Work
Kirtland	July 5 and/or 6, 1835	Probably 1 day	"Commenced the translation of some of the characters or hieroglyphics"
Kirtland	Remainder of July 1835 (after the 10th)	Possibly 15 to 18 days (16?)	"I was . . . translating an alphabet to the Book of Abraham, and arranging a grammar of the Egyptian language."
Kirtland	October 1, 1835	1/2 day	"I labored on the Egyptian alphabet . . . and during the research, the principals of astronomy as understood by Father Abraham . . . unfolded to our understanding."
Kirtland	October 7, 1835	1/2 day	"This afternoon I re-commenced translating the ancient records."
Kirtland	November 19, 1835	1 day	"I . . . spent the day translating the Egyptian records."
Kirtland	November 20, 1835	1 day	"We . . . spent the day in translating, and made rapid progress."
Kirtland	November 24, 1835	1/2 day	"In the afternoon we translated some of the Egyptian records."
Kirtland	November 25, 1835	1 day	"Spent the day in translating."
Kirtland	November 26, 1835	1 day	"Spent the day in translating Egyptian characters from the papyrus."
Nauvoo	March 8, 1842	1 day	"Recommenced translating from the records of Abraham."
Nauvoo	March 9, 1842	1/2 day	"In the afternoon . . . continued translating and revising" the Book of Abraham.

Total: 23 to 26 days

glyphics readily available, were the Prophet and his scribes honing their skills in an attempt to produce a guidebook for future translators or only making notes for their own benefit?

On November 13, 1843, after a hiatus of eight years, Joseph Smith again mentioned in his journal the Egyptian Alphabet and Grammar: "Called again with Doct[or] Bernhisel and

Clayton [both able historians and secretaries] and read again. Afterwards called again and enquired for the Egyptian grammar."[28] Two days later he noted: "p.m. at the office; suggested the idea of preparing a grammar of the Egyptian Language."[29] When he "enquired for the Egyptian Grammar" on November 13, he may have been asking his secretaries to locate the document for him in the Church records. And when it was suggested on November 15 that "a grammar of the Egyptian language" be prepared, it may be that a dictionary or grammar of the old hieroglyphic language was not readily available in a public library, or that the brethren continued to have difficulty reading the hieroglyphic script.

More than fourteen years earlier, Oliver Cowdery unsuccessfully tried to use the Urim and Thummim for a short time when he desired to translate from the gold plates. The Lord explained:

> Behold, you have not understood; you have supposed that I would give it unto you, when you took no thought save it was to ask me.
>
> But, behold I say unto you, that you must study it out in your mind; then you must ask me if it be right, and if it is right I will cause that your bosom shall burn within you; therefore, you shall feel that it is right.
>
> But if it be not right you shall have no such feelings, but you shall have a stupor of thought that shall cause you to forget the thing which is wrong; therefore, you cannot write that which is sacred save it be given you from me.
>
> Now, if you had known this you could have translated; nevertheless, it is not expedient that you should translate now. (D&C 9:7–10.)

Though Oliver was discouraged that he could not translate the Nephite plates, he also received this promise from the Lord: "Other records have I, that I will give unto you power that you may assist to translate. Be patient, my son, for it is wisdom in me, and it is not expedient that you should translate at this present time." (D&C 9:2–3.) Perhaps Oliver's belaboring over and attempting to translate the Egyptian scrolls with the Prophet and William Phelps was a partial fulfillment of that promise.

While working with the papyri, the brethren purchased a book 8 inches by 12 ¼ inches in size in which to make notes. They titled the ledger book "Grammar and Alphabet of the Egyptian Language." How much of its content reflected Joseph Smith's thinking is difficult to say. Both John C. Bernhisel and William Clayton, his secretaries, were intrigued with foreign languages and may have done much or most of the studying and organizing. The Lord's command was "Study it out in your mind." Whatever they were doing and why they were doing it is unclear. As Dr. Hugh Nibley explained:

> "This afternoon," the Prophet reported, "I labored on the Egyptian alphabet, in company with Brothers Oliver Cowdery and W. W. Phelps, and during the research, the principles of astronomy as understood by Father Abraham and the ancients unfolded to our understanding." Here the Prophet received information on two different levels, according to a procedure prescribed by revelation: ". . . you must study it out in your mind; then you must ask me if it be right. . . ." (D&C 9:8.) The revelation may or may not confirm one's studied conclusions. Joseph Smith's work, here mentioned, on the Egyptian alphabet was never accepted or even presented to the Church as revelation, and no one is bound by it; but the zeal and application of the brethren was rewarded by a revelation that far transcended any intellectual efforts of man. It is this revelation that is comprised in the Pearl of Great Price, and it is by it and others like it that one may judge the Prophet Joseph, and *not* by such preliminary gropings as the so-called Egyptian Alphabet and Grammar, which was never completed, never released for publication, and, so far as we have been able to discover, never even mentioned in public. Granted that diligent searching and study may be a preliminary to receiving revelation, the revelation when it comes is certainly not to be judged by them. We are not only permitted but also instructed to cast about from possible solutions in our minds before the real solution is given us, and if we find Joseph Smith doing just that, we should not rush to point out possible flaws in his preliminary speculations as proof that he was not inspired.

Where translation is concerned, Joseph Smith also operated on two levels, with no danger of confusing the two. At no time did he claim that the gift of tongues is constant or permanent; like all gifts of the Spirit, it is bestowed when and as God chooses. The Prophet stated publicly more than once that he had to study languages the hard way, like anyone else, when not actually receiving revelation. And so we must allow him the luxury of having his own ideas about things, and of making his own mistakes and his own translations, as long as he plays the game fairly and never presents them as binding on others.[30]

Was the Urim and Thummim Used?

It is not clear how or how often Joseph Smith used the Urim and Thummim to aid in the translation of the Book of Abraham. Elder Wilford Woodruff wrote in his journal December 27, 1841: "The Twelve, or part of them, spent the day with Joseph the Seer, and he confided unto them many glorious things of the kingdom of God. The privileges and blessings of the priesthood, etc. I had the privelege of seeing for the first time in my day, the Urim and Thummim."

Elder Woodruff became business manager of the *Times and Seasons* less than six weeks later, and on February 19 he wrote in his personal journal: "The Lord is Blessing Joseph with Power to reveal the mysteries of the Kingdom of God; to translate through the Urim and Thummim Ancient records and Hieroglyphics as old as Abraham or Adam, which caused our hearts to burn within us while we beheld their glorious truth opened unto us."

Many years later, Orson Pratt commented: "One of the first gifts bestowed by the Lord for the benefit of His people, was that of revelation, the gift to translate, by the aid of the Urim and Thummim, the gift of bringing to light old and ancient records."[31]

Parley P. Pratt, upon printing the Book of Abraham in Liverpool, England, a few months later, also stated that the

The Urim and Thummim (from Ogden Kraut, comp., Seer Stones, *p. 22)*

Prophet utilized the Urim and Thummim in translating the writings of Abraham.[32]

Joseph Smith did not leave an explanation of how the Urim and Thummim worked. If it were only a matter of reading an English rendition of the Egyptian hieroglyphics, the Book of Abraham could have been translated, dictated, and recorded in a few hours. If reading a screen with the correct English were all that was required, the Book of Mormon could have been dictated in less than a week instead of the approximate sixty working days that it actually took. The Prophet was required to concentrate, study, and resolve in order to translate (see D&C 9) while using the divine spectacles.

Orson Pratt, speaking of the calling of a seer, stated: "The ability to 'see' by means of a stone is a great gift—the greatest— but the use of a stone is not always necessary. The stone is a means or aid in helping or strengthening the gift and ability of the seer. As a man uses this gift he will develop that power and ability without the use of a stone. Joseph received several revelations to which I was witness by means of the Seer stone, but he could receive also without any instrument."[33]

National Publicity on the Book of Abraham

As the Church continued to grow in size and prominence, the eyes of the world were increasingly focused on its every move. Several prominent newspapers in the Eastern United States kept abreast of the Mormons. Without wire services from which editors could randomly select their stories as is done today, newspaper editors in Joseph Smith's day constantly borrowed articles from other publications, usually documenting their source at the bottom of the article.

A *New York Tribune* article published in the Bellafonte, Pennsylvania, *Democratic Whig* stated on April 23, 1842: "The Mormons have found a new book called the book of Abraham. It purports to have been written by that patriarch, and is said to have been found in the Catacombs of Egypt by an English traveller who brought it away with eleven mummies. Jo [*sic*] Smith is engaged in translating this book for the Nauvoo, 'Times and Seasons.' The first chapter appears in the last number that has reached us.—*N. Y. Tribune.*"

An article in the *New York Herald* dated April 3, 1842, read:

> We give in this day's paper, a very curious chapter from the "Book of Abraham," which we find published in the last number of a weekly journal, called the "Times and Seasons," conducted by Joe Smith the great Mormon Prophet, in the city Nauvoo, Hancock county, Illinois.
>
> The Prophet says that it was found in the catacombs of Egypt, but he is mistaken in this idea.—The article was discovered, we presume by Joseph Smith, the grandfather, near one of the propylons of Medinet Abu in the "City of the Sun," in Upper Egypt. The same city which Homer says had one hundred gates. Champollion, Young, Rosselini and various other antiquarians give notices of the magnificent ruins, in red granite, that are strewn over the banks of the Nile. Be all this

as it may, the Prophet of Nauvoo has given the chapter, and it is set down as a revelation among the Mormons.

This Joe Smith is undoubtedly one of the greatest characters of the age. He indicates as much talent, originality, and moral courage as Mahomet, Odin, or any of the great spirits that have hitherto produced the revolutions of past ages. In the present infidel, irreligious, material, ideal, geological, animal-magnetic age of the world, some such singular prophet as Joe smith is required to preserve the principle of faith, and to plant some new germs of civilization that may come to maturity in a thousand years. While modern philosophy, which believes in nothing but what you can touch, is overspreading the Atlantic States, Joe Smith is creating a spiritual system, combined also with morals and industry, that may change the destiny of the race.—Joe believes himself divinely inspired and a worker of miracles. He cures the sick of diseases—so it is said—and although Joe is not aware of the fact, we have been informed by a medical man that his influence over nervous disorders, arises from a powerful magnetic influence—that Joe is a magnet in a large way, which he calls a power or spirit from heaven. In other respects Joe is a mighty man of God—possessing large stores of human nature—great shrewdness, and as he has taken the management of the Mormon newspaper organ, the "Times and Seasons" into his hand, we look for many revelations, and some curious ones too, pretty soon.

We certainly want some such prophet to start up, take a big hold of the public mind—and stop the torrent of materialism that is hurrying the world into infidelity, immorality, licentiousness, and crime. Professor Lyell, Richard Adams Locke, Dr. Brisband, Master Emmerson, Prophet Brownson, Horace Greely, and all the materialists of the age, ought to take a leaf of common sense out of Joe's book.[34]

Two days later the *New York Herald* added: "Joe Smith, in his last 'Times and Seasons,' gives us another slice of the 'Book of Abraham,' embracing a synopsis of his geology and astronomy, illustrated with a curious map of the Mormon Solar System. Joe also gives his readers a bit of his auto-biography—quite rich it is, too."[35]

The brethren at the *Times and Seasons* office were well aware of the attention being given to the publication of the Book of

Abraham in prominent newspapers. The Prophet, acting as editor, entered the following article in the *Times and Seasons* May 16, 1842:

> It will be seen by several extracts taken from different papers, that the press is changing its tone a little, in regard to the subject of Mormonism; many of the most re[s]pectable, influential, and widely circulated periodicals are beginning to look at Mormonism in its true light: at any rate they are for investigating the subject impartially, and as honest and candid journalists, they speak of it as they find it. Such is Mr. James G. Bennett, of the New York Herald; Mr. William Bartlett, of the Dollar Weekly Bostonian; the New York State Mechanic, published by Mr. Joel Munson; and the Chicago Democrat; published by Col. John Wentworth.
>
> The first cut of a facsimile from the Book of Abraham, has been re-published both in the New York Herald, and in the Dollar Weekly Bostonian, as well as in the Boston Daily Ledger, Edited By Mr. Bartlet; together with the translation from the Book of Abraham. Mr. Bartlett says that he "intends opening a corespondence with us, that he may acquaint himself with our public and private acts." &c. we can assure Mr. Bartlett that we shall be most happy to put him in possession of any information that he may require pertaining to our society, as we have always courted publicity, and investigation, and chose light rather than darkness.—ED.[36]

Joseph Smith quoted the *Dollar Weekly Bostonian* article in the *Times and Seasons*:

> Joe is decidedly the greatest original of the present day. He carries all before him when he undertakes an enterprise—knows no impediment—and never halts in his course till he has accomplished his object. His post, at the head of the Mormons, is a conspicuous one, and in a few years of such advancement as he has met with for the past year, will give him a numberless host of followers. We should not be surprised if Joe should become as omnipotent as ever the Pope was in his palmiest days. He is a genius—and a rare one—and all the armies of Satan, should they confront him in a solid phalanx, would be sure to meet with sore discomfiture, if not with complete annihilation. The true philosophy of *go-aheadity*—the quintessence of concentrated moral and spiri-

tual energy—fears no combat—and although we cannot say it exactly courts danger, it never flies from the post of duty on its approach.—We have so high an opinion of Joe Smith that we intend to open a correspondence with him in order to acquaint ourself with all his secret springs of action, and thus get all the secrets of his success, public and private, worldly and ecclesiastical.

The chapter from the recently recovered Book of Abraham, and the unique cut which illustrates it, on our outside, has occasioned us some expense; but we care not for that so long as we please our patrons, which we mean to do at all hazards, trusting to the good sense of the most enlightened public in this, or any other universe, for suitable remuneration.

The Mormons hold meetings in Boston regularly on the Sabbath, somewhere in commercial street, and are equally successful in saving souls, healing the sick and restoring sight to the blind. Meetings are also held in Chelsea, and the cause is on the increase in that place.—

Will Elder Nickerson, or some of the brethren, furnish us with the statistics?[37]

A *New York State Mechanic* article referring to the Book of Abraham was also included in the *Times and Seasons* for the benefit of the Saints: "*The Times and Seasons,* the Mormon newspaper, published at Nauvoo by Joseph Smith, has commenced the translation of a book written by Abraham, and discovered in the catecombs [sic] of Egypt! This people, from a handful of persecuted outcasts, have become a numerous sect, and are able to protect themselves against insult and oppression; in fact, it is said that they have revolutionized the state of Illinois."[38]

With the incessant borrowing from the larger metropolitan newspapers by the smaller presses, it appears that the Book of Abraham must have received wide notice in the papers of the United States.

13

"CHANDLER WAS ONLY
AN AGENT"

After the Saints had moved to the Nauvoo area, an interesting story was unfolding relative to the mummies back in Ohio.
A brief review will set the stage for this new development.

Michael Chandler spent about a week in Kirtland in 1835,
displaying the four mummies and the papyrus, visiting with
Joseph Smith relative to the interpretation of the hieroglyphs,
and making arrangements for the sale of the antiquities at
$2,400. As indicated earlier, Joseph Coe paid $800, Simeon
Andrews paid $800, and Joseph Smith raised the balance of $800
through contributions from various friends.

Chandler did not return to Pennsylvania to live after he sold
these last four mummies. The next year he and his wife, Frances,
bought two parcels of adjoining land totaling 83.46 acres in
Parkman Township, Ohio, approximately forty miles southeast
of Kirtland and ten miles northeast of Hiram. The land was purchased for $600 on August 10, 1836, in the name of "Frances
Chandler wife of Michael Chandler," from George and Francis
Parkman, who lived in Boston.[1] On August 23, 1839, a little over
three years later, the Chandlers sold their land for $1410.[2]

By 1857 Michael Chandler had purchased a farm from
David Tod about one mile east of his first farm, consisting of
three parcels of ground totaling 100.53 acres.[3] The new farm covered three corners of an intersection that some older residents in
the area still call "Chandler's Corners."

Joseph Coe, the one-time financial assistant to Joseph Smith

*The home of Michael H. Chandler in Parkman, Ohio. Author Donl Peterson is
talking to the Amish family who were living there in June 1989*

who had loaned the Church $800 to assist in purchasing the
mummies and papyrus, apostatized from the Church in 1837 in
Kirtland and remained there while the Saints moved to Missouri
and then to Nauvoo. On January 1, 1844, he wrote to Joseph
Smith in Nauvoo regarding some unresolved financial matters
he claimed to have with the Prophet, and in his letter he mentioned a current lawsuit involving Michael H. Chandler:
"Chandler was only an agent acting under some men in
Philadelphia the mummies when delivered to him for exhibition
were valued at some 2 or 300 dollars, but they sued him and was
allowed the sum which he sold them to me for viz. $2400. It also
appeared on the trial that the out goes while Chandler was
exhibiting them exceeded the income $1550. I suppose the own-
ers are if it not outlawed liable for the fraud thus practiced by
their agent but I have hitherto been unable to attest to the collection of it."[4]

Chandler's statement that he was "only an agent acting under some men in Philadelphia" conflicts with his claim of inheriting the mummies from his Italian uncle, Antonio Lebolo. Coe further stated that Chandler's expenses exceeded his income by $1550 the last two years he was exhibiting the mummies. Since Coe was residing in Kirtland and was aware of the court case, it seems logical that Chandler was being sued by the owners of the mummies in a nearby court. And since Chandler had resided in Parkman, Ohio, since 1836, the setting for the trial would be Chardon, the county seat of Geauga County, which is also where Kirtland was located.

Craig and Sargent vs. Michael H. Chandler

Beginning on October 1, 1838, and ending on October 10, 1853, two prominent Philadelphia maritime merchants, William Craig and Winthrop Sargent, were plaintiffs in a continuation of lawsuits against Michael H. Chandler. At issue was $6,000, which the plaintiffs said the defendant owed them. The trials were held in the Court of Common Pleas in Chardon, Geauga County, Ohio.

The Common Pleas record books at the county courthouse in Chardon contain a summary of the various proceedings of the case:

> Pleas before the Court of Common Pleas within and for the county of Geauga in the State of Ohio at a time of said Court begun and held at the Court House in Chardon, on the twenty-seventh day of April in the year of our Lord one thousand eight hundred and forty-one.
>
> Be it remembered that heretofore, at the November Term of said Court, in the year of our Lord one thousand Eight hundred and thirty Eight, Winthrop Sargent and William Craig, sued out of the office of the Clerk of said Court, a writ of summons against Michael Chandler in the words and figures following, to wit:—"The State of Ohio, Geauga County, Seal
>
> To the Sheriff of said County, Greeting: We command you that you summon Michael Chandler to appear forthwith before our Court of Common Pleas for said County, now setting at the Court House in Chardon, to answer unto Winthrop

Sargent and William Craig in a plea of assumpsit to their damage six thousand dollars as is said, Herein fail not but of this writ and your service make due return. Witness D. D. Aiken, Clerk of said Court at Chardon, this thirteenth day of November A.D. 1838. C. H. Foot, Dep. Clerk"

Upon the writ was the following endorsement, to wit:—"Suit both to recover for work and labour and materials done and found by the plaintiffs for deft, for goods, wares and merchandise sold by plffs to deft. for money paid and expended by plffs for use of deft. for money had and received by deft. for use of plffs, and for money found due on an account stated between them. Amount claimed $3000."

The said writ was forthwith returned to Court, by the sheriff of said county, having thereon endorsed the return of his service of the same, in the words and figures following, to wit:—"The State of Ohio, Geauga County ss

I have executed the command of this writ by leaving a true copy of this writ, at the residence of Michael Chandler, he being absent. N. Webb. Dept Shff."

And it was ordered by the Court, that this cause be continued until the next term of said Court. Afterwards, to wit on the twentieth day of December in the year last aforesaid the said Winthrop Sargent and William Craig filed in the office of the Clerk of said Court, their Declaration, in the words and figures following, to wit:—"The State of Ohio Geauga County ss

Court of Common Pleas, Vacation after November Term A.D. 1838.

Winthrop Sargent & William Craig

vs.

Michael Chandler

Declaration in assumpsit. The said defendant was summoned to answer the said plaintiff, in a plea of assumpsit, and therefore come the plaintiffs by Bolton & Kelley their attorneys, and complain of the said defendant: for that whereas the said defendant heretofore to wit, on the first day of October A.D. 1838 at Philadelphia, to wit, at Chardon in said County of Geauga and State of Ohio was indebted to said plaintiffs in the sum of six thousand dollars, for the work, labour, care diligence and attention of them the said plaintiffs, before that time done, performed and bestowed in and about the business of said defendant and for the said defendant, and at his special instance and request; and also in the further sum of six thousand dollars, for divers goods wares and merchandise and other personal property, before them by said plaintiffs sold and delivered to said defendant, and at His like special instance and request of said defendant: and also in the further sum of six thousand dollars, for so much money before there by said plaintiffs lent and advanced to, and paid laid out and expended for said defendant, and at His like special instance and request; and also in the further sum of six thousand dollars for other moneys before there by said defendant had and received to and for the use of the said plaintiff: and being so indebted he the defendant, in consideration thereof, afterwards to wit, on the same day and year last aforesaid, undertook and then and there faithfully promised the said plaintiffs to pay them the said several sums of money in this court mentioned, when he the said defendant should be thereunto afterwards requested;

And whereas, also, afterwards, to wit, on the first day of October A.D. 1838, at Philadelphia, to wit at Chardon in said Geauga County, the said defendant accounted with the said plaintiffs (of and concerning divers other sums of money, for the said defendant to the said plaintiffs, before that time due and owing and there in arrear and unpaid, and upon such accounting the said defendant was there and there found to be in arrear and indebted to the said plaintiffs in the further sum of six thousand dollars, and being so found in arrear and indebted, he the said defendant in consideration thereof afterward, to wit, on the same day and year last aforesaid, at Philadelphia, to wit, at Chardon aforesaid, undertook and there and there faithfully promised the said plaintiffs to pay them the said further sum of six thousand dollars, in this court mentioned when he the said defendant, should be thereunto afterwards requested. Yet the said defendant his said several promises and undertakings in no wise regarding, but contriving etc. has not as yet paid the several sums of money in this Declaration mentioned, or any or either of them, or any part thereof to the said plaintiffs (although often requested etc.) But the said defendant to pay the said plaintiffs the same, has hitherto wholly neglected and refused, and still does neglect and refuse. To the damage of the said plaintiffs of six thousand dollars and therefore they sue etc.

Bolton & Kelley, Attys for plaintiffs."

Afterwards, to wit, on the twenty-sixth day of December in the year last aforesaid, the said Michael Chandler filed in the

Clerk's office aforesaid, his plea & notice, in the words and figures following, viz.

"The State of Ohio Geauga County ss
Michael A. Chandler
       at suit of
Winthrop Sargent & William Craig
In the Common Pleas, Vacation after November Term 1838
Plea & Notice
And now comes the said Chandler by Tod & Hoffman his Atty's and defends etc. and says that he did not undertake and promise in manner and form as the said Sargent and Craig have above thereof declared against him and of this he puts himself upon the county for trial. etc. Tod & Hoffman, Atty's for deft."

The said plaintiffs or their Atty's will take notice that the defendant on the trial of this cause, will give in evidence and insist that at the commencement of this suit, said plaintiffs were and they still are indebted to said defendant, in the sum of six thousand dollars, for goods before them sold & delivered by said defendant to said plaintiffs at their request, also in the sum of six thousand dollars for work done and materials for the same provided, by said defendant, before them for said plaintiffs at their request. Also in the sum of six thousand dollars for money before them had and received by said plaintiffs to and for the use of money found to be due from the plaintiffs to the defendant, on an account before them stated between them. And that on said trial, the defendant will set off against any demand of said plaintiffs to be proved thereon, so much of said several sums of money due defendant, as will be sufficient to satisfy such demands of the plffs, and the deft will also on said trial ask the Court to give him a judgment for the balance of said sums as per statute.

Respectfully Yours Tod & Hoffman, Atty's for deft.

Afterwards, at the April Term of said Court, in the year of our Lord one thousand Eight hundred and thirty-nine, it was ordered by the Court, that this cause be continued until the next term of said Court. Afterwards, at the June Term of said Court, in the year last aforesaid, it was ordered by the Court that the Plaintiffs give bail for costs twelve days before the next term, or in default that he become now suit, and that this cause be continued until the next term. Afterwards, at the

November Term of said Court, in the year last aforesaid, it was ordered by the Court, that this cause be continued until the next time of said Court, and that the defendant pay the costs of term in sixty days. Afterwards at the April term of said Court, in the year of our Lord one thousand Eight hundred & forty, by consent of the parties, it was ordered that this cause be continued until the next term of said Court. Afterwards at the June Term of said Court, in the year last aforesaid it was ordered by the Court, that this cause be continued at the costs of the plaintiffs, until the next term of said Court. And now at this term of said Court, that is to say, at the term thereof first aforesaid, come the said parties, and thereupon came a Jury, to wit, Enoch Scott, Willes Foot, Stanley Spencer, Lewis Smith, Olney Percival, Zenas Gurney, David C. Osborn, Austin Carver, William Holliday, Linsen T. Patchin, Nathaniel C. Stone and Chester Houghton, who being duly impaneled and sworn to say that the deft did espouse and promise as the plaintiffs have declared against him and assess the plaintiffs damages at Eight hundred and fifty dollars. It is therefore considered that the plaintiffs recover of the defendant, the said sum of Eight hundred and fifty dollars, the damages aforesaid, in manner and form aforesaid assessed, and also their costs & charges by him made in defending this suit, taxed at seven dollars and sixty-Eight cents, and in default thereof that execution issue to collect the same—The defendant gives notice of his intention to appeal to the Supreme Court.—[5]

Pleas before the Court of Common Pleas within and for the County of Geauga in the State of Ohio at a term of said Court begun and held at the Court House in Chardon on the twenty second day of October in the year of our Lord one thousand eight hundred and forty four.

Be it remembered that heretofore to wit on the twenty sixth day of March in the year aforesaid Lyman Cowdery brought into Court and filed his deposition in the words and figures following to wit Geauga Common Pleas April term A.D. 1841

Winthrop Sargent &
William Craig
    vs
Michael Chandler
The State of Ohio, Geauga County SS

Judgment of the Plaintiff Damages $850.00
Plffs costs 42.99
Defts costs 7.68

Lyman Cowdery of lawful age being duly sworn according to law deposes and says that Meprs Boulton and Kelley of Cleveland attourneys for said plaintiffs requested this deponent to obtain from Col. Spencer Sheriff of said County his return to the execution issued the 14th day of December 1841 for the purpose as they said to draw a bill in Chancery against the said defendant that on the first day of the next term of this Court this deponent called on Col. Spencer for said execution for the purpose of copying the return of the same which he delivered to this deponent indorsed on the back "To goods chattels lands or tenements whereon to levy" and officially signed by said Sheriff Spencer by his Dept Atwood Whither this deponent sent said deposition to said Boulton and Kelly or has mislaid or lost the same this deponent cannot state but further says that he has no recollection of returning said Execution to said Sheriff Further this deponent saith not.

Sworn and subscribed before me this 26th day of March 1844

Reuben St. John, Clerk of Geauga Common Pleas

And now at this term of said Court that is to say at the term thereof first aforesaid it appearing to the Court by the affidavit of Lyman Cowdery Esq that the execution issued in this case Dec 11, A.D. 1841 has been lost. It is therefore considered by the Court that a new execution issue and that the plaintiff pay the costs of this motion taxed at one dollar.[6]

Who Were Craig and Sargent?

William Craig and Winthrop Sargent were maritime business partners from Philadelphia. Their names were commonly seen in the classified ads of the prominent Philadelphia papers under "Imports," since they were frequently involved in international trade. They were involved in merchandising numerous and varied products, from lumber to wines, colognes, and hair dressings (pomades). They also leased ocean-going vessels.

Taking people to court was not a new experience for Craig and Sargent. The appearance dockets in the Philadelphia

District Court between March 1833 and December 1836 list the partners ten times as plaintiffs, not once as defendants.

It is possible that the eleven mummies shipped from Trieste to New York City to the combined companies of Maitland & Kennedy and McLeod & Gillespie would be sent on to Philadelphia by water in preference to overland travel. Since Chandler was being sued by Craig and Sargent of Philadelphia, is it possible that these two merchants underwrote Chandlers' acquisition of the eleven mummies? Chandler charged Joseph Smith $600 per mummy. If the $6,000 lawsuit was for the acquisition of the eleven mummies alone, then the price per mummy is close to the same: about $545 per mummy. The Common Pleas records from Ohio do not specify the nature of the merchandise or service being contested.

There is plenty of Irish or Scottish-Irish blood among these merchants with names like Maitland, Kennedy, McLeod, Gillespie, Craig, and Sargent. Could Michael H. Chandler or his wife, Frances F. Ludlow, both Irish born, be related to any of them? Or was Chandler a former employee of Craig and Sargent? Six thousand dollars was a very large sum of money to lend to a stranger in 1833, or even the $850 that was finally resolved.

The original receivers of the mummies in the United States, maritime merchants Maitland, Kennedy, McLeod, and Gillespie, may also have had family ties with the Philadelphia merchants William Craig and Winthrop Sargent. In a Philadelphia Appearance Docket dated September 1839 is a case listing as plaintiffs Davis S. Kennedy, David Maitland, Stuart C. Maitland, and Henry S. Craig, trading as Kennedy Maitland and Co. The defendant is John W. Stitt, trading as John W. Stitt and Co. In December 1839 Henry S. Craig is again listed as a partner and a plaintiff for the firm Maitland, Kennedy and Co.

More Conjecture

Michael Chandler was displaying the mummies in Hudson, Ohio, as early as February 19, 1835, and displaying the four mummies in Cleveland in late March. Three months later he was in Kirtland, Ohio, where he spent a week among the Latter-day Saints. In the *Cleveland Advertiser* of March 26, 1835, the announcement of the mummy and papyri display ends with this sentence: "The collection is offered for sale by the proprietor."

One cannot help wondering why Chandler was in that isolated area of Ohio for over four months. Was he displaying his artifacts up and down the newly opened Ohio Canal? Was he visiting family members in the area? Was he traveling with relatives? Or was he looking for land, since he bought a farm in that region the following year?

About a week before he arrived in Kirtland, an interesting item appeared in the *Daily Cleveland Herald* for June 23, 1835, in a column that listed guests staying in local hotels. On June 22, "S. W. Craig, Philadelphia" registered at the Mansion House. Is this William Craig of the firm of William Craig and Winthrop Sargent? Was he in Cleveland to check on Chandler's overdue loan? It is even more interesting to read that "M. W. Chandler of Stow" registered at the Cleveland House on June 25. And on July 18, "M and F Chandler, [of] Stow," Ohio, registered at the same hotel. This was ten or eleven days after Michael Chandler agreed to sell the four mummies and the papyri to the Church.

The inscription for Michael H. and Frances on the Chandler tombstone in the West Farmington, Ohio, cemetery reads "M. H. and F. Chandler." Why did Michael H. and Frances Chandler list their home as Stow, about thirty miles away? Had the family permanently left Pennsylvania, or were they visiting loved ones?

The letter from Joseph Coe to the Prophet Joseph Smith raises several questions relative to Chandler's dealings with the mummies. Some perceptive historians will someday piece this part of the puzzle together. It appears that this series of court cases further discredits Michael H. Chandler's claims to any blood relationship with Antonio Lebolo.

THE BOOK OF ABRAHAM IS PUBLISHED IN LIVERPOOL

The Book of Abraham was initially published in England in 1842 in the *Millennial Star,* a monthly British Mission publication under the editorship of Elder Parley P. Pratt, the mission president and a member of the Quorum of the Twelve Apostles. The following announcement appeared in the June 1842 edition of the *Millennial Star:* "Also, we expect in next month's 'Star,' to give some extracts from the 'Book of Abraham'—a relick of greater antiquity than the Bible, written on papyrus and taken from the breast of an Egyptian mummy, now in the possession of and translated by Joseph Smith.—Ed."

Joseph Smith first published the Book of Abraham in three installments in the *Times and Seasons:* in the edition dated March 1, 1842, Abraham 1:1–2:18, including Facsimile 1; March 15, 1842, Abraham 2:19–5:21, including Facsimile 2; and May 16, 1842, Facsimile 3. Parley P. Pratt followed a similar schedule in England. Abraham 1:1–2:18 and Facsimile 1 were printed in the July 1842 edition of the *Millennial Star,* and Abraham 2:19–5:21 was printed in the August 1842 edition. Neither Facsimile 2 nor Facsimile 3 was reproduced in the 1842 *Millennial Star.*

In the August 1842 edition, Elder Pratt wrote:

> When we read the Book of Abraham with the reflection that its light has burst upon the world after a silence of three or four thousand years, during which it has slumbered in the bosom of the dead, and been sealed up in the sacred archives of Egypt's moldering ruins; when we see there unfolded our

eternal being—our existence before the world was—our high
and responsible station in the councils of the Holy One, and
our eternal destiny; when we there contemplate the majesty of
the works of God as unfolded in all the simplicity of truth,
opening to our view the wide expanse of the universe, and
showing the laws and regulations, the times and revolutions
of all worlds, from the celestial throne of heaven's Kings, or
the mighty Kolob, whose daily revolution is a thousand years,
down through all the gradations of existence to our puny
earth, we are lost in astonishment and admiration, and are led
to exclaim, what is man without the key of knowledge? or
what can he know when shut from the presence of his maker,
and deprived of conversation with all intelligences of a higher
order? Surely the mind of man is just awaking from the deep
sleep of many generations, from his thousand years of mid-
night darkness. The morning of celestial light has dawned
upon a benighted world—

"The opening seals announce the day

By prophets long foretold."

No doubt, many will startle at the term "Gods," or deity in
the plural number; yet it is a fact that the bible calls them Gods
to whom the world of God came. And in the beginning of
Genesis, and throughout the bible, the Hebrew word *Elohim*
(Gods), is actually in the plural, though the translators have
rendered it (God) in the singular.[1]

Either Elder Pratt relied too heavily on his memory or he
had been given some new information as to the origin of the
Egyptian text, because he published an account that contains
several puzzling statements not mentioned or confirmed elsewhere:

We have much pleasure this month in being able to give an
illustration and extract from the Book of ABRAHAM; a book
of higher antiquity than any portion of the bible. Singular is
the providence by which this ancient record fell into the hands
of the servant of the Lord, JOSEPH SMITH. A gentleman, travelling in Egypt, made a selection of several mummies, of the
best kind of embalming, and of course in the best state of
preservation; on his way to England he died, bequeathing
them to a gentleman of the name of CHANDLER. They
arrived in the Thames, but it was found the gentleman was in

Elder Parley P. Pratt, who published the Book of Abraham in the Millennial Star *in England in 1842*

America, they were then forwarded to New York and advertised, when Mr. CHANDLER came forward and claimed them. One of the mummies, on being unrolled, had underneath the cloths in which it was wrapped, lying upon the breast, a roll of papyrus, in an excellent state of preservation, written in Egyptian character, and illustrated in the manner of our engraving, which is a copy from a portion of it. The mummies, together with the record, have been exhibited, generally through the States, previous to their falling into our hands.

Mr. CHANDLER was, of course, anxious to find some one who could interpret or translate this valuable relic of antiquity, and, we believe, on one occasion, met with an individual who was enabled to decipher a small portion, or, at least, to give an opinion of what he supposed its meaning to be. He every where heard mention of JOSEPH SMITH and the Book of Mormon, but so generally associated with something slanderous, that he could scarcely think seriously of applying to him. But at length, however, he called upon Mr. SMITH, to inquire if he had a power by which he could translate the ancient Egyptian. Mr. SMITH replied that he had, when Mr. CHANDLER presented the fragment which had been partially interpreted. Mr. SMITH retired into his translating room, and presently returned with a written translation in English, of the fragment, confirming the supposed meaning ascribed to it by the gentleman to who it had been previously presented.

An event, of a nature so extraordinary, was of course soon noised abroad, when a number of gentlemen in the neighbourhood, not connected with the Saints, united together, and, purchasing the record together with some or all of the mummies, made Mr. SMITH a present of them. The record is now in course of translation by the means of the Urim and Thummim, and proves to be a record written partly by the father of the faithful, Abraham, and finished by Joseph when in Egypt. After his death, it is supposed they were preserved in the family of the Pharaohs and afterwards hid up with the embalmed body of the female with whom they were found. Thus it is, indeed, true, that the ways of the Lord are not as man's ways, nor his thought as our thoughts. Here, then, is another subject for the Gentile world to stumble at, and for which to persecute the Saints, not knowing that there is nothing hidden but what shall be brought to light, and nothing secret but what shall be discovered. Let us have no revelations is the popular cry of the day; any one's creed but God's. How true were the words of Jesus, "because I come unto you in my father's name ye will not receive me; if another should come in his own name, him ye will receive."

The language of the present generation is, we can believe in the marvelous works of God in former ages, but not now; how will they be confounded as the mighty purposes of Jehovah roll on unfolding mystery after mystery to his people, while his judgments are pouring out upon the ungodly and the unbelieving.

Let the Saints be faithful and watchful, and be ready to receive all things that God shall be pleased to communicate for their well-being in these the last days; bearing in mind that his great and finishing work, his gathering of the Saints together into one, in order to establish his kingdom, the dominion of which shall be universal, and all powers become subject unto it, will require revelations peculiar to itself, such as were never communicated at any former period of time. Now is the day of the trial of our faith, the day of warfare and of strife against the powers of darkness; but anon shall be the day of triumph, blessed shall they be who endure unto the end, and overcome, and swell the song of victory, for they shall have power over the nations to rule them with a rod of iron, and they shall have given unto them the morning star.[2]

The article contains several puzzling declarations:

1. *"A gentleman, travelling in Egypt made a selection of several mummies."*

This statement implies that a tourist or perhaps a business-man went to Egypt to procure some antiquities. It has some ring of truth but it is also misleading, since Antonio Lebolo had been employed in Egypt as an excavator and antiquities dealer for several years.

2. *"On his way to England he died."*

No evidence has been found that Lebolo ever planned to go to England. Some Italian families by the name of Lebolo did live in England at that time, or Antonio may have had business interests there, but evidence is lacking. Did a Lebolo family member travel to England from Trieste with the shipment of the mummies?

3. *"They [the mummies] arrived in the Thames."*

The eleven mummies may have been in England while en route to the United States, since we are unable to determine the specific ship that brought them the states or the exact route it took, but their final destination was New York City.

4. *The mummies were bequeathed to a gentleman by the name of Chandler.*

Michael H. Chandler related a similar story to Joseph Smith and Oliver Cowdery, but Lebolo's will and his son Pietro's letter of authorization to Francesco Bertola seem to disprove this statement. Elder Pratt appears to be recalling some of the Oliver Cowdery report.

5. *"A number of gentlemen in the neighbourhood, [Kirtland] not connected with the Saints, united together, and, purchasing the record together with some or all of the mummies, made Mr. Smith a present of them."*

Several people in the Kirtland area aided in purchasing the antiquities and assisted Joseph Smith in raising his third of the

purchase price, along with Joseph Coe's third and Simeon
Andrew's third, so it is possible that nonmembers may have
assisted in their purchase. However, it seems inconceivable that
only nonmembers would, at Joseph Smith's request to acquire
them, contribute $2,400 and then present them to him as a gift.
Other reports do not support this statement.

6. *"The record is now in course of translation by means of the
Urim and Thummim."*

How extensively did Joseph Smith use the Urim and
Thummim in translating the Book of Abraham? Some writers
believed that he returned the Urim and Thummim to the angel
Moroni along with the plates in 1829 and did not have them
thereafter. Others believed the seer stones were also referred to
as Urim and Thummim. Joseph Smith did have one or more seer
stones after 1829, and a generic terminology may have been
used in calling it (or them) Urim and Thummim. Whether he
used a seer stone or Urim and Thummim while translating the
Abrahamic scrolls is not answered in his personal writings or in
the Church history. Since he spent considerable time on "translating" an alphabet and grammar, it seems doubtful that those
sacred instruments were utilized extensively or at all in the
Abrahamic translation between 1835 and 1841. However, as
noted in chapter 12, Wilford Woodruff wrote that the Prophet
had been using the Urim and Thummim to translate Abraham's
record in February 1842. He also recorded on December 27,
1841, that "the twelve or a part of them spent the day with
Joseph the Seer and he unfolded unto them many glorious
things of the kingdom of God the privilege and blessings of the
priesthood etc. I had the privelege of seeing for the first time in
my day the Urim and Thummim."

Brigham Young's report of the same meeting, however,
leaves it unclear whether the Urim and Thummim or a seer
stone was in Joseph's hands on that date. He wrote: "I met with
the Twelve at Brother Joseph's. He conversed with us in a familiar manner on a variety of subjects, and explained to us the Urim
and Thummim which he found with the plates, called in the

Book of Mormon the Interpreters. He said that every man who lived on the earth was entitled to a seer stone, and should have one, but they are kept from them in consequence of their wickedness, and most of those who do find one make an evil use of it; he showed us his seer stone."[3]

7. *"[The papyrus] proves to be a record written partly by the father of the faithful, Abraham, and finished by Joseph when in Egypt."*

Some accounts refer to two scrolls received by Joseph Smith: the scroll of Abraham and the scroll of Joseph. This account is another possibility.

8. *The family of the Pharaohs preserved the prophetic writings that later were "hid up with the embalmed body of the female with whom they were found."*

This account in the *Millennial Star* states that it was a pharaonic line of dignitaries that preserved the sacred documents, and that the final resting place was in the sarcophagus of an embalmed female. Other accounts refer to the parchments' having been found accompanying the body of a male.

The Pearl of Great Price Is Published in England

The writings of Abraham were published in England nine years later, in 1851, in a mission publication entitled *The Pearl of Great Price.* Many important events had transpired between the time the Book of Abraham was published in the *Millennial Star* and this new publication.

The Church in Great Britain grew at a phenomenal rate between 1837, the year the gospel was first introduced there, and 1851, when emigration to the United States caused the membership to decline. The following figures indicate the rapid rate of growth of the Church between 1837 and 1851:

1840	2,544	1844	7,797	1848	17,902
1841	5,814	1845	9,032	1849	26,012
1842	7,514	1846	10,894	1850	30,747
1843	7,975	1847	12,139	1851	32,894[4]

Usually when students are asked, "Where did the majority

of Latter-day Saints live in 1850 or 1851," most respond, "In Utah." Others, remembering that many members were still gathering to Utah from the eastern states, may say, "Utah along with the immigrants heading west along the Mormon trail." Neither answer is correct.

The 1850 census indicates there were 5,779 members of the Church in Salt Lake City; about 11,000 in all of the Utah territory, including Salt Lake City; and 15,531 scattered elsewhere in the United States. Compare this with 30,747 members in Great Britain in 1850, and the total worldwide membership of 57,278 that year, and we can readily see that the majority lived in Great Britain.[5]

In 1850 and 1851 the Church in Great Britain faced several major problems:

1. *Church headquarters located thousands of miles away in the American West.*

The Saints in the West had many problems of their own to resolve, such as inclement weather; a short growing season; lack of adequate irrigation systems and other challenges related to agriculture; a shortage of essential equipment, tools, and supplies; transportation and communication difficulties; Indian relationships; and financial concerns.

2. *Lack of leadership skills among the new converts.*

In England local Church units were administered by recent converts who had little or no experience in observing or managing the affairs of the kingdom. Over two-thirds of the British members in 1850 had been baptized in the previous four years. Most of these new members were from the laboring classes and had few or no leadership skills prior to joining the Church.

3. *A shortage of gospel literature and adequate means of distribution.*

The Great Basin desert lacked timber, a vital ingredient in papermaking. The little amount of paper available was necessary to carry out the official business of the territorial government and the immediate needs of the Church. There was no excess paper available for printing materials to send to England.

The Brethren met these needs and overcame these obstacles in the following ways:

1. Strong leaders, including several apostles, were sent to Great Britain to administer and minister to the needs of the membership there.

2. Realizing that the printed word could help inexperienced converts to learn better their duties as well as the gospel, the Book of Mormon, the Church hymnbook, and many tracts were printed in England. England, with a concentrated population of about 27 million in the 1840s, was the dominant world power, while the United States had a population of about 23 million scattered over an immense area of land. The printing presses and paper quality in England were state of the art, and because the geographical area was small, it was fairly easy to reach the Saints there.

A Mission Pamphlet Is Proposed

With the rapid growth of the Church in England and the shortage of the printed word, most British Saints in 1850 did not own a copy of the Book of Mormon, the Doctrine and Covenants, or any of the many pamphlets the missionaries used in proselyting. President Franklin D. Richards of the European Mission encouraged them "to read Elder [Orson] Pratt's pamphlets, and lend them to others, so the people might know that Mormonism included all that is good."[6]

On February 1, 1851, President Franklin D. Richards wrote to his uncle Levi Richards, who was serving a mission in Swansea, south of Liverpool, and proposed that he (Franklin) compile selected quotations from the writings of Joseph Smith for the British Saints. He listed some material he had collected and asked Levi if he thought the proposal had merit. This letter is a follow-up to previous discussions or correspondence on this proposal:

> You will perhaps recollect my naming to you that I thought of issuing a collection of revelations, prophecies &c., in a tract form of a character not designed to pioneer our doctrines to the world, so much as for the use of the Elders and Saints to

arm and better qualify them for their service in our great *war*. The order of the work which I had thought to adopt so far as I have considered is about as follows:

First the revelation to Moses then the translation of the first chap of Genesis. Then perhaps the revelation to Enoch after which or perhaps before it, items of revelation informing of Gods second law to Adam, viz faith repentance &c. as given to him by ministration of an Angel. The particular place could perhaps be better determined after close examination. Then perhaps, Mr. Chandler's letter about the mummies containing an account of the sale of them to the Church &c. &c. followed with a fac simile of the plates and the translation of the Book of Abraham. I have not particularly determined in my own mind as to the consecutive order of the other items such as translation of 24th Matthew. The destiny of the American Union &c., any further that I had thought it might perhaps be as well to close up with the Key to Revelation. Giving the whole a general feature of chronological order except it be Joseph's prophecy of the Union.

Will you please to give me your views upon the matter in full with any suggestions which may occur to your mind relative to the subject at your earliest convenience. I desire that the whole thing may bear the dignity and weight of character which justly belongs to the revelations of God.[7]

As far as is known, the name of the new publication was first mentioned on May 8, 1851, when Levi Richards wrote in his journal: "With Franklin at 15 Wilton, Liverpool, reading proof sheets of Pearl of Great Price."[8] The Pearl of Great Price was announced to the British Saints on July 15, 1851, in the *Millennial Star*:

Pearl of Great Price, is the title of a new work which will soon be ready for sale, containing 64 pages on beautiful paper of superior quality, and on new type of larger size than any heretofore issued from this office. It contains

Extracts from the prophecy of Enoch, including a revelation of the Gospel to our first parents after their expulsion from the Garden of Eden.

The Words of God, which he spake unto Moses at the time when Moses was caught up into an exceeding high mountain, and saw God face to face, and talked with him, and the Glory

Elder Franklin D. Richards, president of the European Mission, who compiled the materials in the Pearl of Great Price

of God was upon Moses, so that he could endure the presence of the Lord. Including also the history of the creation of this heaven and this earth, together with the inhabitants thereof, and many historical items until the time of the flood, being items from the new translation of the scriptures by the Prophet Joseph.

The Book of Abraham—a translation of some ancient records that fell into the hand of the Church a few years since from the catacombs of Egypt, purporting to be the writings of Abraham while he was in Egypt, called the Book of Abraham, written by his own hand upon Papyrus; translated from the Papyrus by Joseph Smith. Connected with this translation are three fac-similes from the Papyrus.

An extract from a translation of the Bible—being the Twenty-fourth chapter of Matthew, commencing with the last verse of the Twenty-third chapter, by the Prophet, Seer, and Revelator, Joseph Smith.

A Key to the Revelations of St. John, in a series of questions and answers. By the same.

A Revelation given December, 1832, which has never before appeared in print.

Extracts from the History of Joseph Smith, containing an

account of the First Visions and Revelations which he received, also of his discovery and obtaining the Plates of God which contain the Record of Mormon; its translation, his baptism, and ordination by an Angel; items of doctrine from the revelations and commandments to the Church, &c.

This little work though not particularly adapted nor designed as a pioneer of our faith to unbelievers of present revelation, will be a source of much instruction and edification to many thousands of the Saints, who will by an acquaintance with its precious contents, be more abundantly qualified to set forth and defend the principles of our Holy Faith before all men. The PEARL OF GREAT PRICE will recommend itself to all who appreciate the revelations of truth as hidden treasures of Everlasting Life. Prices printed on the covers.[9]

The first edition was not sixty-four pages, as announced, but fifty-six pages. The book included the following preface by President Richards:

The following compilation has been introduced by the repeated solicitations of several friends of the publisher, who are desirous to be put in possession of the very important articles contained therein. Most of the Revelations composing this work were published at early periods of the church, when the circulation of its journals was so very limited as to render them comparatively unknown at present, except to a few who have treasured up the productions of the Church with great care from the beginning. A smaller portion of this work has never before appeared in print; and altogether it is presumed, that true believers in the Divine mission of the Prophet JOSEPH SMITH, will appreciate this little collection of precious truths *as a Pearl of Great Price* that will increase their ability to maintain and to defend the holy faith by becoming possessors of it.

Although not adapted, nor designed, as a pioneer of the faith among unbelievers, still it will commend itself to all careful students of the scriptures, as detailing many important facts which are therein only alluded to, or entirely unmentioned, but consonant with the whole tenor of the revealed will of God; and, to the beginner in the Gospel, will add confirmatory evidence of the rectitude of his faith, by showing him that the doctrines and ordinances thereof are the same as were revealed to Adam for his salvation after his expulsion from the garden, and the same that he handed down and caused to be taught to his generations after him, as the only means appointed of God by which the generations of men may regain His presence.

Nor do we conceive it possible for any unprejudiced person to arise from a careful perusal of this work, without being deeply impressed with a sense of the Divine calling, and holy ordination, of the man by whom these revelations, translations, and narrations have been communicated to us. As impervious as the minds of men may be at present to these convictions, the day is not far distant when sinners, as well as Saints, will know that JOSEPH SMITH was one of the greatest men that ever lived upon the earth, and that under God he was the Prophet and founder of the dispensation of the fullness of times, in which will be gathered together into one all things which are in Christ, both which are in heaven and which are on earth.

This first edition of the Pearl of Great Price contained the entire published text of the Book of Abraham and the three facsimiles as printed in the *Times and Seasons* in 1842. The facsimiles are listed in the table of contents under the heading "Index to Wood-Cuts."

The mission publication was not intended to be used as a proselyting tool, as was the Book of Mormon, but it was, as stated in the preface, intended to convince "true believers in the Divine mission of the Prophet Joseph Smith ... [in order to] increase their ability to maintain and to defend the holy faith by becoming possessors of it."

I studied quite carefully the personal journal entries of President Richards for this time period and concluded that to him, the compiling of the Pearl of Great Price was not considered a monumental accomplishment. My colleague, Dr. Richard O. Cowan, came to a similar conclusion. He wrote:

> Perhaps President Richards and his associates did not fully realize the significance of what had been done. He did not refer to the publication of this future canonized scripture in his journal, nor does the Star's enumeration of his accomplishments as mission president mention it (MS 14:168). Nevertheless, the Saints immediately recognized President

Richards's work as a major contribution to their literature, and as early as 1857 President Brigham Young included the *Pearl of Great Price* among the few books he placed in the foundation stone of the Salt Lake Temple, which was then under construction (JH 13 Aug. 1857).[10]

President Young presented a copy of the Pearl of Great Price to the Harvard College Library on September 1, 1864, along with the Book of Mormon and the Doctrine and Covenants. Although the Pearl of Great Price was not a canonized book of scripture in 1864, this gift indicates the respect the leading brethren had for the British Mission publication.[11]

DISPLAYING THE ANTIQUITIES
IN NAUVOO

In Nauvoo, as in Kirtland, the temple construction and the mummies and papyri were high on the list of things to see while visiting the headquarters of the Church. The Egyptian antiquities were displayed in three locations in Nauvoo: (1) on the second floor of Joseph Smith's two-story log cabin; (2) for a time at his mother's log cabin; and (3) at the "Mansion House," a combination hotel and home for the Prophet that was completed in 1843. The Prophet was murdered before the Nauvoo Temple was completed, and it appears that the antiquities were never housed there as they had been in the Kirtland Temple.

As a young girl, Elizabeth Clements Kendall recalled visiting Joseph Smith's log-cabin home to deliver some laundry. He asked if she would like to see the Egyptian mummies. According to an account of the incident written by her daughter, Elizabeth reported that

> she was very thrilled at the thought and of course very curious, but she felt it a great privilege to be allowed to see them. The mummies were kept in the attic where they wouldn't be destroyed and in those days there weren't any stairways in the houses such as we have now, and in order to get to the attic one had to climb a ladder which was straight up along the wall.
>
> She told Joseph in a very timid voice that she would like to see them, but was a little frightened while climbing the ladder to the attic. But when at the top she saw the room with the curious looking things, and Joseph seeing she was a little

COURTESY RLDS CHURCH

Joseph Smith's two-story log cabin in Nauvoo, Illinois, is depicted
in a painting by Jack Garnier, ca. 1840

frightened stepped to her side, laid his hand on her shoulder
and said, "come little one, do not be afraid." He took her by
the hand and led her to them saying, "touch them and you
will never be afraid of the dead." It was then that he placed his
hands on her shoulder and head and gave her a blessing. He
told her that when she grew up she would be a nurse and
would care for the sick and the dead all her life.[1]

The following report, which appeared in the *Quincy* (Illinois)
Whig under the title "A Glance at the Mormons," described a
writer's visit to Nauvoo in late April 1840:

After [Joseph Smith] had shown us the fine grounds around
his dwelling; he conducted us, at our request, to an upper
room, where he drew aside the curtains of a case; and showed
us several Egyptian Mummies, which we were told that the
church had purchased, at his suggestion, some time before, for
a large sum of money.

The embalmed body that stands near the centre of the case,
said he, is one of the Pharaohs, who sat upon the throne of
Egypt; and the female figure by its side was probably one of
the daughters.

It may have been the Princess Thermutis, I replied, the same that rescued Moses from the waters of the Nile.

It is not improbable, answered the Prophet; but my time has not yet allowed me fully to examine and decide that point. Do you understand the Hebrew language, said he, raising his hand to the top of the case, and taking down a small Hebrew Grammer of Rabbi Seixas.

That language has not altogether escaped my attention was the reply.

He then walked to a secretary, on the opposite side of the room, and drew out several frames, covered with glass, under which were numerous fragments of Egyptian papyras, on which, as usual, a great variety of hieroglyphical characters had been imprinted.

These ancient records, said he, throw great light on the subject of Christianity. They have been unrolled and preserved with great labor and care. My time has been hitherto too much taken up to translate the whole of them, but I will show you how I interpret certain parts. There, said he, pointing to a particular character, that is the signature of the patriarch Abraham.

It is indeed a most interesting autograph, I replied, and doubtless the only one extant. What an ornament it would be to have these ancient manuscripts handsomely set, in appropriate frames, and hung up around the walls of the temple which you are about to erect at this place.

Yes, replied the Prophet, and the translation hung up with them.[2]

Catherine Hulet Winget related in her history that in the fall of 1840 she attended the "first conference ever held in Nauvoo. It was held out of doors. There was considerable sickness there that fall and many of the people attending the conference were pale and sickly. While there, I went to the house of the Prophet Joseph Smith. He had three Egyptian mummies in his room. I saw them standing against the wall."[3]

On February 19, 1843, a girl named Charlotte visited Joseph and Emma Smith, then called on Lucy Mack Smith, Joseph's mother. In a magazine article entitled "A Girl's Letters from Nauvoo," she wrote about the visit:

Madame Smith's residence is a log house very near her son's. She opened the door and received us cordially. She is a motherly kind of woman of about sixty years. She receives a little pittance by exhibiting The Mummies to strangers. When we asked to see them, she lit a candle and conducted us up a short, [narrow] stairway to a low, dark room under the roof. On one side were standing half a dozen mummies, to whom she introduced us, King Onitus and his royal household,—one she did not know. Then she took up what seemed to be a club wrapped in a dark cloth, and said "This is the leg of Pharaoh's daughter, the one that saved Moses." Repressing a smile, I looked from the mummies to the old lady, but could detect nothing but earnestness and sincerity on her countenance. Then she turned to a long table, set her candle-stick down, and opened a long roll of manuscript, saying it was "the writing of Abraham and Isaac, written in Hebrew and Sanscrit," and she read several minutes from it as if it were English. It sounded very much like passages from the Old Testament—and it might have been for anything we knew—but she said she read it through the inspiration of her son Joseph, in whom she seemed to have perfect confidence. Then in the same way she interpreted to us hieroglyphics from another roll. One was Mother Eve being tempted by the serpent, who—the serpent, I mean—was standing on the tip of his tail, which with his two legs formed a tripod, and had his head in Eve's ear. I said, "But serpents don't have legs."

"They did before the fall," she asserted with perfect confidence.

The Judge slipped a coin in her hand which she received smilingly, with a pleasant, "Come again," as we bade her goodby.[4]

The Prophet posted a sign on the front of his house on September 15, 1843, that read:

NAUVOO MANSION

In consequence of my house being constantly crowded with strangers and other persons wishing to see me, or who had business in the city, I found myself unable to support so much company free of charge, which I have done from the foundation of the Church. My house has been a home and resting-place for thousands, and my family many times obliged to do without food, after having fed all they had to visitors; and I

The Mansion House in Nauvoo, where visitors were shown the Egyptian antiquities

could have continued the same liberal course, had it not been for the cruel and untiring persecution of my relentless enemies. I have been reduced to the necessity of opening "The Mansion" as a hotel. I have provided the best table accommodations in the city; and the Mansion, being large and convenient, renders travelers more comfortable than any other place on the Upper Mississippi. I have erected a large and commodious brick stable, and it is capable of accommodating seventy-five horses at one time, and storing the requisite amount of forage, and is unsurpassed by any similar establishment in the State.[5]

Many hundreds of visitors to Nauvoo stayed at the Mansion House, which was the social center of the city. The mummies were kept there, readily available for those who chose to see them. One visitor wrote: "After supper [we] were introduced to Mr. Smith the prophet. Suffice it to say we were agreeably disappointed in his person, appearance, and manners. He seemed to be very sociable and ready in conversation upon any subject. Upon his warm solicitation, we spent the night at his house. The morning was spent in examining some very curious ancient records found with a number of mummies in good preservation, in ancient Thebes. They contain some very curious representations."[6]

Josiah Quincy, a prominent nineteenth-century American who later became mayor of Boston, visited Nauvoo in the spring of 1844 in his attempt to personally unscramble the enigma of Joseph Smith and the controversial Mormons. The much publicized report of his visit in company with Charles Francis Adams, son of U.S. President John Quincy Adams, contains the following about the mummies and parchments:

> "And now come with me," said the prophet, "and I will show you the curiosities." So saying, he led the way to a lower room, where sat a venerable and respectable-looking lady. "This is my mother, gentlemen. The curiosities we shall see belong to her. They were purchased with her own money, at a cost of six thousand dollars;" and then, with deep feeling, were added the words, "And that woman was turned out upon the prairie in the dead of night by a mob." There were some pine presses fixed against the wall of the room. These receptacles Smith opened, and disclosed four human bodies, shrunken and black with age. "These are mummies," said the exhibitor. "I want you to look at that little runt of a fellow over there. He was a great man in his day. Why, that was Pharaoh Necho, King of Egypt!" Some parchments inscribed with hieroglyphics were then offered us. They were preserved under glass and handled with great respect. "That is the handwriting of Abraham, the Father of the Faithful," said the prophet. "This is the autograph of Moses, and these lines were written by his brother Aaron. Here we have the earliest account of the Creation, from which Moses composed the First Book of Genesis." The parchment last referred to showed a rude drawing of a man and woman, and a serpent walking upon a pair of legs. I ventured to doubt the propriety of providing the reptile in question with this unusual means of locomotion. "Why, that's as plain as a pikestaff," was the rejoinder. "Before the Fall snakes always went about on legs, just like chickens. They were deprived of them, in punishment for their agency in the ruin of man." We were further assured that the prophet was the only mortal who could translate these mysterious writings, and that his power was given by direct inspiration.[7]

As Joseph Smith and his distinguished guests left the room that housed the mummies, he told his visitors, "Gentlemen . . .

those who see these curiosities generally pay my mother a quarter of a dollar."[8]

Though some errors are noted, such as the price paid for the mummies and some of the writers of the parchment, Josiah Quincy, a Harvard scholar, did state that the hieroglyphics "were preserved under glass and handled with great respect," and that Joseph's abilities to translate were not in consequence of any scholastically attained skills but by "direct inspiration."

Who Were the Mummies?

When the mummies were purchased in 1835, rumors were so rampant as to their identification that Oliver Cowdery was compelled to publish a disclaimer: "It has been said that the purchasers of these antiquities pretend to have the bodies of Abraham, Abimelech, (the king of the Philistines,) Joseph, who was sold into Egypt, etc., etc., for the purpose of attracting the attention of the multitude, and gulling the unwary; which is utterly false. Who these ancient inhabitants of Egypt were, I do not at present say."[9] If Joseph knew who the mummies were at the time they were in Kirtland, he didn't say.

The writer of the article "A Girl's Letters from Nauvoo" stated that Lucy Mack Smith claimed the mummies were "King Onitus and his royal household." The author of the article entitled "A Glance at the Mormons" recorded that according to Joseph Smith, one of the mummies "is one of the Pharaohs, who sat upon the throne of Egypt; and the female figure by its side was probably one of his daughters." When the visitor suggested that the daughter might be Princess Thermutis, who was believed to have rescued Moses from the Nile, it is reported that the Prophet answered, "It is not improbable . . . but my time has not yet allowed me fully to examine and decide that point." At the time he had had the mummies in his possession for more than five years.

William I. Appleby visited the Prophet in Nauvoo in June 1841 and wrote that he "viewed four Mummies, one male and three females brought from Ancient Thebes in Egypt,—saw the

Roll of Papyrus, and the writings thereon, taken from off the bosom of the Male Mummy, being some of the writings of ancient Abraham and of Joseph that was sold into Egypt." He noted that "the Male mummy was one of the Ancient Pharaoh's of Egypt, and a Priest, as he is embalmed with his tongue extended,—representing a speaker. The females were his wife and two daughters, as a part of the writing has been translated, and informs us who they were, also whose writings it is, and when those mummies were embalmed, which is nearly four thousand years ago."[10]

Many years later Jerusha Walker Blanchard, the oldest granddaughter of Joseph Smith's brother Hyrum, remembered playing hide and seek with her cousins Joseph, Frederick, Alexander, and David Smith. Her favorite hiding place, she said, "was in an old wardrobe which contained the mummies." She recalled that there were three mummies: "the old Egyptian king, the queen and their daughter," and that "in the arms of the Old King, lay the roll of papyrus from which our prophet translated the Book of Abraham."[11]

In a lengthy handwritten account entitled "When the Mormons Dwelt among Us," Eudocia Baldwin Marsh wrote that when she visited Nauvoo with some members of her family, they dined at the "Mansion House Smiths large Hotel. After dinner," she said, "we were told that in an adjoining room some Egyptian mummies were exhibited for a small sum—Some of the party expressing a wish to see them, we were ushered into the room where we found them presided over by the mother of the Prophet, a trim looking old lady in black silk gown and white cap and kerchief."

According to Mrs. Marsh, Lucy Mack Smith, using a "long wand," pointed out to the visitors "old King Pharaoh of old Egypt himself, with wife and daughter and gave us a detailed account of thier [sic] lives and doing three thousand years before." When asked how she obtained this information, "she replied in a severely virtuose tone and a manner calculated to repress all doubt and further question—'My Son Joseph Smith has recently received a revelation from the Lord in regard to these people and times—and *he* has told all these things to *me.'"* [12]

The written accounts of visitors to Nauvoo seem to be in general agreement that those who displayed the mummies said the male mummy was one of Egypt's pharaohs and the female figures were members of his family. However, there are several inconsistencies in the various accounts: the time frame, the names of the mummies, the gender of the mummies, and even the number of mummies. With boxes around the room where the mummies were exhibited, it is easy to see why some writers assumed there were bodies still inside. Also, sometimes a mummy or two might have been on loan for display elsewhere, accounting for differences in the number of antiquities. Assuming that the visitors received correct information during the exhibit, if considerable time elapsed between the visit and the recording, faulty memories might also have played a major role.

Mother Lucy Mack Smith, Curator

As has been noted, several of the visitors who saw the mummies in Nauvoo commented that Joseph Smith's mother, Lucy Mack Smith, appeared to be in charge of the Egyptian artifacts in the log cabin and later in the Mansion House. When Joseph Smith was home, he apparently showed them on occasion, but more frequently his mother would conduct the tours and answer the questions, for which she charged a fee of twenty-five cents per person.

After the deaths of three of her sons within a few weeks of each other—Joseph and Hyrum at Carthage Jail on June 27, 1844, and Samuel five weeks later—leaving William as her only surviving son, Mother Smith continued to manage the small museum to help maintain herself. More than fifty years later Joseph Smith III, Joseph and Emma's eldest son, reflected back upon the Nauvoo period and reported: "The papyrus from which the Book of Abraham, was said to have been translated by Father, was with other portions found in a roll with some

Egyptian mummies, pasted on either paper or linen and put into a small case of flat drawers, some dozen or sixteen in number. This case, with two cases of mummies containing five persons, one much smaller than the others, were in the keeping of Grandmother Lucy Smith, Father's mother, for some time before Father's death, and were still in her possession both at the time he was killed and after."[13]

Some highlights of Lucy Mack Smith's life after the deaths of her sons until her demise have been recorded as follows as a note in her family history:

> Of the life of Lucy Smith, familiarly called Grandmother Smith, after the Martyr's death, little need be written. At the time of the tragedy at Carthage, Grandmother Smith was living with Joseph, and continued living with Emma until in September following, when she removed with her son-in-law, Arthur Millikin, and her daughter Lucy, into a house known as the Ponson house, hired for them by the Church, which also hired a girl to wait upon her and help generally. Sometime that fall, the fall of 1844, she commenced her history, the work now being republished, Mr. and Mrs. Corey writing for her.
>
> She completed this work sometime in 1845, the copyright being secured for her by Elder Almon W. Babbit, in that year, or in the early part of 1846. The family moved into the house owned by Elder William Marks in 1845, but remained only till the next year, when they settled in a house bought for Grandmother, by the Church. In the fall of 1846, under the pressure of the mob coming against the city, they moved to Knoxville, Illinois, remaining over the winter, and in the spring of 1847 returning to Nauvoo, again. Here they remained till the fall of 1849, when they moved to Webster, in the same county, staying there two years, when they removed to Fountain Green. In the Spring of 1852 Grandmother Smith, and a grand child, a daughter of Samuel H. Smith, Mary Bailey Smith by name, went to Nauvoo to live with Major Lewis C. Bidamon, whom Emma Smith had married in 1847. She remained with them, until her death, which occurred on the farm owned by the prophet before his death, two and a half miles east of Nauvoo, on the road to Carthage. The farm was then being carried on by Sr. Emma and her boys; and here, on May 8th, 1855 [actually May 14, 1856], watched over

and ministered to by Emma, the wife of her son Joseph, her grand son Joseph 3rd, and the young daughter of a neighboring farmer, Elizabeth Pilkington by name, this noble-hearted mother in Israel went to her rest.

Her grand daughter, Mary B. Smith, had some months before her death, married a Mr. Edward Kelteau, and had taken up her battle with the things of this life for herself. Major Bidamon was always kind to Grandmother Smith, and being a skillful workman in wood, constructed for her use a chair and carriage, upon which she was wheeled about the house and grounds, she being a bed-ridden invalid for years, helpless to a great extent.

For a time she derived a little income from the exhibition of some mummies and the papyrus records found with them, which had been left in her care by the Church for this purpose.[14]

William Smith and the Mummies

In 1846 William Smith, Joseph's brother, mentioned the mummies in two letters to James J. Strang, a self-appointed leader of a group that had broken off from the Church. In a letter dated December 2, 1846, William wrote: "You in quire what may be the pleasure of Mother Smith it is to see her Children prosperous all gathered to Voree in the spring as soon as the roads & weather will permit, & teams & money sent to remove us the Mumies and records are safe etc., etc."

In a follow-up letter postmarked December 19, 1846, from Knoxville, Illinois, to "Brother Strang" at Burlington W. T., William wrote, ". . . to remove us it will require 7 teams, and one extra Carriage for Mother Smith to ride in. She is quite feeble and I feel anxious that she may be removed to [Vroe or Vree] and see the Prophet before that she is—gathered to the Land of her fathers the mummies & records are with us and will be of benifit to the Church."[15]

William was excommunicated from the Church on October 12, 1845, by Brigham Young and the Quorum of the Twelve Apostles. Several of his business dealings were questionable, and on his missions, "the course of conduct he pursued toward the females subjected him to much criticism."[16] At the time he

wrote the letters to Strang, he was making himself available to
the apostate leader, who attempted to organize a church of his
own. Apparently in William's mind, possessing the mummies
and records added status to his claim that he was a viable
church officer or patriarch.

There is an interesting account extant that William Smith
displayed the mummies and parchments during a lecture series.
Joseph Smith III, his nephew, reported that when Lucy Mack
Smith returned to Nauvoo to live with her daughter Lucy, she
did not bring with her "the mummies and case of drawers." He
continued: "We learned that while living near Galesburg, Uncle
William undertook a lecturing tour, and secured the mummies
and case of records, as the papyrus was called, as an exhibit and
aid to making his lectures more attractive and lucrative. Uncle
William became stranded somewhere along the Illinois River,
and sold the mummies and the records with the understanding
that he might repurchase them. This he never did." He also
wrote: "Uncle William never accounted for the sale he made,
except to state that he was obliged to sell them, but fully intended to repurchase them, before the fire [the Chicago fire of
1871]; and of course could not after they were burned."[17]

Brigham Young was apprised of the fact that William had
taken control of the mummies. Almon W. Babbitt, who was in
charge of the Church's affairs in Nauvoo after the apostles left,
wrote to President Young on January 31, 1848, and told him,
"William has got the mummies from Mother Smith and refuses
to give them up."[18]

THE ELUSIVE TRAIL OF
THE MUMMIES

Did William Smith have the mummies, as Almon Babbitt reported to Brigham Young? This account is puzzling, since the four mummies and the papyrus were previously presumed to be in Lucy Mack Smith's possession when she died on May 14, 1856.

Twelve days later, the "four mummies and records of them" were sold by Emma Smith Bidamon, Lewis C. Bidamon (the man Emma married in 1847), and Joseph Smith III to a man who certainly had no special feelings for what these sacred records and the mummies had meant to Joseph Smith and to members of the Church. The bill of sale, dated May 26, 1856, stated:

> This certifies that we have sold to Mr. A. Combs four Egyptian Mummies with the records of them. This mummies were obtained from the catacoms of Egypt sixty feet below the surface of the Earth by the antiquaritan society of Paris & forwarded to New York & purchased by the Mormon Prophet Joseph Smith at the price of twenty four hundred dollars in the year eighteen hundred thirty five they were highly prized by Mr. Smith on account of the importance which attached to the record which were accidentaly found enclosed in the breast of one of the Mummies. From translations by Mr. Smith of the Records these Mummies were found to be the family of Pharo King of Egypt. they were kept exclusively by Mr. Smith until his death & since by the Mother of Mr. Smith notwithstanding we have had repeated offers to purchase which have invariably been refused until her death which occurred on the fourteenth day of May last.[1]

The document was signed "L. C. Bidamon, Emma Bidamon, Joseph Smith [her son]."

The statement that the antiquities were "highly prized by [Joseph] Smith on account of the importance which attached to the record" is particularly interesting. Some of Emma Smith's descendants in the leadership of the Reorganized Church of Jesus Christ of Latter Day Saints (RLDS) have minimized the worth of the message of the scrolls and Joseph Smith's respect for them. Joseph Smith III and Heman C. Smith, who co-authored a multivolume history of the church in 1898, wrote: "The church has never to our knowledge taken any action on this work, either to endorse or condemn; so it cannot be said to be a church publication; nor can the church be held to answer for the correctness of its teaching. Joseph Smith, as the translator, is committed of course to the correctness of the translation, but not necessarily to the endorsement of its historical or doctrinal content."[2]

RLDS President Israel A. Smith stated, "We have no record that Joseph Smith, Jr., ever endorsed its contents or teachings. He merely translated on the basis of his own learning and study. He referred to it as a 'purported' record."[3]

In 1970, RLDS President W. Wallace Smith made it even clearer with his disclaimer of the Abrahamic writings: "The Book of Abraham, published by Joseph Smith, Jr., in 1842 at Nauvoo, Illinois, and canonized by the Utah Mormon Church in 1880, provides much of the rationale for the Mormon Church's denial of priesthood to the black man. I do not consider the Book of Abraham to be anything other than the speculative writings of its author, and certainly neither intended by him nor endorsed officially by the Reorganized Church at any time since its founding in 1852 to qualify as 'inspired' writing."[4]

Curiously, Joseph Smith III published the following statement, which was written in Lamoni, Iowa, on October 24, 1898, and is addressed to "Bro. Heman C. Smith, Lamoni, Iowa":

> The papyrus from which the Book of Abraham, was said to have been translated by Father, was with other portions found

in a roll with some Egyptian mummies, pasted on either paper or linen and put into a small case of flat drawers, some dozen or sixteen in number. This case, with two cases of mummies containing five persons, one much smaller than the others, were in the keeping of Grandmother Lucy Smith, Father's mother, for some time before Father's death, and were still in her possession both at the time he was killed and after. She took them from our house, some time after Father's death, and had them at her daughter Lucy Millikin's, when they moved into Knox County, Illinois, not far from Galesburg. I cannot give you dates, but during a part of 1846–7 Mother and family were away from Nauvoo and Grandmother was at Lucy Millikin's. Grandmother finally came back to Nauvoo with Lucy's family, but came without the mummies and case of drawers. We learned that while living near Galesburg, Uncle William undertook a lecturing tour, and secured the mummies and case of records, as the papyrus was called, as an exhibit and aid to making his lectures more attractive and lucrative. Uncle William became stranded somewhere along the Illinois River, and sold the mummies and the records with the understanding that he might repurchase them. This he never did. Part of the stock, one case of mummies and part or all of the cases of drawers, found their way to Wood's Museum, Chicago, and a part to St. Louis, where, we never learned.[5]

The bill of sale also affirms that the mummies "were kept exclusively by Mr. Smith until his death." This does not mean that Joseph Smith did not allow other responsible people to display them. We know that they were displayed in and around Kirtland by Frederick G. Williams of the First Presidency, guides in the Kirtland Temple, and Lucy Mack Smith, the Prophet's mother. But these trusted people were personally responsible to Joseph for keeping the mummies safe. In the same vein, the letter confirms that the mummies had been kept by "the Mother of Mr. Smith" since the Prophet's death. The document also helps establish Lucy's death date as May 14, 1856, there being several incorrect dates in print.

Who Was A. Combs?

The purchaser of the antiquities was "Mr. A. Combs." Who was he? How did he know that the mummies and papyri were for sale? Is it possible that he lived in the vicinity of Nauvoo and was aware of Lucy Smith's failing health and death and the availability of the antiquities? Did Emma and the family advertise that they were for sale? How much did Combs pay for the antiquities? What did he intend to do with them?

Through some excellent research carried out by Brigham Young University Family History Services personnel, A. Combs was located. His given name was Abel, and he was born in the state of New York about 1823. He is first located in 1844, when, on April 4, he married Eliza Jane Johnson in Trumbull County, Ohio. On their marriage license, both Abel and Eliza Jane, who was born in Virginia in 1824, listed Bristol, Trumbull County, as their place of residence. One child, a son whom they named Oscar, was born in 1845. Another fact we have learned—one whose significance is not yet known—is that between 1844 and 1855, Abel and Eliza owned land in Southington, Ohio, about thirty miles from Kirtland and just ten to fifteen miles from Michael H. Chandler's farm.

We do not know if Combs lived in Trumbull County as a boy. If he did, he might have visited Kirtland sometime between 1835 and 1838, when the mummies and papyri were on display there, or Rochester, Portage County, Ohio, where Joseph Smith Sr. kept the mummies at the Woolley home when their safety was threatened by radical apostates in Kirtland. If Combs did not personally see the antiquities in Kirtland as a young man, he surely would have learned while living there that Michael H. Chandler, the Irish farmer who lived but a few miles from his home, was the one who had sold them to the Mormon prophet.

Combs is listed in census records for Trumbull County as a "hardware plater." He and Eliza sold a thirty-nine–acre farm in Farmington, Trumbull County, on January 7, 1855,[6] and where they went after that time is unknown. They are not listed in Trumbull County in the 1860 census. Whether they moved to the

Nauvoo area sometime after leaving Ohio is also unknown. Their son, Oscar, married a "Nellie" Ellen Donovan from Illinois in 1863. Many years later, from 1874 to 1892, Abel lived in Philadelphia, where the city directory listed his business as "lamps" and later as "artist."

How Combs learned of the death of Lucy Mack Smith and the availability of the mummies and papyri remains a mystery. There is no evidence that he toured and displayed the mummies as did Michael Chandler. We also do not know at this time how much he paid for the antiquities, since the price was not recorded on the bill of sale. Perhaps William Smith had entered into an agreement months or even years before the items were sold, and the bill of sale merely made the transfer of ownership official.

Two Mummies and Some Records in St. Louis

Dr. James R. Clark, my mentor at BYU and author of *The Story of the Pearl of Great Price,* was well aware that some of the antiquities were in the Wood's Museum prior to the great Chicago fire of 1871. After examining the Chicago Museum catalog of 1863, he learned that the two mummies on display had been acquired from the St. Louis Museum.[7] Through his initial research and the combined efforts of several later researchers, the story of the antiquities following their sale to Abel Combs is coming into sharper focus.

In a St. Louis newspaper on August 2, 1856, an interesting advertisement appeared under the title "Museum and Concert!" The ad stated that a "Floating Palace" containing upwards of one hundred thousand curiosities—including "Ancient Relics from Egypt, Greece, Rome, Pompeii and Herculaneum"— would be exhibited at the Steamboat Landing on August 7, 8, and 9.[8] This information is possibly unrelated but at least it is noteworthy because of an announcement that appeared in the local newspaper twelve days later. On August 14, 1856, the St. Louis Museum released the following story under the heading

"A Combination of Exhibitions! Third Story Wyman's Hall, (opposite the court house)":

> This establishment is now open for exhibition, under the management, and for the benefit of Mr. J. P. BATES, practical naturalist, and contains
>
> FIRST—The finest and most unique collection of Birds, Quadrupeds, Reptiles, Fish, and other illustrations of Natural History in the West, and unrivalled for its choice and rare specimens, (about 2,000 in number,) and the style and beauty displayed in their preparation and arrangement.
>
> SECOND—The greatest geological wonder in the world, the CETACEAN SAURIAN OPHIDIAN MONSTER,
> **ZEUGLODON MACROSPONDYLUS,**
> Of Muller, discovered by Dr. Koch, in Alabama, a complete skeleton 96 feet in length, and set in natural position.
>
> THIRD—**TWO MUMMIES** from the Catacombs of Egypt, which have been unrolled, presenting a full view of the RECORDS enclosed, and of the bodies which are in a remarkable state of preservation.
>
> FOURTH—Vance's great collection of panoramic views of towns, cities and places of note in California—about 200 in number, and exhibited to thousands of persons in New York, at a charge of 25 cents.
>
> FIFTH—A fine collection of MINERALS, FOSSILS, SHELLS, CHOICE PAINTINGS and CURIOSITIES.
>
> Admission fee to the whole 25 cents—and refunded if satisfaction is not given.
>
> Open every day (Sunday's excepted) from 9 A.M., to 6 P.M., and on Tuesday and Saturday evenings from 7 to 10 P.M.
>
> Contributions solicited and carefully preserved.
>
> Taxidermal work executed as usual.[9]

In the same edition of the newspaper, the editor, in a column entitled "Amusement Notices," encouraged readers to visit the museum, confirming that the mummies were a new addition to the displays: "Lately, we observe a new attraction, consisting of a pair of MUMMIES from the Catacombs of Egypt, which are a great novelty in these parts, and should be seen by all."[10] An entry published on June 12, 1857, in the *St. Louis Daily Missouri Democrat* should quell all doubts that these mummies were from the Joseph Smith collection, a premise that had apparently been challenged:

> THE MORMON PROPHET'S MUMMIES—Not long since, we stated that the mummies and accompanying Egyptian manuscripts at the museum were the identical mummies and manuscripts formerly found by Smith the mormon prophet. They were purchased by the proprietor of the museum from Mr. A. Combs, who bought them at Nauvoo city on the 26th of May, 1856. In a work published by "the saints" is a facsimile of the manuscripts with the information added that they were written by the great Jewish patriarch, Abraham himself. Doubt having still been expressed that they were the prophet's mummies, etc., we now append the certificate with which the sale of them to Mr. Combs was accompanied.[11]

The bill of sale, with a few grammatical, spelling, and punctuation corrections and changes, followed this announcement. The article stated that the mummies were purchased "by the proprietor of the museum from Mr. A. Combs, who bought them at Nauvoo city on the 26th of May, 1856." It is not clear whether Edward Wyman of the St. Louis Museum purchased the mummies from Abel Combs in Nauvoo or somewhere else, or whether Combs traveled to St. Louis via the "Floating Palace" or by some other means. What *is* apparent is that two of the four mummies and some papyri from the Mormon collection were in St. Louis just ten weeks after Combs purchased them in Nauvoo.

Dr. Stanley B. Kimball, a professor of history who lives in the St. Louis area, searched the local newspapers for any mention of the mummies. He discovered an article in the *St. Louis Daily Missouri Democrat,* dated May 13, 1857, that read, "Some of the brethren have had the hardness to deny that these were the patriarchal manuscripts and relics. But an unanswerable confirmation of the fact has lately occurred; certain plates issued by the elders as facsimiles of the original having fallen into Mr. Wyman's hands, which plates are also facsimiles of the hieroglyphics in the museum."[12]

Dr. Kimball hypothesized that Wyman had seen a copy of

the 1851 edition of the Pearl of Great Price, which apparently confirmed that one or more of the facsimiles reproduced therein were on display at the St. Louis exhibit. This is a logical conclusion. The producing of the bill of sale a month later apparently settled the misunderstanding. This episode indicates that the local Saints or some who were traveling through St. Louis were aware that the two mummies and the papyri were being exhibited at Wyman's Hall and had raised some questions about Wyman's claim to their authenticity.

Professor Seyffarth and the Papyri

Another piece to the puzzle is found in New York City, where Professor Gustavus Seyffarth was lecturing on Egyptian archaeology at the same time that Abel Combs bought the mummies in Nauvoo. Dr. Seyffarth, a professor of archaeology and exegesis at Concordia Lutheran theological seminary in St. Louis between 1855 and 1871, was born in Saxony in 1796 and studied in Paris in 1820 under Champollion, the celebrated French Egyptologist. He became well known as a decipherer of Egyptian hieroglyphics. Between 1825 and 1855 he was professor of Oriental archaeology at the University of Leipzig.[13]

Dr. Seyffarth, who differed from Champollion on how to interpret Egyptian hieroglyphics, emphasized in his New York lectures his own correctness in deciphering the glyphs. A promotional article in a New York City newspaper, under the headline "Lectures on Egyptian Archaeology," stated:

> The first of a series of three lectures on this recondite subject,—interesting because of the relation to the authenticity of Biblical literature,—was delivered at Stuyvesant Institute, last evening, before a numerous and intelligent auditory. The lecturer is Professor G. SEYFFARTH, M. A., Phil. Doct., who has long enjoyed a distinguished reputation, both in the New and Old Worlds. These lectures will prove of great value, as they will serve as a commentary upon the hidden stores of Egyptian lore contained in the Abbott Museum of the institute, one of the most valuable and interesting collections of that kind in the world.
> The general drift of the first lecture was the assertion and

proof that the Egyptian hieroglyphics, dispersed over the world and found upon an immense number of ancient monuments, are all susceptible of a *syllabic* or *alphabetic* interpretation.

DR. SEYFFARTH afforded sufficient indications that the principal upon which CHAMPOLLION had proceeded was radically insufficient, and, therefore, incorrect. The idea of the French *savan* was that the greater part of these inscriptions and characters were susceptible of a *symbolic* interpretation, or that they contained symbolic signs. He admitted the existence of the alphabet, but his admission of determinatives, and sometimes of symbolic characters, was so blended as to present a system radically differing from that of DR. SEYFFARTH, a system which, when tested by efforts at translation, presents in the one case an unintelligible complication of words—in the latter a rhetorical sense.

At the conclusion of the lecture the Doctor recited a translation of the first sacred book of the ancient Egyptians, the "Turin" papyrus, of which several copies are extant, three of which were in the Abbott Museum. The theology which that document involves is by no means inconsistent with received Christianity, pointing clearly to the fact of a flood, the doctrine of reward and punishment, and more especially of the existence of a Triuno Divinity and the observance of the Sabbath.

We cannot follow these matters in detail. To those who are especially interested in the inquiry, (as who indeed, is not?) these lectures will prove highly interesting and valuable.[14]

Seyffarth's theory was later proven wrong and Champollion's skills have prevailed, but during his lifetime Seyffarth was recognized as a capable—though controversial—scholar.

Professor Seyffarth returned to St. Louis and visited the exhibit at Wyman's Hall in September 1856. Dr. Kimball states that Seyffarth reported, " . . . visitors will find also some large fragments of Egyptian papyrus scrolls, with pieratic [hieratic] (priestly) inscriptions, and drawings representing the judgment of the dead, many Egyptian gods and sacred animals, with certain chapters from the old Egyptian sacred books."[15]

The 1859 catalog of the St. Louis Museum quotes Seyffarth as saying, "The papyrus roll is not a record, but an invocation to the Deity Osiris . . . and a picture of the attendant spirits, introducing the dead to the Judge, Osiris."[16] Dr. Seyffarth may have been looking at two fragments now known as IIIA, Court of Osiris (on the throne), or perhaps Facsimile 3 in the Book of Abraham, or some other fragment presently unknown.[17]

Two Mummies and Some Papyri Move to Chicago

When Edward Wyman established his school in St. Louis in 1843, he also established a museum of natural history and hired J. P. Bates, called by one writer "a naturalist of no mean ability," to head it. In the ads announcing that the Mormon mummies were in the St. Louis Museum, "Mr. J. P. Bates" is listed by various titles and assignments, such as "manager" and "under the personal supervision and management of Mr. J. P. BATES, Practical Naturalist."[18] According to an 1863 museum guide, Bates "has devoted his life, with the enthusiasm of an artist, to this branch of [natural] science and now stands without fear of rivalry, at least in America. . . . He has made frequent journeys to Europe, South America and the tropical regions, in order to obtain the best and rarest birds and quadrupeds which these continents afford."[19] A notice in the *St. Louis Daily Missouri Democrat* on July 3, 1863, noted that the St. Louis Museum would soon be moving from St. Louis. An announcement in the newspaper six days later stated: "The St. Louis Museum WILL POSITIVELY CLOSE on Saturday, the 11th inst. AND IT IS BEING REMOVED TO CHICAGO. J. P. BATES Manager."

On July 6, the *Chicago Tribune* announced "with pleasure that through the liberality of two of our worthy and public spirited citizens the Saint Louis Museum has been purchased, and will soon be removed, and permanently located in this city. This museum is much the largest in the West, and in several features the choicest one in the United States." Five weeks later, on August 10, 1863, the *Chicago Times* stated: "There are the two mummies which in the hands of Joe Smith were made to give a revelation and still they bear the original tablets with the cabalistic or coptic characters thereon."

"A Complete Guide to the Chicago Museum," dated 1863,

gave the same description of the two mummies as appeared in the 1859 St. Louis Museum Catalogue:

> These Mummies were obtained in the Catacombs of Egypt, sixty feet below the surface of the earth, for the Antiquarian Society of Paris, forwarded to New York, and there purchased, in the year 1835, by Joe Smith, the Mormon Prophet, on account of the writings found in the chest of one of them, and which he pretended to translate, stating them to belong to the family of the Pharaohs'—but, according to Prof. Seyffarth, the papyrus roll is not a record, but an invocation to the Deity, Osirus, in which occurs the name of the person, (Horus) and a picture of the attendant spirits introducing the dead to the Judge, Osirus. The body of one is that of a female, about forty; the other, that of a boy about fourteen. They were kept by the Prophet's mother until his death, when the heirs sold them, and were shortly after purchased for the Museum.
>
> The art of embalming is, in a measure, lost, and its details are not known or practiced as among the ancients. With the poor it was a very simple process, and the principle articles used were salt and asphaltum. The rich spent large sums in embalming the dead, using the most costly spices and perfumes. The practice was not confined to Egypt: several examples have been found in the Western States of this country, showing that it was in use to some extent among the aborigines.[20]

Wood's Museum in Chicago

The original buyers of the Chicago Museum did not maintain ownership for very long. They sold their property to Joseph H. Wood about six months later, in 1864, and he changed the name to Wood's Museum. Wood's Museum expanded as did the city itself in the next few years. When Nauvoo was the largest city in Illinois in 1844, its population was between 10,000 and 12,000, compared to Chicago's 5,000. By 1871, the year of the great fire, the population of Chicago was 334,270 and it had become America's fourth largest city, surpassed only by New York, Philadelphia, and Brooklyn.[21]

A few interested parties reported seeing the two mummies and some papyri on display in Wood's Museum between 1864

*Col. Wood's Museum
(Chicago Museum),
1862–1871*

and 1871. C.C.A. Christensen, a Utah artist, wrote: "As this writer, in the year 1865, along with fifty other missionaries from Utah, were on our way to our destination after having visited different towns, some of us got together in New York where we signed up for the boat going to Liverpool, and one of these brethren, I believe it was Elder Penrose, who told me that he had visited the museum in Chicago, and there saw the original papyrus rolls from whence Abraham's book had been translated into English, and to the side of it was a written declaration from Mr. Chandler."[22] Michael Chandler's certificate attesting to Joseph Smith's ability to translate the papyrus was then quoted.

The *Salt Lake City Directory and Business Guide for 1869* under the heading "Chicago, Its Trade and Growth," noted that the museum had numerous and sundry items on display, including "the mummies around which the papyrus was rolled on which the Book of Abraham—published with the Pearl of Great Price—was inscribed, from a collection of specimens worthy of attention of all and the admiration of the students of nature. The mummies were sold by those who had them in charge after the death of the Prophet, Joseph Smith, and were afterwards obtained for the museum—so the printed catalogue states."

President Joseph Smith III of the RLDS church wrote in 1898:

> I personally, in company with Elder Elijah Banta, of Sandwich, Illinois, saw the mummies and case of drawers in the museum in Chicago, before the great fire, in 1871; in which they undoubtedly perished with the rest of the accumulated relics and curiosities. . . .
>
> So far as anything is known by us about the fate, or final disposition of the papyrus, the foregoing is correct, and I was knowing to the facts as they occurred; and saw the mummies and case of drawers in Wood's Museum, Chicago, not long before the fire of October 1871. I was at the time living at Plano, Illinois, fifty-three miles west from Chicago, and did business in the city in behalf of our Publishing Department and *Herald*, and visited the city frequently.[23]

On the evening of October 8, 1871, a fire in Chicago "broke out on the corner of DeKoven and Twelfth streets, at about 9 o'clock on Sunday evening, being caused by a cow kicking over a lamp in a stable in which a woman was milking. An alarm was immediately given but owing to the high southwest wind, the building was speedily consumed, and thence the fire spread rapidly."[24]

The fire, coming after an excessively dry summer and autumn and fanned by high winds, quickly devoured an area of more than two thousand acres, destroying some 18,000 buildings—two-thirds of the city's structures—and property valued at about $196 million. Approximately 90,000 people were left homeless, and it is estimated that at least three hundred died in the conflagration.[25]

The *Chicago Tribune* for October 19 reported that "the only article spared from the immense collection of curiosities which were stored in Wood's Museum is a silver mounted revolver."[26]

The mummies and manuscripts were not popular attractions at Wood's Museum and were seldom, if ever, mentioned after their acquisition in 1863. If they were on display or in storage in the museum that fateful night of October 8, they were undoubtedly destroyed. If they survived the fire, they were either on loan at the time or were stored somewhere beyond the reach of the devastating flames. Colonel Wood, still a showman at heart, placed a sign amid the blackened ruins of his smoldering building: "Col. Wood's Museum, Standing Room Only."[27]

SEARCHING FOR THE ORIGINAL MANUSCRIPTS

In 1969 I was preparing an article relative to the canonization of the Pearl of Great Price, which took place on October 10, 1880, and wrote to Joseph Anderson, secretary to the First Presidency, for related information. I specifically inquired if Elder Orson Pratt had been given explicit instructions by the Brethren as to what to include or exclude in the 1878 edition—the first American edition—of the Pearl of Great Price, which he was preparing for publication and canonization. The following reply arrived about three weeks later:

> Dear Brother Peterson:
> Referring to your letter of May 21, 1969, as per your request I have looked into the minutes covering the period mentioned but find no information on the subject of the Book of Abraham or the anticipated preparation of the American edition of the Pearl of Great Price published in 1878 other than the statement that Elder Pratt, under date of September 2, 1878, mentioned to the brethren the desirability of obtaining the manuscript of the books of Abraham and Joseph which were at the time in the Woods Museum in Chicago, and authorization was given by President Taylor to take the necessary steps to obtain these manuscripts if possible.
> I regret that I cannot be more helpful to you in the matter.[1]

My initial reaction to Elder Anderson's reply was to smile and set it aside, since it did not add anything to my meager knowledge on the preparation of the 1878 American edition of the Pearl of Great Price. I also felt that he had looked in the minutes for the wrong year, since the writings of Abraham and Joseph were apparently destroyed in the Chicago holocaust of 1871.

After I reread the letter several hours later, it slowly dawned on me that Elder Anderson's reply might contain some valuable information on the possible survival and whereabouts of the Egyptian manuscripts after the devastating inferno of 1871. Surely President John Taylor and the General Authorities were well aware of the tragedy in Chicago and the incineration of Wood's Museum seven years before. True, Chicago had suffered a great tragedy, but like the legendary phoenix, out of the ashes had grown a great city.

Had Wood's Museum been rebuilt? Was it possible that through some miraculous means, the sacred records had survived the great inferno? Many questions came to mind as I walked across the BYU campus to the Harold B. Lee Library to resolve whether the revitalized Chicago of the early 1870s included a newly constructed Wood's Museum. I soon discovered that Colonel Wood did rebuild his popular museum, and also built a museum in Philadelphia in 1872.

I had been granted sufficient research funds to allow me to travel to Chicago to pursue this fascinating new development, but I wanted to ascertain the exact wording of President Taylor's counsel to Elders Orson Pratt and Joseph F. Smith prior to their departure for Chicago to learn if it contained additional information that might help me in my research. With permission, I went to the Church Office Building to visit with Brother Anderson.

While I was waiting to see him, President N. Eldon Tanner's secretary asked if I would care to talk personally to President Tanner, since he had been overseeing Pearl of Great Price matters in recent years. I was elated with the opportunity to visit with President Tanner about my research. After a pleasant visit, he sent for Brother Anderson and asked him to allow me to see the journal entry in the First Presidency's minute book pertaining to the proposed trip of Elders Pratt and Smith. Brother

Elder Joseph F. Smith and Elder Orson Pratt, who went on a special mission to the Midwest and eastern states in 1878. Elder Pratt prepared for publication the first American edition of the Pearl of Great Price

Anderson reminded President Tanner that this request was irregular, but I was allowed to follow him to a room where I was seated at a table, and Elder Anderson brought out the ledger containing the minutes for September 2, 1878.

Elder Anderson located the particular entry and covered up the rest of the page with books so that I could read only the relevant material. Because he hovered so closely over my shoulder as I began to copy the entry for September 2, I jokingly said to him, "Brother Anderson, promise you won't leave me alone in here," to which he quietly but firmly replied, "Rest assured you won't be left alone."

Looking through the hastily constructed rectangular peep hole that Elder Anderson made, I copied the following entry:

> An informal meeting of the Council was held after Elders Orson Pratt and Joseph F. Smith had been set apart for their mission to the United States. Present—Pres. John Taylor and

Elders Wilford Woodruff, Orson Pratt, George Q. Cannon, Joseph F. Smith and A. Carrington.

Brother Orson Pratt spoke of the desirability of obtaining the mss. of the Books of Abraham and of Joseph now in Woods Museum, Chicago.

Brother Taylor considered it to be well to do so though he thought it would be well not to appear too anxious, or advantage might be taken if such a feeling were manifested. He felt that anything that would throw light on the subjects, embraced in the mission of Bros. Pratt and Smith should be encouraged.[2]

The Mission to the States

The calling of Elders Pratt and Smith to go east was referred to as "a mission to the States." The entry in the Historical Department Journal dated September 2, 1878, reads: "Elder O. Pratt was set apart by Pres. John Taylor, and Elder Joseph F. Smith by Elder W. Woodruff, in the President's office this morning on a mission to the States."[3] What was the objective of their "mission to the States"?

Elder Wilford Woodruff made this personal journal entry under that same date:

Joseph F. Smith and W. Woodruff set apart 6 missionaries to Scandinavia and in the afternoon 6 of the twelve set apart Orson Pratt and Joseph F. Smith for a mission to visit Jackson County and other parts of Missouri to visit David Whitmer and John Whitmer family to see if they can obtain the early history of the Church in the hands of John Whitmer family and to perform any other acts that may be necessary upon the mission. John Taylor was mouth in blessing Orson Pratt and W. Woodruff in blessing Joseph F. Smith.[4]

Elder Smith's journal entry dated Monday, September 2, 1878, emphasized the importance of acquiring records along with oral histories: "Brother Orson Pratt and I were set apart by President John Taylor, Wilford Woodruff, George Q. Cannon, and A. Carrington, to take a mission to the states to gather up records and data relative to the early history of the Church."[5]

After he returned to Utah about a month later, Elder Smith

reported at the October general conference that "the chief object of their mission east, was to obtain, if possible, some dates and facts that pertained to the early history of the Church, which, for the want of more correct records in that early date, were lacking, supposing that some things might be gleaned from the old settlers still living in that neighborhood, but they found no one who could give them any information, or who knew as much as ourselves on these matters."[6]

Elder Pratt had just finished preparing the first American edition of the Pearl of Great Price, an assignment that would constantly remind him how grossly limited the historical records of the Church were. Over half of the material in the Pearl of Great Price—selections from the Book of Moses (Moses 1–8) and Joseph Smith–Matthew—is extracted from Joseph Smith's inspired corrections of the King James Version of the Bible, which is now commonly referred to as the Joseph Smith Translation of the Bible (JST). The original handwritten pages and the large family Bible from which Moses 1–8 and Joseph Smith–Matthew came remained in the possession of Emma Smith and her family, who refused to let the apostles take them west with them. Professor Robert J. Matthews, in his book *A Plainer Translation: Joseph Smith's Translation of the Bible,* explained that Orson Pratt used the RLDS 1867 edition of the Joseph Smith Translation to prepare the 1878 edition of the Pearl of Great Price.[7]

Elder Pratt and other leading Brethren who had worked closely with Joseph Smith while he made the changes in the Bible were satisfied that the RLDS church had been honest in their 1867 printing of the revisions.

When the Saints moved west to the valleys of the mountains, the original manuscripts and the papyri were left in Emma's home, the Mansion House in Nauvoo.

The last book in the Pearl of Great Price, Joseph Smith–History, covers the life of Joseph Smith between the time of the First Vision in 1820 and the restoration of the Aaronic Priesthood through John the Baptist in 1829. As Elder Woodruff reminded us in his September 2, 1878, journal entry, the two apostles were to visit the families of David and John Whitmer to see if they could "obtain the early history of the Church." Elder Pratt, the Church historian, did not have access to even one primary source from which to prepare the first American edition of the Pearl of Great Price.

Upon returning to Salt Lake City, the brethren reported their "mission to the States," and it was published in the *Deseret Evening News* in two installments, on November 16 and November 23, 1878. In summary it began:

> Left Salt Lake City Sept. 3rd 1878
> Arrived at Independence, Mo. Friday Sept. 6th AM, 1878 Stayed at the Merchants Hotel – Visited the Temple Lot. Visited Mr. Eaton who had some years before purchased part of the Temple site. Mr. Eaton was in "feeble health." His wife was the widow of John E. Page. Mrs. Eaton was hospitable. The Eatons informed them that there were "Some 70 families gathered in and around Independence, who are awaiting the Redemption of Zion, etc." [All RLDS][8]

At Independence, the brethren met with William E. McLellin, one of the original members of the Quorum of the Twelve. "He seemed pleased to see us, and urged very strongly for us to prolong our visit," they said. They also visited a family named Humphreys who "still claimed to belong to the Church of Jesus Christ of Latter-day Saints. Called on Brother Humphreys at his shop where they found him pleased to meet with us."

Then the two apostles boarded the train for Richmond, where they stayed at the Shaw House. On Saturday morning, September 7, they met with David Whitmer, "the last remaining one of the three witnesses of the Book of Mormon." "He seemed wonderfully pleased as well as surprised at seeing Elder Orson Pratt," they reported. They spent many hours with Whitmer, and detailed accounts were kept of the interviews. In the company of several others, Whitmer bore strong testimony of the appearance of Moroni, seeing the gold plates, and hearing the voice of the Lord "as distinctly as I ever heard anything in my

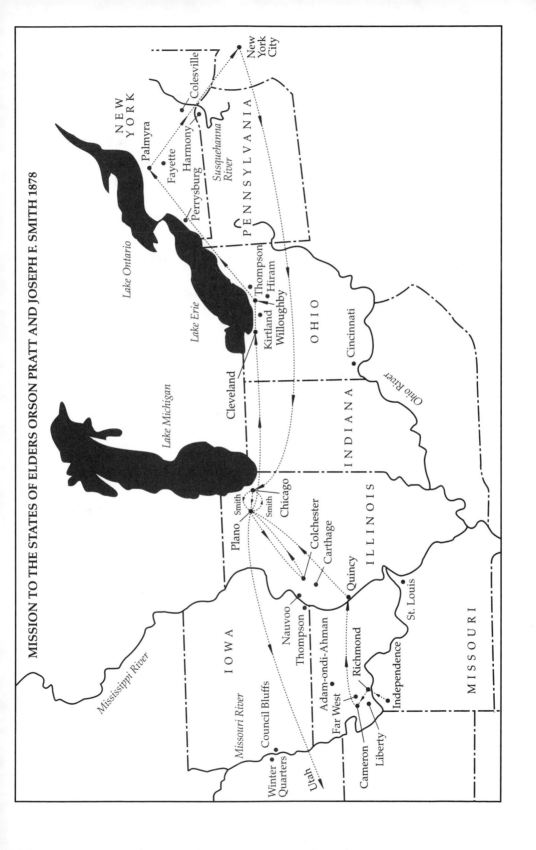

MISSION TO THE STATES OF ELDERS ORSON PRATT AND JOSEPH F. SMITH 1878

life, declaring that the records of the plates of the Book of Mormon were translated by the gift and power of God."

When Elder Pratt inquired whether David Whitmer had in his possession the original manuscripts of the Book of Mormon, he replied that "they are safe and well preserved."

Elder Pratt asked, "Would you not part with them to a purchase?"

Whitmer replied, "No. Oliver charged me to keep them, and Joseph told my father's house to keep the records. I consider these things sacred, and would not part with nor barter them for money."

Elder Smith clarified that he and Elder Pratt were not there to barter for the manuscripts, but wished to see them preserved in some institution "that will not die as man does."

Philander Page, a son of Hiram Page, was present and remarked, "Do you think that the Almighty cannot take care of his own?"

On Sunday, September 8, in the presence of several onlookers, David Whitmer displayed the manuscript of the Book of Mormon. After carefully perusing it, Elder Pratt again raised the issue of procuring the manuscripts, but, he said, "we found that nothing could move him on this point."

That evening David Whitmer called on the two apostles at their hotel. Aware of Oliver Cowdery's rebaptism at Council Bluffs, he stated that "Oliver died the happiest man I ever saw[;] after shaking hands with the family and kissing his wife and daughter, he said, 'Now I lay me down for the last time, I am going to my Savior' and [he] died immediately with a smile on his face."

David Whitmer's parting words to Elders Pratt and Smith were: "This may be the last time I shall ever see you in the flesh so farewell."

On Monday, September 9, Elder Pratt and Elder Smith went to Far West, Missouri, to visit with several members of the Whitmer family, but they found a cold reception. When Elder Pratt inquired about the manuscript that John Whitmer had kept as Church historian, John's son replied, "We've got no history here, all father's papers have gone to Richmond long ago." Elder Pratt told him they had interviewed his uncle David Whitmer in Richmond and had seen the manuscript of the Book of Mormon, but that David had said nothing about having any other papers. John's son repeated, "We have got no papers here." The brethren were convinced that further efforts would be unproductive "where the spirit of bigotry and opposition was so intense."

The apostles then went to Cameron, a railroad station ten miles from Far West, where they booked passage to Quincy, Illinois. They had intended to visit Nauvoo the next day, September 10, but on arrival at Quincy they found that there were no convenient railroad connections to Nauvoo. Early on the morning of September 11, they took a train to Colchester about fifty miles away, en route to Plano and Chicago. During a two-hour wait at Colchester, they met with Lucy Milliken, Joseph Smith's youngest sister, and her husband, Arthur, and family. They also met with the only daughter and the granddaughter of the Prophet's eldest sister, Sophronia McCleary, who was deceased. The reception there was warm.

The evening of September 11 the two brethren went to the house of the president of the RLDS church, Joseph Smith III, in Plano, Illinois, but he was attending a meeting in Iowa. The next day, Thursday, they again visited at President Smith's home and had a "pleasant visit" with his wife and her father. They also called at the printing and publishing office of the RLDS church. When they stated their business, the workers said they could not assist them without Joseph Smith III's permission. They subsequently telegraphed this message to Iowa: "Joseph F. Smith and Orson Pratt here, wish to examine the MS of the new translation. When can you come? Is MS here?" They expected an answer that afternoon "but none came." The next morning a postal card arrived announcing that the conference in Iowa would not be completed until Sunday. The two brethren chose to continue their journey, leaving behind their address in New

York and their request to see the transcript of the Bible. If it was in Plano and could be seen, one or both would call back upon their return home.

The brethren both spoke at an RLDS meeting that evening, and Orson Pratt reviewed his experiences in the early days of the Church, including Joseph Smith's means of receiving revelation and the circumstances surrounding his receiving the revelation on "plural or celestial marriage."

Next the two apostles visited Kirtland, Ohio, going by way of Chicago to Cleveland and then to Willoughby, about three miles from Kirtland. They reported that the Kirtland Temple was in an ill state of repair. They also visited several significant sites and several residents of the town who recalled its early history.

Leaving Kirtland, the brethren decided to visit the Hill Cumorah. They were so impressed with the area, Elder Smith said, that they knelt down in a grove of trees on the hill and "each pronounced upon the other a blessing by the spirit of inspiration and prophecy."[9]

On Tuesday, September 17, after a fourteen-hour train ride from Palmyra, they arrived in New York City and were met by two elders. They spent several days in New York, where they "attended to much church business in regard to immigration and missionary work."[10] Then they started on their homeward journey on September 21. The two-part report in the *Deseret Evening News* ends with their arrival in New York on September 17.

In his journal, Elder Smith noted that he sent a telegram from New York to his cousin Joseph Smith III asking for the opportunity to stop in Plano while en route home to examine the manuscripts of the Inspired Version of the Bible. The reply: "Cannot tell till I see you." Though the answer was less than encouraging, Elder Smith desired to have a friendly visit with his cousin.

According to Elder Smith's journal, when the brethren arrived in Chicago, he (Elder Smith) went on to Plano alone. There, he wrote, the reunion between the sons of the two martyred prophets, Joseph and Hyrum, was "rather strained." Joseph III refused to allow him to see the manuscripts of the Joseph Smith translation of the Bible, although he did give him a printed copy of the work that had been published eleven years earlier. With a feeling of sadness, Elder Smith went back to Chicago and then returned to Utah, arriving home the evening of September 28.[11]

Unresolved Questions

This mission of Joseph F. Smith and Orson Pratt leaves several questions unresolved, including the following:

1. Were the manuscripts of Abraham and Joseph still in existence in Chicago seven years after the great fire, or were the brethren merely checking out a hopeful but unfounded rumor?

Elder Smith's journal indicates he arrived in Salt Lake City on September 28, while an entry in the Historical Department Journal reports that "Orson Pratt returned from his mission to the States" on October 3, five days later. Why did Elder Pratt, who was serving as the Church Historian, spend several extra days in the east, probably in and around Chicago, while Elder Smith returned home?

We learn a little more from a letter written by Elder Smith, dated December 5, 1878, to William E. McLellin in Independence, Missouri. He wrote: "Elder Orson Pratt visited his connexions in Carthage and accomplished his business sooner than he anticipated, so he hurried home to be present at our Semi annual conference commencing October 6th."[12]

It was Elder Pratt who had initially contacted the Church leaders about "the desirability of obtaining the manuscripts of the books of Abraham and Joseph which were at that time in the Woods Museum in Chicago." Elder Smith reported to the October conference that "the entire account of their visit and experience while east, has been written and placed in the possession of President John Taylor."[13]

Elder Franklin D. Richards of the Quorum of the Twelve wrote in his journal on Saturday, October 5, 1878 that he had met at nine o'clock that morning with President John Taylor and ten members of the Quorum of the Twelve, "and heard read— report of O. Pratt and J.F. Smith of their visit to the Whitmers in Missouri and to Young Joseph in Plano, Illinois to Cumorah and City of New York till after one."

2. What about the manuscripts? Did the two apostles believe that the actual papyri containing the writings of Abraham and Joseph were still in existence in Chicago, or that the Prophet Joseph Smith had translated more of the writings of Abraham and Joseph than were published, or both? Elder Pratt had spoken to President Taylor about the desirability of acquiring "the manuscripts." A definition of manuscript is "a written or typewritten composition or document as distinguished from a printed copy." What was his understanding of the word? Without his report of his prolonged visit to Chicago, we are left without answers.

Anxious to pursue the possibility that the ancient papyri containing holy writ or more of its translation might be extant even today, I have spent considerable time pursuing this matter. My research is summarized in a letter dated September 15, 1987, from Richard E. Turley Jr., assistant managing director of the Church Historical Department, to Dr. Robert J. Matthews, then dean of Religious Education at Brigham Young University. Dr. Turley wrote:

> Dear Brother Matthews:
>   . . . In your letter, you enthusiastically endorsed the research of Brother H. Donl Peterson, who has been trying to determine whether any useful information exists about the September 1878 "mission to the states" of Elder Orson Pratt and Elder Joseph F. Smith.
>   A search has been made for information that would supplement data Brother Peterson has already collected. The Historical Department has not been able to locate any documents that would add significant details to what Brother Peterson already knows. As Brother Peterson knows, an October 1878 conference report suggests that Elder Pratt and Elder Smith wrote a full report of their mission to President

John Taylor. This report, if different from the New York letter published in the *Millennial Star,* has not been located.

An inquiry was made to the First Presidency to determine whether such a report might be in the First Presidency's vault. Brother F. Michael Watson, Secretary to the First Presidency, responded that the First Presidency apparently does not have such a report.

We appreciate Brother Peterson's diligent research on the Pearl of Great Price and wish him success in his research efforts. If he has any further questions about this matter, we hope he will feel free to contact us.

Wilford C. Wood Acquires Some Manuscripts

Wilford C. Wood, who died in 1968, was a Latter-day Saint who spent much of his life purchasing property and a large collection of items once identified with Joseph Smith. He often purchased things in his own name and sold them at a great savings to the Church. Since his death, his family has maintained his large collection of Mormon memorabilia at his museum in Woods Cross, Utah, a few miles north of Salt Lake City.

An annotated catalog of the collection mentions that Lewis C. Bidamon's son, Charles E. Bidamon, sold to Wilford C. Wood "several deeds and documents, valuable papers such as an original manuscript of the Book of Abraham" on July 10, 1937. At the time Charles E. Bidamon was living in Wilmette, a suburb of Chicago. The catalog states that "the handwriting is done very neatly and could be possibly that of Oliver Cowdery. The translation includes Chapter 1 (all verses, 1–31) and Chapter 2 (verses 1–18) of our present Book of Abraham . . . and consists of 9 1/2 pages."[14] A facsimile from the Book of Abraham is also listed. Brother Wood deposited the original manuscript in the Church Historian's Office, after he made copies for his own use and a copy for President Heber J. Grant. This 1937 purchase was probably of the material that the two apostles were hoping to find in their "mission to the States."

At this writing, in answer to the question "Did some of the manuscripts of Abraham and Joseph once displayed in the Wood's Museum survive the Chicago Fire," I must answer, "I don't know."

18

THE PEARL OF GREAT PRICE BECOMES A STANDARD WORK

In 1878 the venerable apostle-historian Orson Pratt was preparing the first American edition of the Pearl of Great Price. Several changes from the first edition, published in 1851 in Great Britain, were made in this new edition.

The 1851 edition had two excerpts from the Joseph Smith Translation of the Genesis: "Extracts from the Prophecy of Enoch containing also a Revelation of the Gospel unto our father Adam, after he was driven out from the Garden of Eden. Revealed to Joseph Smith, December 1830" (now Moses 6:43–68 and Moses 7:1–69); and "The words of God, which he spake unto Moses at the time when Moses was caught up into an exceeding high mountain, and he saw God face to face, and he talked with him, and the glory of God was upon Moses; therefore Moses could endure His presence. Revealed to Joseph Smith, June, 1830" (now Moses 1:1–42a; 2:1–4:13a; 4:14–19; 4:22–25; 5:1–16a; 5:19–23a; 5:32–40; and Moses 8:13–30).

In the American edition, the following verses were added to complete the text:

> Moses 1:42b
> Moses 4:13b
> Moses 4:20–21; 26–32
> Moses 5:16b, 17–18, 23b, 24–31, 41–59
> Moses 6:1–42
> Moses 8:1–12

Four partially quoted verses were completed and 102 new

verses were added, making a total of 106 new verses added to the 1878 edition from the Joseph Smith Translation of the Bible. Since the Church did not have the original manuscripts of the Joseph Smith Translation, these additions in the Pearl of Great Price were based on the first edition of the Joseph Smith Translation, published by the Reorganized Church of Jesus Christ of Latter Day Saints in 1867.

Joseph Smith had gone through the King James Bible on three different occasions, each time making additional corrections and clarifications. The original Book of Moses material in the 1851 Pearl of Great Price was based on an earlier manuscript prepared by him, not the one used in the 1867 RLDS publication and reproduced in the American edition. Therefore, there are some variations in the wording in some of the verses.

Orson Pratt and his associates were confident that the RLDS church had been honest in their printing of the Inspired Version in 1867. Because many of the leaders had worked closely with the Prophet in bringing it to light or had read and preached from his corrections for many years, they were assured of the integrity of the RLDS printed text.

No changes were made in the text of the Book of Abraham between the 1851 British edition and the 1878 American edition of the Pearl of Great Price. Both publications were based on the 1842 *Times and Seasons* printing in Nauvoo, which was faithfully reproduced in the 1851 edition. Although Orson Pratt and his assistants did not have the dictated manuscripts of the Book of Abraham in their possession, the *Times and Seasons* reproductions were considered accurate, since they were published in the Church owned newspaper when Joseph Smith was editor and John Taylor was his assistant.

The balance of the 1878 Pearl of Great Price remained the same as the 1851 first edition with one exception: the commandment entitled "A revelation on the Eternity of the Marriage Covenant, Including Plurality of Wives" (now Doctrine and Covenants 132) was added. This revelation was also published in the 1876 edition of the Doctrine and Covenants.

At the time of the printing, the Church and the federal government were in contention over the issue of polygamy. Because of the relevance of this important revelation at the time, it was published in the Pearl of Great Price to make it more accessible to the Saints.

What Constitutes Scripture?

The first American edition of the Pearl of Great Price became the fourth standard work of the Church on October 10, 1880. Prior to reviewing that significant event, it seems appropriate to briefly answer this question: What constitutes scripture?

The Lord explained through the Prophet Joseph Smith that this earth will eventually become a celestial world, that "the poor and the meek of the earth shall inherit it," and that those who "are not sanctified through the law . . . , even the law of Christ, must inherit another kingdom." (D&C 88:17–18, 21.) He further explained that throughout the vast planetary creations, "unto every kingdom is given a law; and unto every law there are certain bounds also and conditions. All beings who abide not in those conditions are not justified." (D&C 88:38–39.)

In order to establish a kingdom of God, four basic components are required: (1) a righteous king (the lawgiver); (2) divine law; (3) subjects who are willing to follow the laws of their king, and (4) a land of inheritance. In speaking of the kingdom of God, it is not difficult to determine who is the king. In order to follow his laws, his people must know what his laws are. The Lord explained: "For I command all men, both in the east and in the west, and in the north, and in the south, and in the islands of the sea, that they shall write the words which I speak unto them; for out of the books which shall be written I will judge the world, every man according to their works, according to that which is written." (2 Nephi 29:11.)

These holy books, these sacred words spoken by the Lord and brought to light by his prophets to whom he has spoken, are referred to as "the standard works." Members of the house of Israel will be judged, as the scriptures teach, by their actions, according to the standards—that is, the measuring rods—established by the Lord. In these last days, those who are obedient to the Lord's counsel "shall be gathered home unto the lands of their possessions." (2 Nephi 29:14.) Following the Millennium, the entire earth will become a celestial world, and the meek—those who have been submissive to divine law—shall eternally inherit the earth, united as one under their king and lawgiver, even the Lord Jesus Christ. (D&C 88:17–20.)

A New Standard Work Is Added

The year 1880 was a jubilee year in the Church, the fiftieth anniversary since its incorporation. At the semiannual general conference in October, three important items of business were transacted: (1) after a three-year interval, a new First Presidency was sustained; (2) twenty-six new sections were added to the text of the Doctrine and Covenants; and (3) the Pearl of Great Price was presented and sustained as the fourth standard work of the Church. All three matters were transacted in the two o'clock session on Sunday afternoon, October 10. The conference ran from Wednesday afternoon to Sunday evening, one of the longest conferences in several years.

The new first presidency, consisting of President John Taylor and counselors George Q. Cannon and Joseph F. Smith, was sustained by the various priesthood quorums, who were grouped and voted by standing vote of the individual quorums. Following this, the congregation as a whole stood and voted in the same manner. A non-Mormon newspaper reporter covering the proceedings confirmed in an interesting way that the sustaining of the new First Presidency and the Quorum of the Twelve had been unanimous: "These [the various quorums] voted in the order above named, by rising to their feet and extended the right hand upwards. Finally, the congregation as a whole voted in the same manner. The votes were unanimously in the affirmative everytime, and though we tried to find a

The First Presidency sustained at the October 1880 general conference:
George Q. Cannon, left, first counselor; President John Taylor;
and Joseph F. Smith, second counselor

single individual who we thought might possess sufficient back-bone to vote in the negative, we did not succeed."[1]

The unanimity was apparently difficult for the reporter to comprehend.

President Cannon stated that to save time, the same order of voting—by individual quorums and then the rest of the congregation as a whole—would not be continued as the other general officers were sustained, but would be done in the customary way, with everyone present voting at the same time.

Following the sustaining of the general officers, President Cannon stated:

> I hold in my hand the Book of Doctrine and Covenants and also The Pearl of Great Price, which books contain revelations of God. In Kirtland, the Doctrine and Covenants in its original form, as first printed was submitted to the officers of the Church and the members of the Church to vote upon. As there

have been additions made to it by the publishing of revelations which were not contained in the original edition, it has been deemed wise to submit these books and their contents as from God, and binding upon us as a people and as a Church.[2]

Following President Cannon's proposal, President Joseph F. Smith said: "I move that we receive and accept the revelations contained in these books, as revelations from God to the Church of Jesus Christ of Latter-day Saints, and to all the world."[3]

The motion of adding twenty-six new sections to the Doctrine and Covenants, and the Pearl of Great Price to the canon of scripture, was sustained by the "unanimous vote of the whole conference." These great truths, recognized as holy from their first hearing, were now added to the sacred texts that we accept as scripture, even the mind and will of the Lord.

19

ELEVEN PAPYRUS FRAGMENTS
ARE DISCOVERED

Latter-day Saints were surprised when the Church issued a press release on Monday, November 27, 1967, that began as follows:

> NEW YORK—A collection of papyrus manuscripts, long believed to have been destroyed in the Chicago Fire of 1871, was presented to The Church of Jesus Christ of Latter-day Saints (Mormon) here Monday by the Metropolitan Museum of Art.
>
> The long-lost manuscripts were presented to President N. Eldon Tanner of the First Presidency, the governing body of the Mormon Church, by Thomas P. F. Hoving, director of the museum.
>
> Accompanying the manuscripts was a letter attesting to the fact that the papyri had been the property of the Prophet Joseph Smith, first president of the Church. The letter, dated May 26, 1856, was signed by Emma Smith Bidamon, widow of the Prophet, and his son.
>
> Included in the papyri is a manuscript identified as the original document from which Joseph Smith had copied the drawing which he called "Facsimile No. 1" and published with the Book of Abraham.
>
> An interpretation of the facsimile was prepared by Joseph Smith, and the Book of Abraham now forms part of the volume known as The Pearl of Great Price.[1]

Before that time, it was generally assumed by historians and members alike that the Chicago fire of 1871 had closed the door

Dr. Aziz Atiya, Dr. Joseph Noble of the Metropolitan Museum of Art staff,
and President N. Eldon Tanner compare Facsimile 1 fragment
with reproduction in the Pearl of Great Price

on that chapter of Church history—the Egyptian mummies and papyri had been burned.

The article continues:

> The Pearl of Great Price is accepted as one of the four volumes of scripture by Church members. The others are the Bible, Book of Mormon, and Doctrine and Covenants.
>
> Included in the museum's presentation are a number of other papyri once in the possession of Joseph Smith.

These include conventional hieroglyphic and hieratic Egyptian funerary texts. Such papyri, including passages from the well-known Book of the Dead, were commonly buried with Egyptian mummies.

The papyri originally came into Joseph Smith's possession in 1835 along with four Egyptian mummies purchased by some church members in Kirtland, Ohio. After his death in 1844, the mummies and papyri were sold by his widow. At least two of the mummies were burned in the Chicago fire of 1871, and it had been assumed the documents were also destroyed at that time. The collection presented to the Church today is only a part of the papyri which Joseph Smith had in his possession.

Dr. Aziz S. Atiya, only recently retired as Director of the University of Utah Middle East Center, said he was electrified when he saw the ancient documents.

"It was one of my most important finds," the distinguished professor said. He is known throughout the academic world as a historian, writer, and teacher. He was instrumental in building the Middle East library at the University of Utah to one of the five finest and most complete in the U.S. For this effort he has been honored by having that library named the Aziz S. Atiya Library for Middle Eastern Studies.

His work in the ancient histories concentrated on Coptic and Arabic scripts. He is a member of the Christian Coptic Orthodox Church but is intensely interested in the Mormon story.

The papyrus documents will be taken to Salt Lake City for further study and research.[2]

Dr. Atiya related his personal account of the discovery for an article that appeared in the Church-owned *Improvement Era:*

> I was writing a book at the time, one that I had started while a professor of world Christianity and eastern Christianity, and I went to the Metropolitan Museum of Art looking for documents, papyri, pictures, and illustrations to serve the book. It must have been in the early spring of 1966. I really forget the date. My book was ready for the press, and I was looking for supplementary material.
>
> While I was in one of the dim rooms where everything was brought to me, something caught my eye, and I asked one of my assistants to take me behind the bars into the storehouse of

documents so that I could look some more. While there I found a file with these documents. I at once recognized the picture part of it. When I saw this picture, I knew that it had appeared in the Pearl of Great Price. I knew the general format of the picture. This kind of picture one can find generally on other papyri, but this particular one has special peculiarities. For instance, the head had fallen off, and I could see that the papyrus was stuck on paper, nineteenth century paper. The head was completed in pencil, apparently by Joseph Smith, who must have had it when that part fell off. He apparently drew the head in his own hand on the supplementary paper. Also, the hands of the mummy, raised as they are, and the leg, raised as it is—usually the mummies lie straight forward—are very peculiar. This papyrus is Egyptian, true enough, but what it stands for, I really don't know.

Now when I saw this, I began to search further. I saw more pieces of papyri stacked together and suspected that Providence had assisted. Another document was found with these documents, signed by Joseph Smith's wife, his son, and someone else, testifying that these papyri were treasured and owned by Joseph Smith.

In 1918 a Mrs. Heusser came to the museum and informed the officials that she had some papyrus, but an understanding was not reached until 1947. They were then acquired by the museum, and then the museum changed curators of Egyptian antiquities and the whole subject was forgotten.

When I saw these documents, I really was taken aback. I know the Mormon community, what it stands for, its scripture, etc., and I said at once that these documents don't belong here. They belong to the Mormon Church. Well, of course, the people in the museum are good friends of mine, and I tried to tempt them into ceding the documents to the Church. I informed my good friend Taza Pierce, who is executive secretary of the Salt Lake Council for International Visitors, and we discussed the manner in which I should acquaint the Mormon community of the find. She suggested I see President Tanner, and she was the intermediary who arranged and attended our first two meetings. Thereafter, I met directly with President Tanner, who had said the Church was very, very interested and would do anything or pay any price for them. Since that time, we worked quietly on the possibility of their transference to the Church.

In these kinds of things, I never push. I take my time. With some kindly persuasions and discussions, the museum ultimately put a memorandum on the subject to the board of trustees of the museum. This took a long time to come to that step. The board discussed the matter at very great length, greater length than you might think, and in the end they thought that since the museum had papyri of this nature in plenty, why should they keep these documents from the Church?

When their generous decision was made, it was telephoned to me by the curator, and he wrote to me also. Then we had a lull in the situation, because the curator had to go to Egypt for a month in order to arrange final steps for the transference to the Metropolitan Museum of another treasure, in which I also had a hand. It concerns a great temple that is being presented by the Egyptian government to the American nation in recognition of the contributions America has made toward the salvage of the Abyssinian monuments.

When the curator came back, he reported very nicely about the subject and said, "The decision has been taken; your Mormon friends are going to get these papyri. So, you go to your friends and the President of the Church and make the necessary arrangements for a ceremony."

Of course, President Tanner was just as excited as I was. He reported to President McKay, who was very enthusiastic about the project also. We then decided the way in which the ceremony would be conducted.

I felt very honored and very, very pleased to be in the center of the picture with such a distinguished person as President Tanner and Mr. Thomas P. F. Hoving, who is director of the museum. He's a very important man, as is his assistant and vice director, Dr. Joseph Noble. He's a very fine man. All of them were there, and to my surprise I found that the papyri were prepared in a very fine box for safekeeping.

But during the morning of that day I made it a point to go in at an early hour, long before the meeting of these magnates, in order to make sure that the papyri were there—not only the papyri, because what is of importance is the document that accompanied the papyri. It was a faded thing, in nineteenth century hand. I found that the museum had photographed it. Well, of course, they had tried to photograph it before, but it wouldn't show because it was very faded blue paper. Now they used infra-red and ultra-violet photography to get the text out, so that now the photograph is very much better than the original.

I was enchanted about the discovery of the papyri, which had been in the hands of Joseph Smith, but the discoveries were not ended there. On the morning of handing over the papyri, I began looking them up and down, up and down, and lo! I found on the back of the paper on which the papyri were glued writings and maps and an enumeration of townships and material of the highest value to Mormon history, made, I think, by Joseph Smith's own hand. Three of the backs were full of notes and maps, which have to be studied by the specialists. I am not a specialist of that, but I have an eye for original documents, and these papyri documents are not fakes; they are original Egyptian papyri of a pre-Christian era. They could be from 3000 B.C. to 300 B.C.—over 300 B.C., at any rate. This is my estimate. The era will have to be decided by the specialists.

I know the kind of ink the Egyptians used and the difference between genuine and fake. Papyrus writings were usually placed with the mummy—papyri of many kinds—but essentially the "Book of the Dead," which would give the mummy safe passage to the world beyond. The papyri were sometimes colored. You find papyri like this with blue, gold, and red colors. This is not out of the ordinary. With regard to the ink used, it was generally made of soot and glue, and that is why it was eternal. I think these scrolls are written in that kind of ink. Usually the priests did the writing—they were most skilled. They used reed pens, and had to sharpen the reed and split it in the middle.

The Egyptians had the papyrus plant, and they used to split it into thin layers and put the layers crisscross on one another, pound them with a wooden hammer, and them glue them together. They cut them to suit the purposes of the documents they wanted to write. Usually long strips were used to make scrolls, and this one was made in that fashion.

In order to protect the papyrus, which becomes brittle with age—for instance, the head of the person fell off simply because the papyrus was brittle—Joseph Smith probably thought that the best thing for its protection was to glue it on paper. When I first discovered these documents, I was so excited about the Egyptian writings that I did not look on the

back of the paper, but when I returned to the museum, I
noticed the writings on the back by Joseph Smith. These writings may not turn out to be of very great importance; however, any footnote one can get in the restoration of Mormon
history is valuable.

The exciting part, which has proved beyond doubt that this
was the papyri that was in Joseph Smith's hand, was established by that document signed by his widow. When I saw
that, I had it transcribed and a copy typewritten to show to
President Tanner.

Do you know that this discovery appeared in the Egyptian
press on the day following the ceremony? On the first page of
the most important paper! You would be surprised at the
attention that was given to this discovery, and apparently the
Egyptians were very pleased about the revealing of these documents. I consider it a great honor to have been able to make
this discovery. Great discoveries are always accidental, and
this one was as accidental as any discovery I have made—and
probably more exciting than all of them. It was an honor to
have been able to persuade such an august body as the
Metropolitan Museum to present it to another body as august
as the Mormon Church. I feel flattered to have been able to do
what I did.[3]

The announcement of the find was widely circulated
throughout the world by radio, television, and the press because
of the respected credentials of Dr. Atiya,[4] and also because of
universal interest in the doings of the Church.

How the Metropolitan Museum Acquired the Papyri

Through the courtesy of officials of the Metropolitan
Museum of Art in New York City, who generously gave me
access to their correspondence file relative to their acquisition
of the eleven papyri fragments, we are better able to piece the
story together.

On January 16, 1918, Dr. A. M. Lythgoe, the museum's first
curator, wrote an in-house memorandum that read in part:

In connection with the effort made by Bishop Spaulding of
Utah about 1912 to obtain confirmation, from various
Egyptian scholars of Europe and America, that Joseph Smith's

supposed translations of sacred Egyptian texts on which he founded his "Pearl of Great Price" were a fraud, an interesting piece of evidence turned up at the Museum today. A Mrs. Alice C. Heusser, of 221 Ralph Avenue, Brooklyn, brought for our inspection some eight or ten fragments of papyri, all from late funerary papyri with small vignettes interspersed throughout the text. With the fragments she had a letter dated 1856 at Nauvoo City, and signed by three persons (one of them the former wife of Joseph Smith, and another Joseph Smith the son of the older Joseph Smith) vouching for the authenticity of these papyri as original Egyptian documents and as having belonged to the "family of one of the Pharaohs," and which they were selling to a Mr. A. Combs.

Mrs. Heusser's mother was a servant in the Combs family and at his death he left these papyri to her.

No transaction took place as a result of that meeting—it was probably intended only for an appraisal of the value of the papyrus fragments—but the memorandum was noticed by Ludlow Bull, the associate curator of the museum, twenty-seven years later. In December 1945 Mr. Bull wrote a letter to Mrs. Heusser inquiring after the papyrus. He sent the letter to the address given in 1918, but it was returned marked "addressee unknown." On December 28, 1945, Mr. Bull wrote to an Edward Heusser in the New York City borough of Brooklyn at an address close to Alice Heusser's old address, but that letter also was returned unclaimed. But Mr. Bull was persistent. On January 7, 1946, he wrote to a Heusser family in Queens, another borough of New York, and received the following short but important reply: "Sorry for the late information. Mrs. A. Heusser has passed away, and her late husband and son reside at 1321 Halsey St., Brooklyn, N.Y. I am Mrs. Heusser's nephew."

On April 29, 1946, Mr. Bull wrote to Edward Heusser: "Our records show that in January, 1918, Mrs. Alice C. Heusser, who we understand, was your wife, brought to the Museum for our inspection eight or ten fragments of ancient papyrus documents. Do you still possess these fragments and, if not, can you tell us where they are at present?"

The next day the following brief handwritten note, signed

by Albin Edward Heusser, was sent to the museum: "I am writing in behalf of my father, Edward Heusser. He is still in possession of the papyrus documents mentioned in your letter of April 29 and is awaiting further word from you."

Mr. Bull replied on May 1: "If your father is inclined to dispose of these papyrus fragments, it is possible that this museum might be interested in them." He invited the Heussers to make an appointment with Ambrose Lanning, the curator of the department, to further discuss the matter.

In a letter dated May 5, 1946, Albin Heusser said that his father was "quite willing to show his documents, which incidentally are in the same condition as they were in 1918." He also asked for an evening or Saturday appointment, explaining that his father was "now in his 80th year and would find it quite difficult to travel alone." He added that he himself had also just returned from military service and hesitated to ask his employer for time off.

Five weeks later, on June 11, 1946, Mr. Bull sent the following offer to Albin Edward Heusser:

> We have looked over the fragments of Egyptian papyri which you recently left with us. They all come from a late period in Egyptian history and are fragments of four different Books of the Dead. We have a number of complete funerary papyri in excellent condition in our collection and do not really need these pieces. Such fragments can also be found in all museums which do not possess important collections of Egyptian antiquities. Never-the-less, if you wish to dispose of these fragments, we are prepared to offer you [a certain dollar amount].[5]
>
> A former member of our staff, now retired, who was in the Museum at the time your mother first brought the papyri here, has told us that he thought your mother also brought a circular piece of either linen or wood, or possibly metal, bearing hieroglyphic inscription, perhaps eight inches in diameter. This was the type of object that was placed under the head of the mummy in its coffin. Do you recall having such a piece in your family? It may be that our friend's recollection is at fault after so many years.
>
> Our records of your mother's visit also suggest that you

had some papers referring to the acquisition of the papyri and indicating who some of the previous possessors of them were. If you have these papers, we should be glad to see them.[6]

On July 30, 1946, Albin Heusser responded to the offer, stating: "My father has decided to accept your offer . . . . for his Egyptian relics. . . . I know that somewhere on the premises we have the papers pertaining to the acquisition of the papyrus, and when I locate them I shall gladly forward them to you."

More than twenty-one years after the museum acquired the eleven papyrus fragments from the Heusser family, Thomas P. F. Hoving, director of the Metropolitan Museum of Art, sent to President N. Eldon Tanner of the First Presidency the following letter, dated November 1, 1967:

Dear President Tanner,

It is a very great pleasure for me to inform you that the Metropolitan Museum is prepared to give the Latter Day Saints Church a group of Egyptian Funerary papyri formerly in the possession of Joseph Smith, one of which is illustrated in *The Pearl of Great Price.*

We should be very happy to receive you and other delegates of the Church to effect the transfer of these documents. I shall myself be present, as will our Curator of Egyptian Art, and we hope that Professor Aziz Atiya can attend as well. As a tentative date for the ceremony, I propose that we meet on Monday, November 27, at midday.

President Tanner replied in a letter dated November 7, 1967:

Dear Mr. Hoving:

It is impossible for us to express in words our appreciation for the very generous action on the part of the Metropolitan Museum in giving the Church of Jesus Christ of Latter-day Saints a group of Egyptian funerary papyri formerly in the possession of Joseph Smith, one of which is illustrated in the Pearl of Great Price.

Monday, November 27, at midday as a time to receive these documents is most satisfactory. Dr. Atiya, and probably one or two delegates of the Church, will be in attendance on this occasion. We are so happy that you and your Curator of

Egyptian Art and others, as you wish, will be present to make the transfer.

Professor Aziz Atiya, who has been most kind, considerate, and helpful in this matter, will be coming to New York preceding this ceremony and will arrange to see you or Dr. Fisher early Monday morning, the 27th.

Again on behalf of the First Presidency of the Church I wish to express our sincere and deep appreciation to you and those associated with you for this most generous gift.

Abel Combs Returns to Center Stage

In his memorandum of January 16, 1918, Dr. Lythgoe, the museum's first curator, mentioned that the Heusser family had acquired the eleven fragments from Mrs. Heusser's mother, who was "a servant in the Combs family and at his death he left these papyri to her."

Many interested parties have attempted to piece this part of the puzzle together without success. I was fortunate to engage the services of one of the finest genealogical researchers in the Church to aid me in this project. With great effort, skill, and a unique intuition that some would call inspiration, Preston J. Owens, an analyst at the Brigham Young University Family History Services, struck pay dirt. There are still some gaps in the story, but considerably fewer than before.

As we learned in chapter 17, Abel Combs lived in Farmington, Ohio, and owned land in Southington, Ohio, just a few miles from Michael H. Chandler's home in Parkman, in the 1840s and early 1850s. He sold his farm on January 7, 1855, and next we hear of him buying the four mummies and papyri from Emma Smith Bidamon, Joseph Smith III, and Lewis C. Bidamon in Nauvoo on May 26, 1856. A few weeks later, Combs was in St. Louis, where he sold two mummies and some papyri to the St. Louis Museum.

We lose track of Combs between 1856 and 1874. Eighteen years later, he and his wife, Eliza Jane, with their son Oscar, are living in Philadelphia. In Ohio he had listed his occupation as a plater. In the Philadelphia city directory, he was listed between 1875 and 1893 as "A. Combs and Son Oscar—lamps"; and in 1888 and 1889, as an artist. Oscar, at the same address, was listed as a lather in 1888; as a machinist in 1889; and again as a lather in 1891 and 1892.

Although they moved to several different locations in Philadelphia, the father and son continued to work together at each location. The listings in *Gospill's Philadelphia City Directory for 1892* reads: "Combs Abel, artist, 454 Glenwood av. and Combs Oscar, lather h. 454 Glenwood av." Abel died July 5, 1892, when he was sixty-nine years of age. His brief obituary states that "relatives and friends are invited to attend the funeral services, at his late residence, No. 454 Glenwood avenue, on Friday morning at 9 o'clock."[7]

In his 1918 memorandum, Mr. Lythgoe mentioned that Alice C. Heusser's mother had worked as a servant for the Combs family, and that at his death Combs left the papyri to her. After considerable searching for Alice's mother's name, Preston Owens found two documents of relevance: (1) Alice C. Heusser's certificate of death in Brooklyn, which listed her parents' names as Henry H. Weaver and Charlotte Benecke; and (2) an 1896 application for a marriage license for Edward Heusser and Alice Combs Weaver.

From this document we learn that the married name of the "servant" who attended Abel Combs during the latter part of his life was Charlotte Benecke Weaver and that her daughter was Alice Combs Weaver. It seems very unlikely that Alice would be given the middle name of Combs unless she were related in some way to Abel Combs. Instead of the title *servant*, Charlotte (Lottie) E. Benecke Weaver Huntsman listed her occupation as a private nurse in the 1910 census of New Jersey, where she then resided. That was probably her role in relation to Abel Combs during the last months of his life. And as a result of the experience, she acquired the eleven papyri fragments that were eventually returned to the Church by way of the Metropolitan Museum in 1967.

Abel Combs had sold two mummies and some papyri to the St. Louis Museum in 1856, but the disposition of the other two mummies and any other papyri aside from these eleven fragments still remains a mystery.

20

READY ANSWERS AND AREAS
FOR FURTHER RESEARCH

In 1912–13 the Reverend Franklin S. Spaulding, Episcopal Bishop of Utah, sent photographs of the three facsimiles in the Book of Abraham, along with Joseph Smith's explanations of them, to several renowned Egyptologists. The interpretations of the scholars were compared with the explanation of Joseph Smith, and a controversy began that lasted for several years but subsided with the passage of time.

When Dr. Aziz Atiya's discovery of the eleven papyrus fragments in 1967 became public, the embers of controversy again flared up. Facsimile 1 of the Pearl of Great Price was a part of the reclaimed collection. There was no doubt that these eleven fragments had once been in the hands of the Church, because included with them was the bill of sale that Emma Smith Bidamon and her associates negotiated with Abel Combs. To prevent their continued disintegration, the papyrus fragments had been glued to recognizable maps and floor plans that had at one time been in the hands of the early Saints. Claims and counterclaims were soon exchanged between opposing sides. The war of words that began again in late November 1967, though less intense today, still continues.

Over the years instructors and students of the Pearl of Great Price, knowing the claims and counterclaims, have asked about the historical background of the Book of Abraham. Following are some of their questions and my responses.

Question One: I read in an anti-Mormon publication that if

Joseph Smith were really a seer, he would have been able to read unknown languages, such as that found on the papyri, as a gift from God. Is that correct?

Answer: No! A prophet is the Lord's servant. Aside from his inherent abilities and his acquired skills, he is able to do only what the Lord calls him to do and enables him to do. When translations have been necessary, the Lord has inspired various prophets to read unknown tongues and translate them for the Saints, even by "him that is not learned." (Isaiah 29:12.) This was the case with the translation of the Book of Mormon. It is the Lord alone who determines why, when, where, and how new truths are revealed or translated through his prophets. Even with the aid of such sacred instruments as the Urim and Thummim or a seer stone provided by the Lord, a prophet is obligated to work within the bounds the Lord has established for its usage. (See D&C 9:7–9.)

Question Two: The author of an anti-Mormon publication stated that the eleven fragments returned to the Church in 1967 constituted most, if not all, of the papyri that Joseph Smith bought from Michael H. Chandler in 1835. Is that correct?

Answer: Some anti-Mormon writers reason that the eleven papyri fragments returned to the Church in 1967 contained most, if not all, of the fragments Joseph Smith bought from Michael Chandler. They further reason that since the eleven pieces of papyri are the source of the Book of Abraham, and yet are identified by Egyptologists as fragments from the Book of Breathings—and not the writings of Abraham—Joseph Smith was a deceiver and a fraud. Therefore, the Book of Abraham is a product of his creative imagination and is not based on an ancient text as he claimed it was.

This claim is false. A careful reading clearly shows that at least two and probably three scrolls of unknown length were purchased by the Church, in addition to several flat pieces that were not a part of any of the scrolls.

Question Three: Does the Church claim that the papyri containing the writings of Abraham were actually "written by his own hand, upon papyrus," as a subtitle to the Book of Abraham reads?

Answer: Dr. Hugh Nibley, a gifted linguist who has made a lifelong study of ancient Near Eastern documents written in many languages and dialects, has explained: "Two important and peculiar aspects of ancient authorship must be considered when we are told that a writing is by the hand of Abraham or anybody else. One is that according to Egyptian and Hebrew thinking any copy of a book originally written by Abraham would be regarded and designated as the very work of his hand forever after, no matter how many reproductions had been made and handed down through the years. The other is that no matter who did the writing originally, if it was Abraham who commissioned or directed the work, he would take credit for the actual writing of the document, whether he penned it or not."[1]

So, when we read "the Book of Abraham, written by his own hand upon papyrus," we are to understand, as the Saints always have, that this book, no matter how often "renewed," is still the writing of Abraham and no one else. He commissioned it or, "according to the accepted Egyptian expression," wrote it himself—with his own hand. And when Abraham tells us, "That you may have an understanding of these gods, I have given you the fashion of them in the figures at the beginning," we do not need to imagine Abraham himself personally drawing the very sketches we have before us. It was the practice of Egyptian scribes to rephrase obscure old passages they were copying to make them clearer. Then, when this was done, the scribe would add his own name to the page, which shows how careful the Egyptians were to give credit for original work only—whatever the first author wrote remained forever "by his own hand."

Question Four: Did Joseph Smith ever identify the four mummies that he acquired in 1835?

Answer: Many non-LDS newspapers published articles that stated the Church leaders in Kirtland claimed to have the bodies of various ancients, such as Abraham, Abimelech, and Joseph of Egypt. In his article published in the December 1835 issue of the *Messenger and Advocate,* Oliver Cowdery disclaimed all the unfounded rumors by stating, "Who these ancient inhabitants of Egypt were, I do not at present say." (See HC 2:348.) Five years later a visitor to Nauvoo reported that Joseph Smith identified one mummy as "one of the Pharaohs, who sat upon the throne of Egypt, and the female figure by its side was probably one of his daughters." The visitor suggested to Joseph Smith that the daughter might be Princess Thermutis, who rescued Moses from the Nile. Joseph is reported to have replied, "It is not improbable . . . but my time has not yet allowed me to examine and decide that point." (See page 193.)

According to another visitor to Nauvoo, Lucy Mack Smith said that her son Joseph had received a revelation from the Lord in regard to the mummies and their times and had shared the information with her. (See chapter 16.) She claimed that the mummies were a king and his wife and daughter. Emma Smith Bidamon also affirmed on the bill of sale, "From translation by Mr. Smith of the records these mummies were found to be the family of Pharo King of Egypt." (See page 203.)

Initially the Prophet did not identify the mummies, but later he is reported to have said that at least three were of Egyptian royalty. (See chapter 16.) No writings of Joseph Smith or his scribes are known to confirm the identity of the mummies.

Question Five: Michael H. Chandler originally had eleven mummies. The Church purchased four of them. Where are the other seven mummies?

Answer: Chandler initially acquired eleven mummies in New York City in the winter or early spring of 1833. He was displaying only six mummies in Baltimore that July and in Harrisburg, Pennsylvania, in September. Two of the seven mummies were sold in the summer of 1833 to Dr. Samuel George Morton at the Academy of Natural Science in Philadelphia, where they were dissected as cadavers at the medical school on December 10 and 17. Two more mummies were sold between September 1833 and February 1835. Chandler explained on his placard that "the seven have been sold to gentlemen for private museums, and in consequence are kept from the public." Since they were purchased by private collectors, it has been and will be very difficult to trace them. Two of the four mummies purchased by the Church in 1835 were in Wood's Museum in Chicago prior to the fire; those two may still be in existence. Without a bill of sale or some other evidence, it will not be possible to identify a mummy as one possessed by Chandler or the Church.

Question Six: Are Joseph Smith's explanations of the three facsimiles in the Pearl of Great Price in harmony with the interpretations of Egyptologists?

Answer: Several of Joseph Smith's explanations are similar to interpretations of some Egyptologists, but some are not. Remember that Egyptology is not an exact science. Our understanding will be faulty until we have the entire text with which Joseph Smith was working and understand the Lord's way of working through his prophet. Did a later copyist insert the facsimiles in order to give readers a general idea of the accepted usage in his day? Facsimiles 2 and 3 are not mentioned in the written text, and we do not know who placed them in the texts that are currently dated many hundreds of years later than the events described. The inspired text of the Book of Abraham, as attested by the Holy Ghost, is a witness of its divine source. Someday this dilemma, along with many others, will be solved. (See D&C 101:32–34.)

Question Seven: I've heard it said that Pietro Lebolo, Antonio Lebolo's son, was a Chandler. What is significant about that? What is meant?

Answer: In considering different ways that Antonio Lebolo might have ties with an Irish nephew named Michael H. Chandler, this story has developed. Pietro Lebolo, Antonio's son, died at thirty-five in Castellamonte, Italy. By occupation he had been a wax dealer. In the English language a wax dealer, primarily one who makes candles, is called a chandler. It is an interesting similarity that has caused me many hours of double-checking, but I am confident this relationship is only coincidental.

Question Eight: I understand that an Irish genealogist made an interesting observation about Michael H. Chandler's wife's name, Frances F. Ludlow. Would you relate the experience?

Answer: While researching the Chandler and Ludlow genealogical lines in Dublin several years ago, I spoke to a prominent genealogist at the institution where I was studying. He said that it was unusual for the Irish to give females a middle initial, but that it was "common among certain Latin countries, such as Italy." "Her name may be an anglicized name from an Italian origin," he said. "Her original name would probably be Francesco and the closest name to Ludlow [Lebolo] in their language." I was extremely interested, since Antonio Lebolo had several female relatives named Francesco Lebolo. Again, a coincidence or a major clue?

Areas for Further Research

If writers waited for all the facts to be in before they published, there would be far fewer books. I have chosen to publish now what I have collected and observed over the past three decades. Future students will advance this research as new information is found and new discoveries are made. That is what research is all about. Following are some unresolved questions. I am hopeful, even confident, that this publication will help to solve some unresolved questions.

Question One: In what tomb on the West Bank of the Nile were the writings of Abraham and Joseph found?

Answer: I don't know. I would continue to look for tombs on the West Bank (Thebes) where Lebolo's name may be inscribed and that fit the description. Pit Tomb 32 has Lebolo's name chiseled in the passageway, but several other tombs may also be inscribed with his name. Some diaries, correspondence files, and journals of early travelers may yet be located in various European or Egyptian libraries and museums and family collections to assist in locating the tomb.

Question Two: What were the date and the circumstances around which the eleven mummies were excavated from the West Bank?

Answer: It must have happened between 1817 and 1822. Lebolo may have kept notes or copies of his correspondence, or Drovetti's official correspondence file with Lebolo may yet surface. It was listed as Sardinian file number 60. I would recheck the state archives in Turin, the former capital of Sardinia, and then Castellamonte. The tomb in El Gurna (or Gourneh), where he lived, may have his name carved on it.

Question Three: When did the eleven mummies enter and leave the harbor at Trieste?

Answer: They may have been in Albano Oblasser's care after being shipped from Alexandria between 1822 and 1830. Oblasser, the shipping magnate, must have shipped them to New York City shortly before Chandler acquired them (1832 or early 1833). Shipping records in Trieste and mercantile, customs, and newspaper records in New York City must have something to add. I searched through them, but obviously I missed something. What route they took between Trieste and New York City is unknown.

Question Four: Which ship transported the eleven mummies from Trieste to New York City?

Answer: I checked many documents in the National Archives in Washington, D.C., and the New York Historical Society, as well as newspaper accounts in the New York Public Library and some shipping records, but I was unable to locate specifics. Some customs records were burned in Washington, D.C., in 1833, but the chances are good that the documents missed the destruction. Do the shipping records of Maitland & Kennedy and McLeod & Gillespie still exist in some warehouse or archive or maritime firm?

Question Five: Who wrote the account that Michael Chandler gave of Lebolo's excavation of the mummies and their shipment to New York City?

Answer: Chandler had access to documents that gave him

specific information concerning the mummies, Drovetti, Lebolo, Trieste, and the West Bank. It might have been a document prepared by Pietro Lebolo based on his father's or stepmother's recollections. The Trieste–Dublin–New York City story concerning Chandler and the shipping of the mummies appears to be a fabrication. I checked the newspapers in Dublin without success. The incorrect dating of Lebolo's excavations and death by two years remains a mystery.

Question Six: Were notices of upcoming auctions advertised in New York City other than in newspapers?

Answer: It still seems strange to me that if newspapers were the primary or only way to announce upcoming auctions, we've missed that column where the eleven mummies were listed. Several researchers have checked the New York City newspapers but nothing has been found. That forces me to presume that Chandler had an inside track with the receivers if the mummies were not announced for auction.

Question Seven: Who was Michael H. Chandler?

Answer: Michael H. Chandler, as listed in the Ohio censuses of the 1840s to 1860s, claimed to be Irish born. His wife, Frances F. Ludlow, and their first four children were also reported as Irish born. He claimed to live in Philadelphia at the time he acquired the mummies, but no tax records, Methodist Episcopal records, or documents of any kind have been located in Philadelphia to confirm his residency there. Further research ought to be done in and around Philadelphia, especially of port records and employees. Between 1836 and 1895, the Chandlers lived in Parkman, Geauga County, Ohio. Chandler died in 1866 in Parkman. His wife remained in Parkman, where she died in 1895.

Question Eight: Where were Chandler and the mummies between the middle of September 1833 and June 27, 1835?

Answer: We know Chandler displayed the mummies in Hudson, Ohio, in February 1835 and in Cleveland in late March 1835, but his whereabouts for the rest of the twenty-one months is unknown. Dogged researchers in Pennsylvania, Ohio, and surrounding areas will surely locate other towns where he exhibited the antiquities. Local newspapers and antique stores with old posters are prime targets.

Question Nine: Was Michael H. Chandler a nephew of Antonio Lebolo, as he claimed?

Answer: It is painful to conclude, but my research leads me to believe that Chandler fabricated that part of the report. Perhaps researchers will someday locate Chandler's and his wife's family records in Ireland. Michael was born about 1797 or 1798, and Frances was born between 1798 and 1800. Their Irish-born children and years of birth are Thomas C., 1820; Ann C., 1822; William H., 1825; and George W., 1827. Genealogists can solve the Lebolo/Chandler relationship, or lack thereof, if records surface. The Lebolo records are available for comparison.

Question Ten: What does the untranslated portion of the Book of Abraham contain?

Answer: I don't know, but we may hypothesize a few possibilities. The subtitle of the Book of Abraham reads in part "the writings of Abraham while he was in Egypt." Likewise, after Abraham was shown the planetary system in all its grandeur, the Lord told him: "Abraham, I show these things unto thee before ye go into Egypt, that ye may declare all these words." (Abraham 3:15.) Facsimile 3 portrays Abraham in the king's court "reasoning upon the principles of astronomy." These statements allow me to surmise that the unpublished part of the Book of Abraham speaks of astronomical matters and their relationships to God's design in organizing his enormous family in all three stages of their existence. In chapters 3 through 5, Abraham merely introduces the concept. Prophets are commanded to preach the gospel as occasion permits. Surely the untranslated portion of the Book of Abraham would contain many great eternal truths that Abraham would be able to share, including temple preparation or related insights. (See Facsimile 2.)

Question Eleven: What does the unpublished Book of Joseph contain?

Answer: The Book of Joseph appears to contain some material that is similar to sacred teachings in the temple. Perhaps it was not written for general consumption. Perhaps these documents are still in existence.

Question Twelve: When translated, how large will the Books of Abraham and Joseph be?

Answer: In the two accounts given in chapter 2, Oliver Cowdery spoke of "volumes" and William West stated that he was told that the printed text would exceed the Bible in length.

Question Thirteen: Where did William Smith display the mummies and records, and why did he allow them to be taken from his hands?

Answer: It appears that William Smith was displaying the antiquities for money. He was in western Illinois when he became financially troubled and pawned them in exchange for daily expenses. The particulars are very sketchy. Joseph Smith III reported that William never reclaimed the antiquities. Newspaper and personal histories in that area may have more answers. Perhaps some court records mention the mummies being pledged for a price.

Question Fourteen: What happened to the two mummies and any papyri that were purchased by Abel Combs from Emma Smith Bidamon and not sold to the St. Louis Museum?

Answer: Abel Combs retained some papyri, since he gave at least eleven fragments to his nurse, Charlotte Benecke Weaver, in 1892 in Philadelphia. What happened to the two missing mummies and any other papyri fragments is unknown. Combs died in Philadelphia in 1892. Additional fragments may be in museums in Philadelphia, Chicago, or elsewhere. They are probably glued to old maps cut to fit the fragments. Watchful researchers may locate something with this lead. With transportation made convenient by the great inland waterways of the United States, they could be almost anywhere.

Question Fifteen: Isn't it unusual that a bill of sale such as that which was drawn up between Emma Smith Bidamon, et al., and Abel Combs did not mention the amount of money involved for the sale of the Egyptian antiquities?

Answer: As long as both parties agree to the terms of the document, a dollar amount seems unnecessary. This document has caused me to wonder if A. Combs is the person to whom William Smith was beholden several years before when someone gave William money in exchange for the antiquities left behind as security. Combs was last known to be in Ohio in 1855 when he sold a farm just a few miles from Michael H. Chandler's farm. He was next known to be in Nauvoo on May 26, 1856, when he bought the four mummies and "the records." This is an unsolved mystery. Abel Combs lived in Philadelphia between 1874 and 1892, when he died. He had kept at least eleven fragments from the Joseph Smith collection, those that were returned to the Church in 1967.

Question Sixteen: What would lead the General Authorities to expect that the manuscripts of the writings of Abraham and Joseph were still in existence in 1878, seven years after the destruction of Wood's Museum?

Answer: We do not know what report the brethren had received that would lead them to send two apostles to several eastern states in hopes of obtaining information concerning the manuscripts of Abraham and Joseph. Orson Pratt spent several days in the Chicago area, but there is no report of his activities in available records. In the 1930s, Wilford C. Wood, an avid LDS collector of Mormon memorabilia, purchased some of the manuscripts of the writings of Abraham from Lewis C. Bidamon's son Charles in Wilmette, a suburb of Chicago. Even to hope that some of the writings of Abraham and his great-grandson Joseph are still in existence today, nearly four thousand years later, is amazing. To accept the idea that Joseph Smith had translated some of Joseph's writings and that someday they may be located is a marvelous expectation.

21

CONCEPTS, CHALLENGES,
AND TESTIMONY

The contents of the Book of Abraham are far more valuable to mankind than any historical account of the mummies and papyri identified with the book. This work partially fills a previous historical void in our understanding, but it is of minimal consequence when compared to the actual words of the prophet Abraham, one who was authorized to speak the words of the Lord. Even though we have only a few introductory pages of this important work preserved in the Pearl of Great Price, we learn that the Book of Abraham contains many significant concepts and alludes to others that are logically in the balance of the lengthy manuscript. In brief, here are some significant concepts that are mentioned in the 5,552 words that we call the Book of Abraham. Most of this material is not contained in the Bible.

1. As the account begins, Abraham's extended family was bitterly apostate. Terah, his father, and other close relatives had consented to have Abraham publicly murdered upon an altar of sacrifice.

2. Abraham sought for blessings from on high in his time of great frustration and became "a rightful heir, a High Priest, holding the right belonging to the fathers (the Holy Prophets)." He was ordained by Melchizedek, the great high priest. (D&C 84:14.)

3. Abraham desired to become a "prince of peace." Only four men are identified with this title in the standard works: Adam, Melchizedek, Abraham, and Jesus. The title is mentioned

in the scriptures pertaining to *Adam* (D&C 107:54–55) when Jesus himself blessed Adam and called him "Michael, the prince, the archangel." President John Taylor was more specific when he stated that Jesus called Adam "Michael, the Archangel, the Prince of Peace."[1] *Melchizedek,* who ordained Abraham, also held that holy title (Alma 13:18). It is assumed that Abraham, in his desire for greater blessings as a patriarch, achieved his goal to become "a prince of peace." The Lord changed Abram's name to *Abraham,* which means "father of a multitude." *Jesus* is the one most frequently identified with this title. (See Isaiah 9:6.) When Joseph Smith Jr. ordained his own father to the office of patriarch, he said that Joseph Smith Sr. "shall be called a prince over them, and shall be numbered among those who hold the right of Patriarchal Priesthood, even the keys of the ministry." After quoting Doctrine and Covenants 107:53–55, relative to Adam being a prince forever, the Prophet declared: "So shall it be with my father; he shall be called a prince over his posterity, holding the keys of the Patriarchal Priesthood."[2] The title apparently has a patriarchal connotation of eternal importance.

4. Several pagan gods and practices of the Chaldeans are documented in Abraham's writings.

5. Human sacrifice was practiced in Abraham's day. At that time, not only were males offered upon the pagan altars, but women and children were also offered as sacrifices. Abraham was to be offered as a public example as one who dared to challenge the popular apostate notions of his day.

6. The Lord made a series of covenants with Abraham, based on obedience, that we refer to as the Abrahamic covenant. This is the gospel covenant. Abraham, among other things, was promised a land of inheritance for his posterity, that Jesus the Christ would come through his lineage, that eternal marriage would be possible, and that all the righteous from then on would be known as Abraham's seed.

7. Jehovah or Jesus personally intervened to save Abraham's life on the pagan altar. The death of the wicked priest of pharaoh who was wielding the sacrificial knife is noted.

8. The records of previous prophets, the sacred scriptures, were entrusted to Abraham's care and keeping, including genealogical records and information on the creation, the planets, and the stars.

9. A brief genealogy of the Canaanites' lineage prior to the flood and in early Egyptian history is given, including the lineage of pharaoh.

10. A widespread famine of great severity prevailed in Chaldea, Haran, Jershon, and Canaan. Haran, Abraham's brother, died as a result of the famine.

11. Abraham and Lot's journey from Ur to Haran is mentioned. Terah followed after them to Haran.

12. Abraham and his associates preached the gospel while they were in Haran. When they left, they invited the "souls that they had won" to leave with them. Terah, having returned to his idolatrous ways, remained behind.

13. While Abraham's party was traveling from Haran toward Egypt, Jesus appeared and gave the land of Canaan to Abraham for his inheritance.

14. The Lord commanded Abraham to represent Sarah as his sister to the Egyptians. This was a means by which Abraham was introduced into the pharaoh's court and by which Sarah was assured of her safety.

15. Abraham was given a great vision of the planetary system through the Urim and Thummim, which he received while living in Ur. The residence of God, or the throne of God, and our master star Kolob were both visualized.

16. Abraham again talked face to face with the Lord, who further explained his creations. The creations, without end, multiplied before Abraham's eyes. He was promised that his posterity would be as plenteous.

17. Abraham was shown that the Lord's organization of the planetary system is similar in many ways to God's organization of his pre-earth children.

18. New insights not found in other scriptural texts are given relative to man's pre-earth life and foreordination.

19. The purpose of mortality, man's second estate, is stated: "We will prove them herewith, to see if they will do all things whatsoever the Lord their God shall command them."

20. The six days of creation were planned by the council of the Gods.

21. The creation of the earth near our master star Kolob was concluded.

22. Adam and Eve were placed on the earth. The animals and fowls were brought to Adam, and he named them.

23. "The grand key-words of the Holy Priesthood" were revealed to Adam in the Garden of Eden, and later they were revealed "to Seth, Noah, Melchizedek, Abraham, and all to whom the Priesthood was revealed."

24. God is portrayed sitting upon his throne and revealing through the heavens the grand key-words of the priesthood (Facsimile 2).

25. The Lord also refers to some writings that are not to be revealed except in the temple.

26. Several new words are introduced into our scriptural vocabulary, such as *Kolob, Kokob, Olea, Shinehah, Kokaubeam, Olibish, Gnolaum, intelligences, Kae-e-vanrash,* and *Enish-go-on-dosh.*

All of these concepts are recorded in five brief chapters. The entire text of the Book of Abraham will someday be made available and will be of great worth to those who cherish the writings of this great prophet and patriarch.

More Scriptures and Warnings of Counterfeits

This last dispensation of the gospel will be flooded with great and eternal truths that have been withheld to come forth in this era. As we review the voluminous amount of information that the Lord has promised will be revealed in these last days, we stand in awe and wonder at its magnitude. Without the forerunners of printing presses, modern transportation, duplicators, microfilms, computers, fax machines, and other modern inventions, the management and synthesis of these pending documents would be nearly impossible.

All dispensations culminate in this dispensation. This is the time of restoration, when records of the past, both scriptural and genealogical, will be made available. Peter explained that Jesus will return after the "restitution of all things, which God hath spoken by the mouth of all his holy prophets since the world began." (Acts 3:21.) The chart on pages 269–71 projects the magnitude of the restoration of scriptures and genealogies that will yet come forth.

We are also told that in the last days, false Christs and false prophets shall arise, and they will be effective in their deceit. The Lord warned that even the very elect, according to the Abrahamic covenant—that is, those married in holy temples, even active members of the Church—may be deceived by the signs and wonders these false prophets will be able to perform. (See Joseph Smith–Matthew 1:22.) False prophets have brought forth spurious teachings, prophecies, and histories as a part of their deceptive arsenal throughout history. Surely Satan will not let this moment in history pass without launching forth his most sophisticated weapons.

Our Father's teachings are eternally the same. If the restored records teach the same doctrines as the standard works and as the living prophets do, and they are confirmed in our souls by the Holy Ghost, they are undoubtedly from the same source as the standard works that are not in our possession.

My Testimony

Though my research on this topic is primarily over, I will be interested in this work as new information surfaces and this publication raises new questions. My active field work is no longer possible. My formal classroom days are over. My university teaching has been challenging and rewarding, and now younger professors with excellent credentials are fielding the questions and providing excellent answers as intelligent young scholars, armed with testimonies, continue to probe for answers.

After spending many years teaching the great doctrines of the Pearl of Great Price, I can honestly say that it has been a marvelous experience. Some things in the scriptures I do not yet fully understand, but the things that I do understand give me peace and assurance that these unknown truths will yet be received with awe and appreciation.

I know that God lives and that Jesus is the Christ. I know that an apostasy necessitated a restoration of the gospel to enable us to enjoy God's teachings and ordinances in these last days. I know with great certainty that the Book of Mormon is a divine record containing the fullness of the gospel. It is truly "the keystone of our religion"—that which holds it all together as far as testimony and doctrine are concerned. I know that each of the standard works is true. I fell in love with the Bible while I was serving as a missionary, when it was our primary scripture for proselyting. I anxiously await the day when the complete text of Father Abraham, and all other scriptures that are to come forth, will be revealed to those who honor Abraham as our exemplar, prophet, and patriarch. My major concern now is to live the truths that have already been revealed.

APPENDIX A

EARLIEST PRINTED SOURCES
OF THE PEARL OF GREAT PRICE

1851 Edition Chapter Headings	1981 Edition Scripture References	Original Printed Source
"Extracts from the Prophecy of Enoch . . . "	Moses 6:43–68	*Evening and Morning Star* (Mar. 1833)
	Moses 7:1–69	*Evening and Morning Star (Aug. 1832)*
"The Words of God, which he spake unto Moses at the time when Moses was caught up into an exceeding high mountain . . . "	Moses 1:1–42a*	*Times and Seasons*, 4 (16 Jan. 1843): 71–73
	Moses 2:1–4:13a	*Millennial Star*, 13 (15 Mar. 1851): 90–93
	Moses 4:14–19	Probably Pearl of Great Price (1851 ed.)
	Moses 4:22–25	Probably Pearl of Great Price (1851 ed.)
	Moses 5:1–16a	*Evening and Morning Star* (Apr. 1833)
	Moses 5:19–23 32–40	*Lectures on Faith,* 2:26; Doctrine and Covenants (1835 ed.)
	Moses 8:13–30	*Evening and Morning Star* (Apr. 1833)

* The first half of the verse.

1851 Edition Chapter Headings	1981 Edition Scripture References	Original Printed Source
"The Book of Abraham—A Translation of some Ancient Records, that have fallen into our hands from the Catacombs of Egypt . . . "	Abraham 1:1–2:18 Abraham 2:19–5:21	*Times and Seasons*, 3 (1 Mar. 1842): 704–6 *Times and Seasons*, 3 (15 Mar. 1842): 719–22
"An Extract from a Translation of the Bible . . . "	Matthew 23:39–24:55	Printed as a broadside in Kirtland, Ohio, in 1836 or 1837
"A Key to the Revelations of St. John . . . "	Doctrine and Covenants 77	*Times and Seasons*, 5 (1 Aug. 1844): 595–96
"A Revelation and Prophecy by the Prophet, Seer, and Revelator, Joseph Smith. Given December 25th, 1832 . . . "	Doctrine and Covenants 87	Pearl of Great Price (1851 ed.)
"Extracts from the History of Joseph Smith . . . "	Joseph Smith–History 1:1–14 Joseph Smith–History 1:15–29 Joseph Smith–History 1:30–49 Joseph Smith–History 1:50–65 Joseph Smith–History 1:66–67 Joseph Smith–History 1:68–75	*Times and Seasons*, 3 (15 Mar. 1842): 726–28 *Times and Seasons*, 3 (1 Apr. 1842): 748–49 *Times and Seasons*, 3 (15 Apr. 1842): 753–54 *Times and Seasons*, 3 (2 May 1842): 771–73 *Times and Seasons*, 3 (1 Jul. 1842): 832 *Times and Seasons*, 3 (1 Aug. 1842): 865–66

1851 Edition Chapter Headings	1981 Edition Scripture References	Original Printed Source
"Commandment to the Church Concerning Baptism"	Doctrine and Covenants 20:71, 37, 72–74	Doctrine and Covenants (1835 ed.) 2:21, 7, 22
"The Duties of the members after they are received by Baptism"	Doctrine and Covenants 20:68–69	Doctrine and Covenants (1835 ed.) 2:18–19
"Method of administering the Sacrament of the Lord's Supper"	Doctrine and Covenants 20:75–79	Doctrine and Covenants (1835 ed.) 2:23–24
"The Duties of the Elders, Priests, Teachers, Deacons, and Members of the Church of Christ"	Doctrine and Covenants 20:38–44	Doctrine and Covenants (1835 ed.) 2:8
	Doctrine and Covenants 107:11	Doctrine and Covenants (1835 ed.) 3:6
	Doctrine and Covenants 20:45–59, 70, 80	Doctrine and Covenants (1835 ed.) 2:9–11, 20, 25
"On Priesthood	Doctrine and Covenants 107:1–10, 12–20	Doctrine and Covenants (1835 ed.) 3:1–5, 7–10
"The Calling and Duties of the Twelve Apostles"	Doctrine and Covenants 107:23, 33	Doctrine and Covenants (1835 ed.) 3:11a, 12
"The Calling and Duties of the Seventy"	Doctrine and Covenants 107:34–35, 93–100	Doctrine and Covenants (1835 ed.) 3:13, 43–44
"Extract from a Revelation given July, 1830"	Doctrine and Covenants 27:5–18	Doctrine and Covenants (1835 ed.) 50:2–3
"Rise of the Church of Jesus Christ of Latter-day Saints"	Doctrine and Covenants 20:1–36	Doctrine and Covenants (1835 ed.) 2:1–6
"Articles of Faith"	Pearl of Great Price, pages 60–61	Times and Seasons, 3 (1 Mar. 1842): 709–10
"Truth"	Hymns, no. 272	Millennial Star, 12 (1 Aug. 1850): 240

1851 Edition Chapter Headings	1981 Edition Scripture References	Original Printed Source
Fac-Simile No. 1 from the Book of Abraham	A Facsimile from the Book of Abraham, No. 1	Times and Seasons, 3 (1 Mar. 1842): 703
Fac-Simile No. 2 from the Book of Abraham	A Facsimile from the Book of Abraham, No. 2	Times and Seasons, 3 (1 Mar. 1842): 720–22
Fac-Simile No. 3 from the Book of Abraham	A Facsimile from the Book of Abraham, No. 3	Times and Seasons, 3 (16 May 1842): 783–84

APPENDIX B

SACRED WRITINGS
YET TO COME FORTH

Names of Writing/Writer	Comments	Reference
Sealed portion of Book of Mormon	Written by Moroni. If two-thirds of plates are sealed, 1,062 pages to come forth; if one-third of plates are sealed, 266 pages to come forth	Ether 4:5–7 2 Ne. 27:10
Large plates of Nephi	Records written by the Nephite prophets, of which the Book of Mormon is an abridgment by Mormon	1 Ne. 9:1–6
Lost 116 pages—"Book of Lehi"	Translated by Joseph Smith, assisted by Martin Harris; replaced in the Book of Mormon by the small plates of Nephi	D&C 3, 10
Book of remembrance	Started by Adam and continued for several generations	Moses 6:5, 6, 45–46; Abr. 1:28, 31
Brass plates	Larger than the Bible (1 Ne. 13:23). An early writer was Joseph of Egypt; last writer was Laban, c. 600 B. C.	1 Ne. 5:17–19; Alma 37:3–5
Records of the lost ten tribes	This could be a record of great size, but little is said about it	2 Ne. 29:13
"The fulness of the record of John"	Possibly John the Baptist or John the Apostle	D&C 93:6, 18[1]
Book of Abraham "while in Egypt," in addition to records written elsewhere	Abraham's complete writings may be voluminous	Book of Abraham heading (Pearl of Great Price)

Names of Writing/Writer	Comments	Reference
Record of Enoch	Seventh generation from Adam; had a unique ministry; was translated at 430 years of age	D&C 107:57
Jaredite gold plates (24 plates)	Could this be 24 sets of plates or 24 sheets of metal? Covered a period of about 2,000 years	Written by Ether
Book of Joseph in Egypt	Joseph's posterity should be thrilled with this release— part or all of his writings— accompanied by Abraham's writings	See chapters 2 and 3 of this book
Book of the covenant	Moses read to the people from this book	Ex. 24:4, 7[2]
Book of the wars of the Lord	Mentioned in the Bible but missing	Num. 21:14
Book of Jasher	Mentioned in the Bible but missing	Josh. 10:13; 2 Sam. 1:18
A book of statutes	Mentioned in the Bible but missing	1 Sam. 10:25
Acts of Solomon	Mentioned in the Bible but missing	1 Kings 11:41
Books of Nathan and Gad	Mentioned in the Bible but missing	1 Chron. 28:29; 2 Chron. 9:29
Prophecy of Ahizah and visions of Iddo	Mentioned in the Bible but missing	2 Chron. 9:29; 12:10; 13:22
Book of Shamaiah	Mentioned in the Bible but missing	2 Chron. 2:15
Book of Jehu	Mentioned in the Bible but missing	2 Chron. 20:34
Acts of Uzziah, written by Isaiah	Mentioned in the Bible but missing	2 Chron. 26:22
Sayings of the seers	Mentioned in the Bible but missing	2 Chron. 33:19
Missing epistles of Paul	Mentioned in the Bible but missing	1 Cor. 5:9; Eph. 3:3; Col. 4:16

Names of Writing/Writer	Comments	Reference
Missing epistle of Jude	Mentioned in the Bible but missing	Jude 3
Prophecies of Enoch	Whether this is the same as the record of Enoch is unclear	Jude 14
God shall "reveal all things"	Contents include things of the earth by which earth was made; the purpose and end thereof—things precious—above and beneath, in, and upon the earth and in heaven	D&C 101:32–34
Scriptures or genealogy or both?	He "shall speak unto all the nations of the earth and they shall write it"	2 Ne. 29:5, 12, 14
All authorized records	"My words shall be gathered in one"	2 Ne. 29:12, 14

THE ELEVEN PAPYRUS FRAGMENTS FOUND IN THE METROPOLITAN MUSEUM OF ART

Number 1

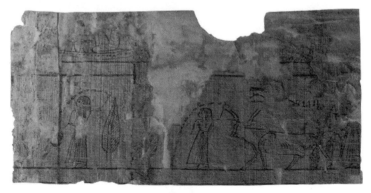

Number 2

Number 3A

Number 3B

Number 4

Number 5

Number 6

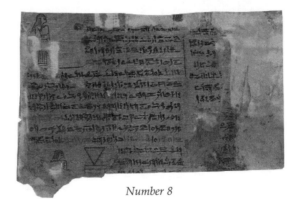

Number 7

Number 8

Number 9

Number 10

Number 11

NOTES

Preface

1. This paper was published under the title "Antonio Lebolo: Excavator of the Book of Abraham," in *BYU Studies* 31 (Summer 1991): 5–7.

2. Jay M. Todd, "Egyptian Papyri Rediscovered," *Improvement Era,* January 1968, 12–16.

3. Jay M. Todd, *The Saga of the Book of Abraham* (Salt Lake City: Deseret Book Co., 1969), 63–70.

Chapter 1: Antiquities in Kirtland, Ohio

1. Jean Francois Champollion first published his groundbreaking findings on the meaning of the hieroglyphic script in his *Lettre à M. Dacier* (Paris, 1822). This was incorporated into a more detailed study entitled *Précis du système hiéroglyphique des anciens égyptiens* (Paris, 1827–28). These publications would have given American scholars a rudimentary understanding of hieroglyphic script. Champollion died in 1832, and an Egyptian grammar and Egyptian dictionary were published posthumously in 1836 and 1841, respectively (*Grammaire égyptianne, ou Principes généraux de l'écriture sacrée égyptienne* [Paris, 1836]; *Dictionnaire égyptien, en écriture hiéroglyphique* [Paris, 1841]). His findings were basically correct, but they were disputed by many scholars for three decades before a scholarly consensus on the meaning of the hieroglyphic script emerged; see Johannes Friedrich, *Extinct Languages,* F. Gaynor, trans. (New York: Philosophical Library, 1957), 24–25.

2. Orson Pratt in *Journal of Discourses,* 26 vols. (Liverpool: 1854–86), 20:65. Hereafter cited as JD.

3. *History of the Church of Jesus Christ of Latter-day Saints,* 7 vols. and index (Salt Lake City: Deseret Book Co.), 2:350. Hereafter cited as HC.

4. "Egyptian Antiquities," *Times and Seasons* 3 (May 2, 1842): 774. Joseph Smith was editor of the *Times and Seasons* in 1842, when the two placards were quoted in the LDS newspaper. He published the following explanation beneath the copies of the placards: "The above is a copy of the original placards published by Mr. Chandler, whilst they were yet in his possession."

5. Edward W. Tullidge, "History of Provo City," *Tullidge's Quarterly Magazine* 3, no. 3 (July 1884): 283. This is the Dr. Charles Anthon to whom Martin Harris took a copy of some of the writings of the gold plates to interpret. See HC 1:19–20.

6. Oliver Cowdery, "Egyptian Mummies—Ancient Records," *Messenger and Advocate* 2, no. 3 (December 1835): 235.

7. HC 2:235.

8. Leah Y. Phelps, "Letters of Faith from Kirtland," *Improvement Era* 45 (August 1942): 529.

9. Cowdery, op. cit.

10. HC 2:235.

11. Cowdery, op. cit.

12. JD 20:64–65.

13. *Cleveland Advertiser*, March 26, 1835.

14. Cited in Jay M. Todd, *The Saga of the Book of Abraham*, 159.

15. N. L. Nelson, "The Book of Abraham," *BYU Academic Review*, March 1885, 46.

16. Josiah Quincy, *Figures of the Past from the Leaves of Old Journals* (Boston, 1883), 386.

17. Joseph Coe, letter to Joseph Smith, January 1, 1844, in the Joseph Smith Collection, Church Historical Department, Archives Division, The Church of Jesus Christ of Latter-day Saints, Salt Lake City, Utah. Microfilm copy available in Special Collections, Harold B. Lee Library, Brigham Young University.

18. Jay M. Todd, "Egyptian Papyri Rediscovered," 16.

19. Courtesy of Dr. Rulon Pope, Department of Economics, Brigham Young University, intercampus memo dated June 1993.

20. "Editorial Remarks," *Millennial Star* 3, no. 3 (July 1842): 47.

21. HC 2:236.

22. Joseph Coe, letter to Joseph Smith, January 1, 1844.

23. HC 2:236.

Chapter 2: Abraham and Joseph in Egypt

1. HC 2:17; also Joseph Fielding Smith, comp., *Teachings of the Prophet Joseph Smith* (Salt Lake City: Deseret Book Co., 1976), 60–61.

2. Bruce R. McConkie, *Mormon Doctrine*, 2nd ed. (Salt Lake City: Bookcraft, 1966), 13.

3. Flavius Josephus, *Antiquities of the Jews* 1:7:2; see William Whiston, trans., *Josephus: Complete Works* (Grand Rapids, Mich.: Kregel Publications, 1981), 32.

4. Josephus, *Antiquities* 1:8:1; see Whiston, 33.

5. Ibid.

6. "Grammar and Alphabet of the Egyptian Language," second part, 1 degree. Transcript and copies of the original available in Special Collections, Harold B. Lee Library, Brigham Young University.

7. See the entries "Abraham" and "Sarah" in the Bible Dictionary of the LDS edition (1979) of the Bible.

8. Oliver Cowdery, "Egyptian Mummies—Ancient Records," *Messenger and Advocate* 2, no. 3 (December 1835): 236.

9. William S. West, *A Few Interesting Facts, Respecting the Rise, Progress and Pretensions of the Mormons* (Warren, Ohio, 1837), 5.

Chapter 3: The Writings of Abraham and Joseph in Egypt

1. A jar in which the ancient Egyptians preserved the entrails of a deceased person for burial with the mummy. Figures 5 through 8 of Facsimile 1 are examples of canopic jars.

2. *The Egypt of Herodotus Being the Second Book, Entitled Euterpe, of the History, in the English Version of the Late Professor George Rawlinson*, with preface and note by E. H. Blakeney (London: Mailin Hopkinson and Co., Ltd., 1924), 45–46.

3. M. Broderick and A. A. Morton, *A Concise Dictionary of Egyptian Archaeology* (Chicago: Ares Publishers, 1924), 124.

4. Richard A. Parker, "The Joseph Smith Papyri: A Preliminary Report," *Dialogue: A Journal of Mormon Thought* 3, no. 2 (Summer 1968): 86.

5. "A Translation," *Times and Seasons* 3 (March 1, 1842): 704.

6. "The Book of Abraham," *Millennial Star* 3, no. 3 (July 1842): 34.

7. Hugh Nibley, *Abraham in Egypt* (Salt Lake City: Deseret Book Co., 1981), 4–7.

8. See Broderick and Morton, 75.

9. Nibley, 34.

10. In 1967 The Church of Jesus Christ of Latter-day Saints received eleven Egyptian papyrus fragments that had been in the archives of the Metropolitan Museum of Art in New York City. The Church Historical Department already had one piece of papyri in its files at the same time, making a total of twelve pieces. The Church does not have Facsimile 2, the hypocephalus, at the present time (1994).

11. John Ruffle, *The Egyptians* (Ithaca, New York: Cornell University Press, 1977), 153.

12. J. Kip Finch and M. Asce, "The Civil Engineer through the Ages: Egypt, Part 2," *Civil Engineering* 27, no. 3 (March 1957): 63.

13. Elmer D. Johnson and Michael H. Harris, *History of Libraries in the Western World* (Metuchen, N. J., and London: Scarecrow Press, 1984), 6.

Chapter 4: Lebolo and the French Revolution

1. For greater detail on Antonio Lebolo's life, see H. Donl Peterson, "Antonio Lebolo: Excavator of the Book of Abraham," *BYU Studies* 31, no. 3 (Summer 1991): 5–29.

2. A. Bertolotti, *Passeggiate nél Canavese* O.C. (1871), 5:455–56, cited in Michelangelo Giorda, *La Stòria civille religiósa ed econòmica di Castellamonte Canavese* (Ivrea, Italy, 1953), 337.

3. Jacques Bainville, "Napoleon I," *Encyclopaedia Britannica* 16 (Chicago: Encyclopedia Britannica, Inc., 1964): 86.

4. H. Donl Peterson, comp., "Antonio Lebolo: His Roots and Branches" (n.p., 1982), 135–36. These documents are a compilation of the Lebolo family's genealogical records photocopied by Francesco Morozzo of Castellamonte from parish records. They were organized by H. Donl Peterson in 1982. Copies may be found in the Harold B. Lee Library at Brigham Young University; in the Church Historical Department in Salt Lake City; and in the Church's Family History Department, also in Salt Lake City.

5. Stanley Mayes, *The Great Belzoni* (London: Putnam, 1959), 173.

6. Brian M. Fagan, *Rape of the Nile* (New York: Schribner, 1975), 66–68.

7. Bainville, 87.

8. Fagan, 74.

9. Ibid.

10. Ibid., 77–81.

11. Bainville, 94.

Chapter 5: Lebolo—Excavator and Artifacts Dealer in Egypt

1. *The Registry Office Secret Register* (Torino Archives, 1817), letter no. 2094. See H. Donl Peterson, "Antonio Lebolo Papers Collection," 2:56. Photocopies of documents from the Turin State Archives and other documents relative to tne life of Antonio Lebolo were collected by H. Donl Peterson. Copies of the original documents with accompanying English translations are arranged chronologically in the five large binders that comprise this collection, which is being arranged at this writing (1994) for presentation to the Harold B. Lee Library, Brigham Young University.

2. Letter from Spagnolini to General Consulate of His Sardinian Majesty, July 3, 1817, Torino State Archives, no. 109; see Peterson, "Antonio Lebolo Papers Collection," 2:60.

3. G. Belzoni, *Narrative of the Operations and Recent Discoveries . . . in Egypt and Nubia*, 2 vols., 3rd ed. (London, 1822), 1:343.

4. Warren R. Dawson, in his work *Who Was Who in Egyptology* (London: Egyptian Exploration Society, 1951), says of Rosignani "nothing is known of his history" (p. 138).

5. Letter of M. D. Brine to Bernardino Drovetti, March 1818, in Giovanni Marro, *Il Còrpo Epistolàre di Bernardino Drovetti Ordinato ed Illustrato*, vol. 1,

letter no. 141 (Rome, 1940); see Peterson, "Antonio Lebolo Papers Collection," 2:64. Dr. Giovanni Marro collected many hundreds of letters and documents once owned by Bernardino Drovetti. He published one volume of Drovetti's papers, but before the second volume was published, Professor Marro died. I was allowed access to his papers; his collection is kept at the library of the Accadèmia Delle Scìenze Di Torino.

6. M. D. Brine to Bernardino Drovetti, *op. cit.*

7. Fitzclarence, *Journal of a Route across India, through Egypt, to England in the Latter End of the Year 1817 and the Beginning 1818* (London, 1819), 422.

8. Ibid., 424–25.

9. Ibid., 424–25.

10. *Lettère del Conte Carlo Vidua,* published by Cesare Balbo, vol. 2 (Turin, 1834): 175–77, letter no. 34; see Peterson, 5:37.

11. Giovanni D'Athanasi, *A Brief Account of the Searches and Discoveries in Upper Egypt, Made under the Direction of Henry Salt, Esq.* (London, 1836), 50–51.

12. The Journal of Count Carlo Vidua, 1820, Turin Academy of Sciences; see Peterson, "Antonio Lebolo Papers Collection," 3:7.

13. Letter of Roger O. de Keersmaecker to H. Donl Peterson, April 5, 1992.

14. *Lettère del Conte Carlo Vidua, op. cit.*

15. Letter of F. Brouzet to Bernardino Drovetti, August 18, 1820, in the Bernardino Drovetti papers collection, compiled by Giovanni Marro, Accadèmia Delle Scìenze Di Torino; see Peterson, 3:21–23.

16. Letter of F. Cailliaud to Bernardino Drovetti, August 23, 1820, in the Drovetti papers collection; see Peterson, "Antonio Lebolo Papers Collection," 3:24–25.

17. Linant De Bellefonds, *Journal of a Trip in the Lower Nubia* (n.p., n.d.), 45, entry dated July 2, 1821.

18. William John Bankes Journal, British Museum, MS 42, 103; see Peterson, 2:69.

19. *Lèttere del Conte Carlo Vidua,* 2:177.

20. HC 2:348–49.

21. Dawson, *Who Was Who in Egyptology,* 88.

22. Todd, *The Saga of the Book of Abraham,* 63–64.

23. *Webster's Ninth New Collegiate Dictionary,* 797.

24. The incorrect spelling of Lebolo's name as Sebolo in LDS histories is not Chandler's or Oliver Cowdery's fault. In *Messenger and Advocate* 2 (December 22, 1835): 234, Oliver Cowdery spells Lebolo correctly. Most of the early newspaper accounts of Chandler's exhibits also spell Lebolo correctly. The "S" instead of the "L" on the excavator's name appears much later in *History of the Church* and the *Comprehensive History of the Church,* both edited by B. H. Roberts.

25. Richard Pococke, *A Description of the East and some Other Countries, Volume of the First Observations on Egypt* (London, 1743), 100.

26. Lise Mannicke, *The Tombs of the Nobles at Luxor* (Cairo: American University in Cairo Press, 1987), 96.

27. William John Bankes, Esq., ed., *Narrative of the Life and Adventures of Giovanni Finati, Native of Ferrara* (London, 1830), 2:211–13.

28. Laszlo Kakosy, "Hungarian Excavations in Thebes," *Africana Budapest* 2 (1986): 98–104.

29. Lady Lucie Duff-Gordon in Fagan, *The Rape of the Nile,* 14.

Chapter 6: Lebolo Returns to Europe

1. Giovanni D'Athanasi, *A Brief Account of the Researches and Discoveries in Upper Egypt,* 51.

2. L. A. Balboni, *Gl' Italiani nélla Civille Egiziana del Secolo XIX,* 1 (Alexandria, Egypt, 1906): 309; see H. Donl Peterson, "Antonio Lebolo Papers Collection," 3:40.

3. Church of Catecumeni archives, Venice, June 12, 1824; see Peterson, "Antonio Lebolo Papers Collection," 3:74–76.

4. A. Bertolotti, *Passeggiate nél Canavese* O.C., 5:456, cited in Michelangelo Giorda, *La Stòria civile religiósa ed econòmica di Castèllamonte Canavese,* 337.

5. Church of Catecumeni archives; see Peterson, 3:74–76.

6. *Dell' Osservatóre Triestino,* April 24, 1823; see Peterson, 3:51.

7. Ibid., June 17, 1823; see Peterson, 3:56.

8. Letter of J. Rifaud to Bernardino Drovetti, January 28, 1824, in the Bernardino Drovetti papers collection; see Peterson, 3:65.

9. Letter of the General Aide-de-Camp of the King of Wurttenberg to Bernardino Drovetti, October 1824, in the Drovetti papers collection; see Peterson, 3:80.

10. Letter of Filiberto Maruchi to Bernardino Drovetti, February 8, 1825, in the Drovetti papers collection; see Peterson, 4:7.

11. G. B. Brocchi, *Giornale délle osservazióni fatte ne viaggi in Egitto, nélla Sìria e nélla Nubia* (Bassano, 1845), 273–74.

12. Egon Komorzynski, *Das Erbe des Alten Agypten* (Vienna: H. Bauer, 1965), 65.

13. Giovanni Marro, summary of a letter of Francois Gau, May 10, 1820, in the Drovetti papers collection; see Peterson, 3:9.

14. B. H. Stricker, *The Death Papyrus of Sensaos,* Oudheidkundige Mededeelingen van het Rijks museum van Oudheden te Leiden, XXIII (Leyden, 1942), 30–47.

15. Bertolotti in Giorda, 337.

16. Giuseppe Perotti, *Castellamonte e la sua Stòria* (Ivrea, Italy: 1980), 199.

Chapter 7: The Death and Will of Lebolo

1. HC 2:328–49.

2. It is interesting to note that both Lebolo and Maria Catherina, Anna Maria's two-year-old daughter, are mentioned as being ill when they arrived in Trieste in early October 1822. It appears that Marie Catherina was baptized because of her illness. I have wondered if Lebolo was sufficiently ill on the same ship that the final rites of the Catholic church were bestowed upon him. He may have made out a will before or at that time but destroyed it upon his recovery.

3. The last will and testament of Antonio Lebolo is located in the State Archives in Turin, Italy. It was prepared by Giacomo Buffa, notary, from Parella. I was fortunate to be involved in finding the will in 1984. I photographed the will and the lengthy inventory and had the documents translated into English. Copies are found in the Harold B. Lee Library at Brigham Young University and the LDS Church Historical Department in Salt Lake City. The discovery is discussed in chapter 8.

4. H. Donl Peterson, comp., "Lebolo's Will and Inventory Book," 3.

5. Ibid.

6. Ibid., 4.

7. Ibid., 6.

8. Ibid., 5–6.

9. Ibid., 5.

10. Ibid.

11. Ibid., 7.

12. Ibid., 33.

13. Ibid., 35–42.

14. Ibid., 42–44.

15. Ibid., 52.

16. Dan C. Jorgensen, "Research on Antonio Lebolo: 1977." Copies of this work are found in both the Harold B. Lee Library at BYU and the Church Historical Department in Salt Lake City.

17. Peterson, "Lebolo's Will and Inventory Book," 55–56. Emphasis added.

18. See Cavalier Guilio Di S. Quintino, "Interpretazióne e Confrónto di una Bilingue Iscrizióne," in Lezióni Archeològiche (Torino: Stamperia Reale, 1824). The curator of the Egyptian museum at Turin spoke of Lebolo's Greek sepulchre that he located in Thebes and several mummies that men scattered to several museums in Europe. San Quintino stated that "one [mummy] remained intact and is with him [Lebolo] in Trieste, where he has been for a few months [year 1824]. It is, as I have said, of ordinary Egyptian form and is the most beautiful because of the quality of its pictures." The present location of this mummy is unknown.

19. Trieste Archives, 1828; see H. Donl Peterson, "Antonio Lebolo Papers Collection," 4:61.

20. Peterson, "Lebolo's Will and Inventory Book," 85–86; see also Peterson, "Antonio Lebolo Papers Collection," 5:21.

21. Ibid.

22. Ibid., 5:22.

23. Peterson, "Lebolo's Will and Inventory Book," 27.

24. Ibid., 31.

25. Ibid., 40.

26. Ibid., 53.

27. Ibid., 60–61.

28. Ibid., 65–66.

29. Ibid., 59–60.

Chapter 8: Michael H. Chandler and the Mummies

1. In the National Archives in Washington, D.C., a shipping record from Trieste, dated October 15, 1831, reads: "List of Goods shipped on board the American Brig Mary Capt. Foster of New York." In the column entitled "Numbers" are the figures "1" and "2"; under the column "Packages," the figure "2"; in the column entitled "Shippers," "A. Oblasser" and "2 Casks Cross Berries." The shipment was consigned to "R. Gillespie and W. McLeod."

2. Letter is in the personal file of H. Donl Peterson.

3. Letter dated June 7, 1976, from the Civil Archives Division; in the personal file of H. Donl Peterson.

4. Genealogical records in the files of H. Donl Peterson.

5. An account quoted in Jay M. Todd, *The Saga of the Book of Abraham,* pp. 145–48, indicates that this stranger, a non-Mormon in New York City, was a man named Benjamin Bullock. Bullock volunteered to drive Chandler and his mummies and papyri to Kirtland, Ohio, to meet Joseph Smith. According to the account, Chandler agreed, and the two men traveled to Kirtland together to seek Joseph Smith's translation of the papyri. The account also indicates that as a result of this experience, many Bullocks joined The Church of Jesus Christ of Latter-day Saints.

   The story as it is recorded appears to be inaccurate for the following reasons: Surely Joseph Smith would have mentioned that the writings of Abraham and Joseph were in the United States after such a meeting. The *Messenger and Advocate* account by Oliver Cowdery said that after leaving New York City, Mr. Chandler next displayed his antiquities in Philadelphia. It also said that "seven of the said eleven [mummies] were purchased by gentlemen for private museums, *previous to Mr. Chandler's visit to this place,* with a small quantity of papyrus." And finally, the article declared that after Chandler exhibited his antiquities in Philadelphia, he showed them in "Harrisburgh an other places east of the mountains, and was frequently referred to Bro. Smith for a translation of the Egyptian Relic. . . . *He visited this place* [Kirtland] *the last of June, or first of July at which time he presented Bro. Smith with his papyrus. Till then neither myself nor brother Smith knew of such relics in America."* (Cowdery, *Messenger and Advocate* 2:235; emphasis added.)

6. Ibid.

7. *Daily Intelligencer,* April 9, 1833, p. 2. The announcement states that "several rolls of papyrus" were exhibited along with the mummies. Several is generally defined in dictionaries as more than two and less than ten. The importance of this information will be discussed later.

8. "Egyptian Antiquities," *Times and Seasons* 3 (May 2, 1842): 774. The Philadelphia Arcade was the property of a joint stock company. The idea of its erection was borrowed from London's Burlington Arcade, a collection of small retail shops in one building. For the building, the Philadelphia Arcade Company purchased the mansion and grounds of Chief Justice Tilghman, on the north side of Chestnut Street, between Sixth and Seventh. The property extended through to Carpenter (now Jayne) Street.

9. This Baltimore Museum ad ran simultaneously in the *Baltimore Gazette and Daily Advertiser* and the *Baltimore American and Commercial Daily Advertiser* from July 20 to August 16, 1833.

10. *Times and Seasons* 3:774.

11. Diary of David Hudson Jr., son of David Hudson Sr., the founder of Hudson, Ohio. Hudson Library and Historical Society.

12. Ibid.

13. *Messenger and Advocate* 2:236.

14. Samuel George Morton, *Catalogue of Skulls of Man and the Inferior Animals in the Collection of Samuel George Morton, M.D., Penn. and Edinb.,* 3rd ed. (Philadelphia: Merrihew & Thompson, 1849), Entries 48 and 60.

15. Samuel Morton, "Observations on Egyptian Ethnography, Derived from Anatomy, History, and the Monuments," *American Philosophical Society Transactions* 9 (Philadelphia, 1846): 124.

16. For additional information, see the Provo, Utah, *Daily Herald* for Sunday, November 23, 1980, p. 59.

17. Correspondence between the government of Sardinia and the Sardinian Consulate in New York City, State Archives, Torino.

18. Ibid.

19. Ibid.

20. Death certificate of Francesco Bertola Sr., State Archives of Turin; copy in the author's possession.

21. Testamento 14 Luglio 1841, Notary Signoretti—Torino.

Chapter 9: Egyptian Mummies in America, 1823–1833

1. *Palmyra Herald* 2, no. 19 (July 24, 1822).

2. *Massachusetts General Hospital News* 29, no. 10 (December 1970): 8.

3. Ibid.

4. Ibid. The mummy is still the property of the hospital as of this writing. The hospital occasionally allows various institutions to borrow it for display purposes.

5. New York Public Library, *C. p.v. 329 #13.

6. "PADIHERSHEF, Boston newspapers in 1823," in the files of City Life Museums, Baltimore.

7. Leslie L. Luther, *Moravia and Its Past and Adjoining Townships* (Indianapolis: The Frederic Luther Co., 1966), 439–40.

8. HC 1:20.

9. William B. Dinsmoor, "Early American Studies of Mediterranean Archaeology," *Proceedings of the American Philosophical Society* 87, no. 1 (1943): 95.

10. John A. Wilson, *Signs & Wonders Upon Pharaoh: A History of American Egyptology* (Chicago: University of Chicago Press, 1964), 37.

11. *New York Commercial Advertiser,* January 26, 1832.

12. Ibid., February 24, 1832.

13. Ibid., March 2, 1832.

14. Ibid., March 12, 1832.

15. Ibid., March 21, 1833.

16. J. F. Watson, "Annals of Philadephia," Manuscripts Department, Historical Society of Pennsylvania.

17. "Egyptian Mummies," *Cleveland Daily Advertiser,* March 26, 1835.

18. "A Rare Exhibition," *Cleveland Whig,* March 25, 1835.

19. "Mummies," *Painesville Telegraph,* March 27, 1835.

20. *Webster's Ninth New Collegiate Dictionary,* 887.

Chapter 10: Joseph Smith and the Sacred Papyri

1. HC 2:236.

2. HC 2:238.

3. HC 2:286.

4. "Grammar and Alphabet of the Egyptian Language," second part, 1 degree. Transcript and copies of the original available in Special Collections, Harold B. Lee Library, Brigham Young University.

5. HC 5:63.

6. HC 2:287.

7. HC 2:289.

8. HC 2:311.

9. HC 2:321.

10. HC 2:334.

11. HC 2:396.

12. HC 2:347.

13. HC 2:520–21.

14. Dean C. Jessee, ed., *The Papers of Joseph Smith* 2 (Salt Lake City: Deseret Book, 1992), 53.

15. "Another Humbug," *Cleveland Whig,* July 31, 1835.

16. *Cincinnati Journal and Western Luminary,* August 25, 1836, 4.

17. Leah Y. Phelps, "Letters of Faith from Kirtland," *Improvement Era* 45 (1942): 529.

18. *Benjamin Johnson Journal,* 2, in Archives Division, Church Historical Department.

19. *Stephen Post Journal,* in Archives Division, Church Historical Department. 1304 Box 6, Folder 1, April 4, 1836.

20. Caroline Crosby Journal in *Women's Voices: An Untold History of the Latter-day Saints,* ed. Kenneth W. Godfrey, Audrey M. Godfrey, and Jill Mulvay Derr (Salt Lake City: Deseret Book Co., 1982), 52.

21. F. Mark McKiernan and Roger D. Launius, eds., *An Early Latter Day Saint History: The Book of John Whitmer* (Independence, Mo.: Herald Publishing House, 1980), 147–48.

22. John Corrill, *A Brief History of the Church of Christ Latter-Day Saints (Commonly Called Mormons)* (St. Louis, 1839), 3.

23. Dean C. Jessee, "The Kirtland Diary of Wilford Woodruff," *BYU Studies* 12, no. 4 (Summer 1972): 371.

24. Oliver Cowdery, "Egyptian Mummies—Ancient Records," *Messenger and Advocate* 2 (December 1835): 236.

25. James E. Talmage, *The House of the Lord* (Salt Lake City: Bookcraft, 1962), 99–101.

26. Bruce R. McConkie, *Mormon Doctrine,* 2nd ed. (Salt Lake City: Bookcraft, 1966), 779.

Chapter 11: Chaos in Kirtland

1. Milton V. Backman, *The Heavens Resound* (Salt Lake City: Deseret Book Co., 1983), 310–11.

2. Ibid., 328.

3. Oliver Huntington Autobiography, electronic version of journal in Milton V. Backman and Keith W. Perkins, comp., *Writings of Early Latter-day Saints and Their Contemporaries* (Orem, Utah: Infobases, Inc., 1992).

4. Journal History, Church Historical Department.

5. Lucy Mack Smith, *History of Joseph Smith by His Mother* (Salt Lake City: Bookcraft, 1958), 247.

6. Hepzibah L. Richards, 1838 Letters in Godfrey and Derr, *Women's Voices*, 72.

7. Jay M. Todd, *The Saga of the Book of Abraham*, 203.

8. Personal letter from Hazel B. Roese of the Royal Oak Ward, Detroit Stake, to Jay M. Todd. Undated (about 1970).

9. *A History of William Huntington written by Himself*—January 1855, BYU Special Collections, Harold B. Lee Library.

10. "Prominent Mormon Women," *Deseret News*, Church Section, November 30, 1963, as quoted by David Henry Jacobs, Utah State Historical Society Seminar, Weber State College, Winter 1977.

11. Lucy Mack Smith, 217–18.

12. Samuel A. Woolley Autobiography, p. 3, in Backman and Perkins, *Writings of Early Latter-day Saints*.

13. William I. Appleby journal in Backman and Perkins, *Writings of Early Latter-day Saints*.

14. Duane D. Call, "Anson Call and His Contributions Toward Latter-Day Saint Colonization" (master's thesis, Brigham Young University, 1956), 32–33.

15. See James R. Clark, "Joseph Smith and the Lebolo Egyptian Papyri," *BYU Studies* 8 (Winter 1968): 200.

16. William Swartzell, *Mormonism Exposed, Being a Journal of a Residence in Missouri* (Pekin, Ohio, 1840), 9.

17. Ibid., 25.

Chapter 12: The Book of Abraham Is Published

1. William Edwin Berrett, *The Restored Church* (Salt Lake City: Deseret Book Co., 1961), 149.

2. Ibid., 150.

3. "Kirtland Council Minute Book," November 5, 1837, typescript, 259, in Archives Division, Church Historical Department.

4. [Nauvoo High Council Minute Book], 60–62, Archives Division, Church Historical Department.

5. Ibid.

6. HC 4:184–87.

7. HC 4:402–3.

8. HC 4:503.

9. Ebenezer Robinson, "Valedictory," *Times and Seasons* 3 (February 15, 1842): 695–96.

10. Joseph Smith, "To Subscribers," *Times and Seasons* 3 (February 15, 1842): 696.

11. *Wilford Woodruff's Journal: 1833–1898,* typescript, ed. Scott G. Kenney (Midvale, Utah: Signature Books, 1983), entry dated February 19, 1842.

12. HC 4:517–18.

13. Joseph Smith Collection, "Letters of 1842," Archives Division, Church Historical Department.

14. *Times and Seasons* 3:710.

15. HC 4:519.

16. HC 4:542.

17. HC 4:543.

18. HC 4:548.

19. Ibid.

20. HC 5:11.

21. HC 4:524.

22. John Taylor, "Notice," *Times and Seasons* 4 (February 1, 1843): 95.

23. HC 5:293.

24. William S. West, *A Few Interesting Facts, Respecting the Rise Progress and Pretensions of the Mormons* (Warren, Ohio, 1837), 5.

25. T. Edgar Lyon, "The Sketches on the Papyri Backings," *Improvement Era,* May 1968, pp. 18–23. See also Todd, *The Saga of the Book of Abraham,* pp. 351–64.

26. Hugh Nibley, "A New Look at the Pearl of Great Price," *Improvement Era* 71 (March 1968): 17–18.

27. HC 2:238.

28. Joseph Smith Journal, November 13, 1843, in the Joseph Smith Collection, Archives Division, Church Historical Department.

29. HC 6:79.

30. Nibley, "A New Look at the Pearl of Great Price," 18.

31. Orson Pratt, *Journal of Discourses* 20:65.

32. *Millennial Star* 3 (July 1842): 46–47.

33. *Millennial Star* 40:49.

34. "The Mormons—A Leaf from Joe Smith," *New York Herald,* April 3, 1842. This article was reprinted in the *Times and Seasons* 3 (May 2, 1842): 773–74.

35. "More Prophecy," *New York Herald,* April 5, 1842, 2.

36. *Times and Seasons* 3 (May 16, 1842): 790.

37. "The Mormons—Joe Smith, the Prophet," *Times and Seasons* 3 (May 16, 1842): 796–97; reprinted from the *Dollar Weekly Bostonian.*

38. *Times and Seasons* 3 (June 1, 1842): 805; reprinted from the *New York State Mechanic.*

Chapter 13: "Chandler Was Only an Agent"

1. Geauga County Courthouse records, Chardon, Ohio. Copy of documents in author's possession.

2. Ibid.

3. Ibid.

4. Joseph Smith Collection, Archives Division, Church Historical Department.

5. Common Pleas Record Book X, Geauga County Courthouse, Chardon, Ohio. Sargent and Craig vs. Chandler (April 7, 1841), 610–12.

6. Common Pleas Record Book, Geauga County Courthouse, Chardon, Ohio. Sargent and Craig vs. Chandler (October 22, 1844), 464.

Chapter 14: The Book of Abraham Is Published in Liverpool

1. *Millennial Star* 3 (August 1842): 70–71.

2. *Millennial Star* 3 (July 1842): 46–47.

3. *Millennial Star* 26 (February 20, 1864): 118.

4. James R. Clark, *The Story of the Pearl of Great Price* (Salt Lake City: Bookcraft, 1955), 197. The 1851 statistic is in Richard O. Cowan, "Church Growth in England, 1841–1914," in *Truth Will Prevail*, ed. V. Ben Bloxham, James R. Moss, and Larry C. Porter (Solihull, England: The Church of Jesus Christ of Latter-day Saints, 1987), 213.

5. Ibid., 197.

6. British Mission Manuscript History, June 2, 1850, Church Historical Department, Salt Lake City.

7. Used by permission of Mrs. Riley Richards, whose husband was a descendant of Levi Richards.

8. See H. Donl Peterson, *The Pearl of Great Price: A History and Commentary* (Salt Lake City: Deseret Book Co., 1987), 12.

9. *Millennial Star* 13 (July 15, 1851): 216–17.

10. Cowan, *Truth Will Prevail*, 209.

11. See Clark, 194, 205.

Chapter 15: Displaying the Antiquities in Nauvoo

1. Courtesy of Kristin Linebarger, a student in a Pearl of Great Price class at Brigham Young University and a great-great-granddaughter of Elizabeth Clements Kendall, who told the story. The account was written by Bertha Pearl Kendall Molmstrom, Elizabeth's daughter.

2. "A Glance at the Mormons," *Alexandria Gazette,* quoted in the *Quincy Whig,* October 17, 1840.

3. Ida A. Isaacson, "They Knew the Prophet Joseph Smith," *Relief Society Magazine* 53 (July 1966): 507.

4. "A Girl's Letters from Nauvoo," *The Overland Monthly* (December 1890): 623–24.

5. HC 6:33.

6. *Millennial Star* 4 (December 1843): 122–23; quoted from the *Nauvoo Neighbor*.

7. Josiah Quincy, *Figures of the Past from the Leaves of Old Journals*, 386–87.

8. Ibid., 387.

9. HC 2:348.

10. William I. Appleby Journal, electronic version in Backman and Perkins, *Writings of Early Latter-day Saints and Their Contemporaries*, 64–65.

11. Nellie Stary Bean, "Reminiscences of the Granddaughter of Hyrum Smith," *Relief Society Magazine* 9 (January 1922): 9.

12. Eudocia Baldwin Marsh, "When the Mormons Dwelt Among Us," Archives Division, Church Historical Department.

13. Joseph Smith III, "Another Book of Abraham, Apocalypse of Abraham," *The Saints' Herald*, January 11, 1899.

14. Lucy M. Smith, *Biographical Sketches of Joseph Smith the Prophet, and His Progenitors for Many Generations* (1853), note b, 90–91.

15. William Smith letters to James J. Strang, Strang MSS, Quaife Collection, University of Utah Library, Salt Lake City.

16. Andrew Jenson, *LDS Biographical Encyclopedia* 1 (Salt Lake City: Publishers Press, 1971): 87

17. Smith III, *The Saints' Herald*, January 11, 1899.

18. Journal History, January 31, 1848, Archives Division, Church Historical Department.

Chapter 16: The Elusive Trail of the Mummies

1. Jay M. Todd, "Egyptian Papyri Rediscovered," 16.

2. As quoted in Richard P. Howard, "The 'Book of Abraham' in the Light of History and Egyptology," *Courage*, April 1970, 44.

3. "Question Time #63," *The Saints' Herald*, November 1955, 75–76.

4. Howard, 45.

5. Joseph Smith III, "Another Book of Abraham," *The Saints' Herald*, January 11, 1899, 18.

6. General Index to Deeds, Trumbull County, Ohio 1848–1855, January 7, 1855, 67; 73:554.

7. James R. Clark, *The Story of the Pearl of Great Price* (Salt Lake City: Bookcraft, 1955), 158–61.

8. "Museum & Concert!," *St. Louis Daily Missouri Democrat*, August 2, 1856.

9. "St. Louis Museum," *St. Louis Daily Missouri Democrat*, August 14, 1856.

10. "Amusement Notices," *St. Louis Daily Missouri Democrat,* August 14, 1856.

11. "The Mormon Prophet's Mummies," *St. Louis Daily Missouri Democrat,* June 12, 1857.

12. Stanley B. Kimball, "New Light on Old Egyptiana: Mormon Mummies 1848–71," *Dialogue, a Journal of Mormon Thought* 16, no. 4 (Winter 1983): 72.

13. James Grant Wilson and Johne Fiske, *Appleton's Cyclopedia of American Biography,* 6 vols. (New York, 1888–89), 5:474.

14. "Lectures on Egyptian Archaeology," *New York Daily Times,* May 28, 1856.

15. Kimball, 74.

16. Ibid.

17. Doyle L. Green, "New Light on Joseph Smith's Egyptian Papyri: New Fragment Disclosed," and Jay M. Todd, "Background of the Church Historian's Fragment," *Improvement Era,* February 1968, 40, 40B, and 40C.

18. *St. Louis Daily Missouri Democrat,* August 14, 1856, and July 8, 1863.

19. Kimball, 73, note 2.

20. As quoted in Clark, 159.

21. Chicago Director, Census Reports, 1871, 1246. Footed in Alen R. Cooper, "Colonel Wood's Museum: A Study in the Development of the Early Chicago Stage," master's thesis, Roosevelt University, 1974.

22. Translated from Danish, *Bikuben,* Salt Lake City, July 28, 1910.

23. Joseph Smith III, "Another Book of Abraham," *The Saints' Herald,* January 11, 1899, 18.

24. "Extra" edition, *Chicago Evening Journal,* October 9, 1871.

25. Bessie Louise Pierce, "Chicago," *Encyclopaedia Britannica* (Chicago: Encyclopaedia Britannica, Inc., 1964), 5:481.

26. Kimball, 80.

27. Ibid.

Chapter 17: Searching for the Original Manuscripts

1. In the author's personal correspondence file.

2. In the author's personal file. The minutes were recorded by George Reynolds, secretary.

3. Historical Department Journal, Archives Division, Church Historical Department.

4. *Wilford Woodruff's Journal: 1833–1898,* entry dated September 2, 1878.

5. Joseph Fielding Smith, *Life of Joseph F. Smith* (Salt Lake City: Deseret News Press, 1938), 237.

6. *Millennial Star,* October 28, 1878.

7. Robert J. Matthews, *A Plainer Translation—Joseph Smith's Translation of the Bible* (Provo, Utah: BYU Press, 1975), 221–32.

8. Joseph F. Smith and Orson Pratt, "Mission to the States,"*Deseret Evening News*, November 16, 1878. Information in this section regarding the apostles' visit in Missouri and Illinois, prior to their going on to Kirtland, Ohio, and New York State, is from this article.

9. Smith, *Life of Joseph F. Smith*, 251.

10. Ibid.

11. Ibid.

12. Joseph F. Smith, personal (Private Letterbook) C. #3 = 5/6.

13. *Millennial Star*, October 28, 1878.

14. LaMar C. Berrett, *An Annotated Catalog of Documentary-type Materials in the Wilford C. Wood Collection* 1 (Provo, Utah: Wilford C. Wood Foundation, September 1972): 172.

Chapter 18: The Pearl of Great Price Becomes a Standard Work

1. *Salt Lake Tribune*, October 11, 1880.

2. *Deseret News*, October 11, 1880.

3. Ibid.

Chapter 19: Eleven Papyrus Fragments Are Discovered

1. Todd, *The Saga of the Book of Abraham*, 1.

2. Ibid., 3–5.

3. Todd, "Egyptian Papyri Rediscovered," 13–15.

4. Dr. Atiya's credentials are listed in the 1992 *International Who's Who* (London: Europa Publications Ltd.) as follows: "M.A., Ph.D., Litt.D., D.Hum.Litt.; Egyptian historian and writer; b. 7 July 1898; ed. Univ. of Liverpool and London; ... Prof. of Medieval History, Cairo 1938–42, Alexandria 1942–54; ... Pres. Inst. of Coptic Studies, Cairo 1954–56; Medieval Acad. Visiting Prof. of Islamic Studies, Univ. of Michigan, Ann Arbor 1955–56; Luce Prof. of World Christianity, Union Theological Seminary, and Visiting Prof. of History, Columbia Univ., New York, 1956–57; Visiting Prof. of Arabic and Islamic History, Princeton 1958–59; Dir., Middle East Center, Utah Univ. 1959–67; Distinguished Prof. of History, Utah 1967–; ... The Crusade in the Later Middle Ages 1938, Egypt and Aragon—Embassies and Diplomatic Correspondence between 1300 and 1330 1938, ... History of the Patriarchs of the Egyptian Church (2 vols.) 1948–59, Monastery of St. Catherine in Mt. Sinai 1949, The Mt. Sinai Arabic Microfilms 1954, Coptic Historiography and Bibliography 1962, History of Eastern Christianity 1968, Kitab al-Ilman by al-Nuwairy (7 vols.) 1968–76, etc. (all books in either English or Arabic)."

5. The amount of money the Metropolitan Museum of Art paid for the eleven fragments is privileged information; therefore it is omitted from the quoted correspondence.

6. I interviewed Mrs. Hilma Heusser, Albin Edward Heusser's widow,

relative to the Heusser family possibly having Facsimile 2 in their possession. She stated that she was unaware of such an object.

7. *North American*, Philadelphia, July 6, 1892; *Philadelphia Inquirer*, July 6, 1892.

Chapter 20: Ready Answers and Areas for Further Research

1. See chapter 3 for the complete statement of Dr. Nibley, which is taken from his book *Abraham in Egypt.*

Chapter 21: Concepts, Challenges, and Testimony

1. *Journal of Discourses* 26:129.

2. Joseph Fielding McConkie, *His Name Shall Be Joseph* (Salt Lake City: Hawkes Publishing, 1980), 101–2.

Appendix B: Sacred Writings Yet to Come Forth

1. Robert J. Matthews, "The Restoration of All Things," in *The Heavens Are Opened* (Salt Lake City: Deseret Book Co., 1993), 227.

2. The missing books of the Bible found in this list are taken from the "Ready References" section that was published by The Church of Jesus Christ of Latter-day Saints in 1917. For several years this publication was bound in a 112–page supplement between the Old and New Testaments of the missionary edition of the King James Bible.

INDEX

Champollion, Jean Francois, 1, 32, 40, 210, 276n. 1
Chandler, Frances, 167, 176, 253
Chandler, Michael H.: brings Egyptian collection to Kirtland, 1–3; written accounts concerning, 3–6; writes certificate affirming Joseph Smith's translation, 5; sells artifacts to Church, 6, 167; errors in account of, 57–58, 72; acquires mummies in New York, 79; family of, 87–88; purchases land in Ohio, 167; lawsuits involving, 168–75; Parley Pratt's account of, 178–80; questions concerning, 254–56
Chicago, great fire in, 215–16
Christensen, C.C.A., 214
Christensen, Ross T., 55–56
Circumcision, 17
Clark, James R., vii, 207
Clayton, William, 160
Cleonzo, F. Clemente, 83
Coe, Joseph, 6, 7–8, 123–24, 137, 167–69
Combs, Abel, 206–7, 209, 246–47, 257
Combs, Oscar, 246–47
Comollo, Jerrilyn and Adriano, 77–78, 82–83
Copying of ancient records, 28–32
Corrill, John, 127
Cowan, Richard O., 189–90
Cowdery, Oliver: mentions Chandler's arrival in Kirtland, 3; letter of, to William Frye, 4–5, 128–29; on writings of Abraham and Joseph, 25; on Lebolo's discovery of mummies, 54–55; on Chandler's acquisition of artifacts, 72; assists as Joseph's scribe, 119; apostasy of, 135; desires to translate, 159–60; publishes disclaimer regarding mummies' identities, 197, 251
Craig, William, 169–75
Crosby, Caroline, 127

Darfour, Anna Marie, 65
Darfour, Rosina, 65
Darfour, Maria Catherina, 65, 285n. 2
D'Athanasi, Giovanni, 48, 63
Dawson, Warren R., 55, 57
De Bellefonds, Linant, 52–53
De Keersmaecker, Roger O., 51
Denon, Vivant, 39
Dreams of Joseph, 19–21

Drovetti, Bernardino, 41–42, 43–47, 52–54, 68
Duemichen, Johannes, 58
Duns, President, ix

Egypt: Abraham's experiences in, 13, 15–16; Joseph's experiences in, 21–23; embalming and burial processes in, 26–27; writings of, "renewed" by scribes, 28–32; record keeping in, 33–34; ties between Israel and, 34–35; Napoleon invades, 38–39; British army drives French from, 40; "Bonapartists" in, 45; excavations in, were jealously guarded, 59–60
Egyptian alphabet and grammar, 119–20, 157–60, 279n. 1
Egyptian antiquities (Chandler's): are brought to Kirtland, 1–3; purchase of, by Church, 6–8, 167; possible excavation site of, 55–57, 60–62; *Messenger and Advocate* account of, 88–89; advertisements announcing display of, 89–93; mob vows to destroy, 136; protecting, from mob, 138–40; are removed to Missouri, 140–41; Parley P. Pratt's account of, 177–81; confusion in Pratt account of, 181–83; are displayed in Nauvoo, 191–97; William Smith's supposed possession of, 201–2; are sold to A. Combs, 203–4; questions and answers concerning, 248–58. *See also* Mummies, Chandler's collection of; Papyri, Chandler's collection of
Embalming process in ancient Egypt, 26–27
Excommunication of Church leaders, 135

Facsimiles in Book of Abraham, 32, 130, 151–52, 177, 252, 281n. 10
Finati, Giovanni, 59–60
First Presidency statement seeking Saint's support, 144–45
Fitzclarence, Colonel, 45
Frye, William, 4–5

Gau, Francois, 69
Gaylord, John, 135
Gee, Salmon, 135